SOCIAL SERVICE DELIVERY SYSTEMS
An International Annual
Volume 5

LINKING
HEALTH CARE
AND SOCIAL SERVICES

International Perspectives

D0107717

Editors
MERL C. HOKENSTAD, Jr.
and
ROGER A. RITVO

Foreword by PATRICIA ROBERTS HARRIS

SAGE PUBLICATIONS
Beverly Hills / London / New Delhi

For information address:

SAGE Publications, Inc.
275 South Beverly Drive
Beverly Hills, California 90212

SAGE Publications India Pvt. Ltd.
C-236 Defence Colony
New Delhi 110 024, India

SAGE Publications Ltd
28 Banner Street
London EC1Y 8QE, England

Printed in the United States of America

Library of Congress Cataloging in Publication Data

Main entry under title:

Linking service systems.

   (Social service delivery systems ; vol. 5)
   Bibliography: p.
   1. Social service—Addresses, essays, lectures.
2. Public health—Addresses, essays, lectures.
I. Hokenstad, Merl C. II. Ritvo, Roger A., 1944-
III. Series. [DNLM: 1. Delivery of health care.
2. Social work. W1 S01322 v.5 / W 84.1 C756]
HV40.L54   362.1   82-705
ISBN 0-8039-1819-4   AACR2
ISBN 0-8039-1820-8 (pbk.)

FIRST PRINTING

LINKING
HEALTH CARE
AND SOCIAL SERVICES

International Perspectives

SOCIAL SERVICE DELIVERY SYSTEMS

An International Annual

Series Editors

MORTON I. TEICHER

DANIEL THURSZ

JOSEPH L. VIGILANTE

CONTENTS

To our wives and families:
Dorothy, Alene, Laura, and Marta Hokenstad;
Lynn, Roberta, and Eric Ritvo

FOREWORD

Throughout human history, the goal of a decent life for all human beings has eluded mankind. Even as science has reduced illness and increased the lifespan of many people, there remain many for whom poverty, illness, hunger, and hopelessness are standard. Unmet human needs cry out for attention, not only in the underdeveloped world but also in industrial nations. Whether we focus on the "urban condition" or on the plight of the urban and rural poor, scientific progress has not solved the health and social welfare problems of the world. Nor has the single best mechanism emerged to analyze these problems. It is in meeting these analytical needs that a book such as this has potential value.

As a former Secretary of Housing and Urban Development (HUD), Health, Education and Welfare (HEW), and Health and Human Services (HHS), I have a professional and personal interest in this collection of international human service efforts. The United States can learn from the experience of other nations. Within the limits of federal power and revenues, HUD has a record of successful interventions to encourage, augment, and coordinate local community efforts to meet human needs, through such programs as the Community Development Block Grant and the Urban Development Action Grants. HHS's efforts to coordinate programs were widespread, covering health, retirement, and welfare, as well as specific needs such as deinstitutionalization programs for the mentally ill.

Out of these experiences, three major obstacles emerged. Professional domain boundaries often impede coordination of service delivery programs. Without casting blame, the trend toward professional specialization has created turf battles over control, the outcome of which often serves the professional at the expense of the client and the community. Organizational structures often reflect this diversity. HHS by title created distinct units for health, mental health, and human services. The numerous task forces, committees, and joint planning efforts represent cumbersome mechanisms to bridge these gaps. Finally, inadequate financing limits the public sector involvement. It is axiomatic that there are human problems for which neither local nor national government have real solutions.

Three fundamental issues—professional boundaries, organizational structures, and limited resources—emerge as major themes throughout this book. As one who has spent a lifetime considering these areas, I am pleased that this volume sheds new light on the ways in which other national efforts respond to these concerns.

On a personal level, two of my former staff members have made contributions in this book. Bill TenHoor's career in mental health policy and programs has included the development of innovative approaches to these issues. His chapter on linking health and mental health programs develops these themes. Roger Ritvo's efforts on my staff centered on coordinating the HHS health and social welfare programs. His concluding chapter in this book documents the lessons of these varied approaches to linking services in the international community.

The reduced commitment of the United States government's resources to human services leaves little doubt that even fewer of the needy will be served. While efforts to change these policies must continu , energy must also be directed to improving the effectiveness and efficiency of service delivery systems.

The challenge lies before us: All societies must find a more responsive approach to improving the human condition. The obstacles are known. The ability to learn from our mistakes and the successes of others will improve our efforts.

Patricia Roberts Harris
Washington, D.C.

PREFACE

Editing a volume on international approaches to any topic presents challenges far exceeding those of other manuscripts. Not only do the logistical concerns of language, translations, time zones, postal strikes, and closure of the international air traffic lanes present unexpected obstacles, but the content must vary greatly, by definition. The challenge of pulling these chapters together into a coherent, single book falls to the editors. We accepted the opportunity in the belief that this effort would have a significant value to others. For those of us in education, this volume and the entire series provides ready access to alternative delivery systems. For policymakers, it presents different philosophical and political issues for decision making and resource allocation. For the student, it can increase understanding of how selected industrial nations of North America and Europe approach this field. And for those of us who believe that health and social welfare programs and policies must be linked more effectively, these chapters provide evidence that it can work, despite the vast differences in national histories, values, economic conditions, and professional educational systems.

Such a volume would never see the light of day if many people did not contribute. The series editors, Daniel Thursz and Joseph Vigilante, gave us the responsibility and latitude to construct the volume. This trust was accepted and fulfilled. The chapters were written by top professionals in several nations. Their time and effort is reflected in the high quality of these analyses. As a group, they stuck to deadlines, a major concern to any editor. As individuals, they have expressed views that may not be popular but which are grounded in the data they present. This helps make the book stronger because of its analytical nature.

Manuscript preparation falls to the editors and our various support systems. Mrs. Debra Strekal not only typed the manuscript but provided continual commentary on the structure, grammar, and flow of the chapters. This additional input strengthened the book considerably.

It is our hope that this volume will challenge policymakers, strengthen student research and libraries, and enhance the pool of available references for educators and professional delivery personnel in health and social service systems.

Merl C. Hokenstad, Jr.
Roger A. Ritvo
Cleveland, Ohio

1

INTRODUCTION

MERL C. HOKENSTAD, Jr.

Volume 5 of the International Social Service Delivery Systems Annual focuses on a major program area which is receiving increasing attention in most industrialized nations: the relationship between social services and health services. Health and social service linkage is a major challenge to countries and communities seeking to provide adequate service resources to meet client needs and to ensure that those resources reach the client group and are utilized effectively. Policymakers and professionals recognize that program fragmentation and professional specialization produce obstacles to effective utilization of both health and social services. Linkages between the two service systems are hindered by these and other factors inherent in the modern industrial state. Thus, experiences and experiments in social and health service linkage deserve cross-national attention and analysis.

In their introduction to Volume 1 of the Social Service Delivery Systems Annuals, series editors Thurz and Vigilante (1975) identify several key issues confronting administrators and planners. One such issue is the relationship between social services and other social systems. They have asked the editors of Volume 5 to address one major component of this issue in its international context. In doing so, we have in turn asked scholars in eight industrialized Western countries to prepare chapters on health and social service interaction. Countries included in this volume are Canada, France, Denmark, Finland, Israel, Sweden, the United Kingdom, and the United States. Each chapter includes background information about the historical development and contemporary organization of health and social service delivery systems. Linkages between the systems and obstacles to linkage are then explained and examined in detail. Finally, current issues and future directions in health and social service coordination are described and analyzed.

This introductory chapter will identify and explore several dimensions of the health and social service linkage issue which are common to the industrialized nations included in Volume 5. These include developmental, organizational, and professional obstacles to coordinated service provision, as well as provider and consumer roles in shaping the service delivery system. It will then offer a framework for analyzing linkage problems and alternative problem-solving strategies. The concluding chapter of the book identifies a number of common themes which characterize national efforts to link health and social services. It draws on examples from the countries discussed to identify commonalities and variances in the role of government, professional concerns, financial issues, and consumer expectations. Finally, it examines points of departure for future approaches to service linkage.

RATIONALE FOR HEALTH AND
SOCIAL SERVICE LINKAGE

We have earlier summarized the rationale for policy and planning attention to the linking of health and social services as follows:

Universal health care and social services are fundamental building blocks of the modern welfare state. They are invariably discrete organizational and programmatic systems within the structure of government. From an administrative standpoint, this is rational and efficient. But, for the consumer of services this structural arrangement may have negative consequences—particularly where there is little provision for linkage and collaboration between the two systems. The interrelationship of health, mental health, and social well-being is well documented. Emotional problems are frequently converted into health problems and lack of social support is sometimes manifested as a health problem. There is an interrelationship in other areas. For example, there are many physical problems that have psychological and social correlates, and therefore require an integrated approach to the delivery of health and social services. Following a serious injury or debilitating illness, individuals and families often need help in planning and organizing a rehabilitation program. In terminal illness, the emotional and social components are an integral part of the treatment plan. Elderly people who need both physical and social support require a continuum of care [Hokenstad et al., 1979].

Recently, the linkage issue has received growing attention by international bodies as well as scholars and policymakers in several countries. In 1977, the World Health Organization's Regional Office for Europe published a study of health and welfare service coordination in Austria, Italy, Poland, and Sweden. This report identified three major reasons for the current concern with service linkage: (1) service fragmentation resulting from increased program and provider specialization; (2) growing needs of client groups; and (3) demand for agency accountability regarding service efficiency and effectiveness (Kohn, 1977). The Organisation for Economic Co-operation and Development (OECD) published a report in the same year which identified relevant factors to be considered in policies for service sector innovation. The management of integrated delivery systems was one important problem area explored in this study. Functional government bureaucracy and professional specialization were factors cited as requiring attention in attempts to improve service delivery and to meet client needs. (OCED, 1977).

Ultimately, the goal in the provision of human services is to meet the needs of, or provide benefits to, client and consumer groups. The achievement of this goal depends not only on the effectiveness of specific services but also on the coordination of the service system. Too often, the individual or the family requiring help is faced with a confusing array of agencies and professional personnel providing sometimes fragmented and sometimes overlapping services. Differing professional ideologies and organizational requirements lead to confusion, if not consternation, on the part of the help seeker. This is true even within service systems, but it is particularly true between service systems, each with its own organizational structure and professional ideology. The health service and social service systems, while directed at interrelated human needs, often function in isolation from, if not in conflict with, one another.

OBSTACLES TO HEALTH AND SOCIAL SERVICE LINKAGE

The problem of health and social service linkage has several dimensions. The two service systems have developed within different organizational structures and with different professional providers. Although the historical evolution of services has varied among countries, the separate development of the two systems is a constant across nations. Each system has expanded its services in a piecemeal and often fragmented manner as new forms of service provision have been initiated to meet identified problems. Service expansion in response to client needs has been well motivated but often has created new service delivery obstacles as the system has grown more complex and fragmented.

Organizational obstacles to effective service provision include both vertical and horizontal fragmentation. Vertical fragmentation occurs when different departments of the national or state government carry responsibilities for separate service systems. Health services financing and planning are the functions of one department, while another plans and funds the social services. Separate organizational structures, regulations, and reporting mechanisms result from this differentiation of functions. They, in turn, often serve as barriers to, rather than facilitators of, coordinated service delivery at the local level. This is true in several European countries as well as at both the national and state level within the United States.

Horizontal fragmentation occurs when different levels of government are responsible for different types of services. In many European countries, health services are provided by the county and social services by the municipality. It also occurs when functional differentiation of service systems leads to differing geographical boundaries for service sectors within the local community. Both types of structure hinder the effectiveness of coordinating mechanisms established to help link the two systems. Even the most creative experimental projects referred to in the chapters that follow have had difficulty in overcoming such built-in structural barriers.

Most of the chapters in this volume give primary attention to these and other organizational obstacles to service linkage. In addition to the structural and geographical barriers, they consider organizational specialization, bureaucracy, and administrative rigidity as important contributing factors to service fragmentation. The great majority of programs and projects designed to overcome fragmentation also have placed major emphasis on overcoming organizational obstacles. Umbrella health and welfare departments at the national level and multiservice centers at the local level have been utilized in the attempt to combat such problems.

However, it is unlikely that success in the structural-organizational area alone will lead to effective delivery of health and social services. Delivery problems will not be overcome and client needs will not be adequately met until professional as well as organizational obstacles are addressed. Collaboration between provider disciplines is an objective equally important to coordination between service sectors. Multidisciplinary cooperation is a key component in integrated service delivery.

Professional obstacles to service linkage are evident in all of the countries considered in this book. While both the health services system and the social services system include a number of different provider disciplines, each reflects a dominant professional orientation. Medical doctors are the dominant and controlling discipline in the health services system regardless of whether the service is provided under public or entrepreneurial auspices. Social workers are the predominant discipline in the social services system, although their authority and autonomy are more limited in relationship to the organizational and managerial controls of social service agencies. Bureaucratic authority and decision making are preeminent in the social services, while professional authority and collegial decision making are preeminent in the health services. In both sectors, the ethos and orientation of the dominant profession play a major role in problem diagnosis and service provision.

Collaboration among provider disciplines, and in particular between doctors and social workers, is hindered by a number of professional obstacles. These include differing service orientations based on training and professional socialization as well as differing status and public recognition. In many countries, the treatment emphasis of medical training runs counter to the prevention and environmental change emphasis of social work training. Since there are few, if any, opportunities for multidisciplinary training in most educational programs for physicians and social workers, these distinct emphases are well ingrained in the two disciplines at the commencement of professional practice. In most European countries, social work education takes place outside the university. While both types of professional education are university-based within the United States, there is little evidence that this organizational proximity leads to joint training ventures. Thus, with few exceptions, the skills and techniques of professional collaboration must be learned on the job.

Cooperative efforts in service provision are further hampered by status and autonomy differences among the provider disciplines. The medical profession has high status and commands respect as well as the authority to make major decisions in health care. Social workers have less prestige and decision-making power than their medical counterparts. This difference in status and authority is accentuated by different systems of accountability. The physician is responsible to the peer group, while the social worker is responsible to the organization. As we have indicated elsewhere, the limitation in decision-making autonomy reinforces the doctor's view of the social worker as a "semiprofessional" who should perform tasks under the direction of a fully qualified professional. On the other hand, the social worker resists subordination to the physician in projects focusing on coordinated delivery of health and social services. These differences in professional status and accountability reinforce differing orientations to service which have resulted from distinct and separate patterns of training. They are a potential source of conflict which increases the difficulty of collaborative planning and service delivery (Hokenstad et al., 1979).

Organizational and professional obstacles to service linkage require careful attention by educators and practitioners as well as policymakers and planners. These obstacles are seen in differing perspectives by governmental officials, agency executives, provider disciplines and client/consumer groups. They also vary in content and emphasis across nations depending on the history and sociology of the service systems. Still, they are recognized as significant factors influencing efforts to create coordinated, if not integrated, health-social service delivery systems throughout the countries of the industrialized world. Each of the country chapters included in this volume draws attention to these obstacles, as well as efforts to surmount or moderate them.

PROVIDER AND CONSUMER ROLES IN
HEALTH AND SOCIAL SERVICE DELIVERY

Although obstacles to coordinated and collaborative service delivery exist in all countries, there is evidence of progress in improving linkages between health and social services. In addition to a variety of attempts to improve vertical and horizontal coordination, attention is being given to new roles in the delivery of services. These include increased opportunities for interprofessional collaboration in client contacts and growing involvement of consumers in both service provision and organizational decision-making.

Special projects in several nations are demonstrating various approaches to multidisciplinary cooperation and interdisciplinary collaboration among the dominant service providers in health care and the social services. Some of these projects emphasize well-established modes of provider cooperation, such as information exchange, referral mechanisms, liaison personnel, and case conferences involving different professional disciplines. Others utilize newer forms of collaboration, such as interdisciplinary provider teams. Teamwork with multiproblem individuals and families is receiving increased attention as a major device to link provider disciplines in the service delivery process.

Case management and continuity of care are key concepts applied in projects and programs utilizing interdisciplinary collaboration. The assignment of case managers to clients and client groups offers a focal point for addressing problems which have an emotional or social component in addition to a physical component. Such managers serve as diagnosticians and referral agents. In some cases, they also coordinate a team approach to treatment and rehabilitation. Provider teams comprising different disciplines offer a continuity of care by cutting across barriers separating needed services and by linking inpatient, outpatient, and social support services to client needs.

Consumer participation in service delivery is most evident in the variety of self-help groups which are playing an increasingly important role in both the health and social services. Alcoholics Anonymous is perhaps the prototype for such groups which offer peer support in various forms. In addition to education and economic support for individuals and their families, self-help groups also provide a sense of security and belonging. The tangible and intangible benefits of this form of consumer participation are sufficient to make it a significant factor in future planning for effective service delivery. Self-help groups are potential components of a service network which addresses multifaceted problems.

Consumer roles in health and social service delivery also include involvement at various levels of decision-making. Citizen representation on policymaking boards or advisory committees has been a traditional form of consumer input into policymaking and program implementation. More recently, clients are being included in case conferences. In some countries, interprofessional teams have involved clients as active participants in their diagnostic, referral, and treatment planning. Such participation at the point of service provision remains experimental and controversial. Different professions have differing perspectives on the appropriate role for the client in this process. However, a more active role for the client as consumer is an apparent outcome of several demonstration projects. Client/ consumer input in both organization and case decision-making offers another focal point for service linkage.

FRAMEWORK FOR CROSS-NATIONAL ANALYSIS OF HEALTH AND SOCIAL SERVICE LINKAGE

Authors from the various countries represented in this volume identify and discuss a wide variety of problems and programs concerned with service fragmentation and service linkage. While each country has some unique characteristics in the structure and operation of its delivery system, there also are important similarities. Most of the important obstacles and issues which have been identified cut across nations. Although they may vary in form and emphasis from country to country, they are sufficiently alike to provide a basis for generalization. Overgeneralization is always a danger, but this can be avoided if there is a discriminating framework which provides a basis for cross-national comparison.

Cross-national comparisons are needed if we are to move beyond appreciation and understanding of linkage problems and problem-solving strategies in individual countries to the selective application of this knowledge in the improvement of service delivery throughout the industrialized world. While it is not possible to do an in-depth cross-national analysis within the confines of this volume, it is possible to suggest a framework for analysis based on similarities and differences in national experiences. This requires an identification of relevant criteria for cross-national analysis. It also necessitates a typology of problem areas and related program goals. Such a framework can be used as the reader reviews the specific chapters and relates them to the problems and programs in his or her own country.

Criteria which might be utilized in a cross-national analysis of service delivery systems and linkages can be drawn from the above discussion of obstacles, trends, and issues as well as from the country chapters.

Eight such variables immediately come to mind:

(1) *Development of Health and Social Service Systems.* The historical evolution and socioeconomic context of health services and the social services.

(2) *Structure of the Health and Social Service Systems.* The functional and geographical division of the service sectors at both the national and local level.

(3) *Resource Provision for Health and Social Services.* The financial and personnel resources available in the society for health care and for social services.

(4) *Organizational Auspices for the Delivery of Services.* The division of responsibility and authority for service provision.

(5) *Management of Service Delivery.* The task and accountability definitions applied to the delivery of health and social services.

(6) *Provider Disciplines Involved in Service Provision.* The status characteristics and role responsibilities of the professional service providers.

(7) *Educational Backgrounds of Service Providers.* The auspice, focus, and content of training for health and social service professionals.

(8) *Participation of Clients and Consumers in Service Provision.* The expectations and attitudes of client-consumer groups and their influence and involvement in decision-making.

Each of these criteria is useful in the understanding of health and social service provision in one country. Taken together, they provide an overview of the service delivery system as well as the potential for, and problems faced in, service linkages. Further, they provide a basis for comparison across countries. Yet, this comparison is limited to a static view of how the current system operates. The factual data plugged into such a listing of criteria thus gives a useful but limited basis for cross-national analysis. A more in-depth examination of service delivery problems and program goals is required if cross-national comparisons are to provide practical assistance to planners and policymakers.

A major dilemma in goal-setting and program planning is the complexity of linking health and social services. The goal of improved service linkages is directed at overcoming a complex problem with a number of important components. A listing of the criteria to be considered in problem and program analysis provides important background knowledge, but attempts to deal with all the variables at once are doomed to failure. Problem analysis becomes too global and program resources are too limited to achieve major societal improvements in service linkage. Effective intervention requires a more circumscribed problem definition or target area.

One answer to the dilemma for many countries has been to implement demonstration projects. Some of the countries included in this volume have had considerable success in demonstrating the efficacy and efficiency of service linkage through such projects. However, none has been able to translate the results of these circumscribed projects into successful countrywide linkage strategies. Limited resources coupled with organizational and professional resistance have certainly worked against the expansion of local projects to national programs. Still, it might be argued that the breadth of the problem definition is equally responsible for this lack of success.

Another way of targeting linkage strategies is to break down the problem into a number of components and to determine which aspects of the problem can best be addressed locally and immediately and which aspects require more long-term and broad-based intervention strategies. Even when different problem components are interwoven, this approach can be used as an analytic tool to provide a better understanding of problem characteristics and program potentials. It also can help in setting goal priorities and in preventing goal conflicts.

Five problem components can be identified from a review of the obstacles and issues in health and social service linkage: *inadequate services*, *inaccessible services*, *underutilized services*, *fragmented services*, and *discontinuous services.* Most of the discussion on service linkage centers on the problems of service fragmentation and service discontinuity. This is understandable, since coordination and collaboration are the focal points of most efforts to improve linkage. However, service inadequacy, service inaccessibility, and service underutilization are causes as well as components of fragmentation and discontinuity.

(1) Inadequate services: Resource scarcity is a problem which certainly affects the way services are delivered and

linked. If an organization or community does not have sufficient funds or personnel to meet client-consumer demands,
service linkage becomes a low priority, if not a moot issue. Or,
if certain services are missing, the development of efficient
referral systems or effective disciplinary collaboration becomes
frustrated, if not defeated.

(2) *Inaccessible services:* Bureaucratic complexity and insen-
sitivity often prevent client groups from using available services.
The red tape and regulation of large service bureaucracies can be
major roadblocks to effective service delivery. The frustrations
caused by such regulations affect both staff and clients. If
complex procedures and insensitive personnel hinder service
accessibility, coordinating mechanisms are likely to have limited
impact in accomplishing improved service delivery.

(3) *Underutilized services:* Insufficient knowledge about
available services constitutes a major barrier to effective service
delivery. If client groups lack information about services and
knowledge about how to use them, there is little likelihood that
interagency coordination or interdisciplinary collaboration will
result in improved and more effective service utilization.

(4) *Fragmented services:* Poorly coordinated service systems
are of course a major component of the linkage problem.
Limited communication, loosely developed referral procedures,
and conflicting organizational goals serve as barriers to improving health and social service linkages. However, intervention
directed at fragmentation will have the greatest impact in an
already adequate and accessible service system.

(5) *Discontinuous services:* Unintegrated service systems can
exist even when services are well coordinated through information exchange and interagency coordinating mechanisms.
This discontinuity may result from inadequate follow-up and
feedback devices to assure responsiveness to client needs. It also
may be the result of nonexistent or limited collaboration among
provider disciplines. Both organizational and disciplinary barriers must be addressed in order to overcome service discontinuity.

This problem categorization framework provides a tool for
identifying appropriate goals and strategies to overcome linkage

obstacles and improve service delivery. While the problem categories are clearly interrelated, the framework can increase understanding of relationships and thus help in determining the initial point for intervention. For example, the lack of resources may be an important contributing factor to the establishment of regulations and red tape. Or services may be underutilized because they are fragmented. Decisions about linkage goals will need to be based on a careful study of client population characteristics and service utilization patterns. With this information, such decisions can be aided by informed judgment about the underlying problem which must be initially addressed.

Effective health and social service linkage can be facilitated by a systematic approach to goal-setting based on such problem identification. If services are inadequate or underdeveloped, additional resources will be necessary before interagency coordinating committees or case managers will be effective. If, on the other hand, services are available but not fully utilized, improved information and referral mechanisms may be the appropriate answer to improved service delivery. System linkages require adequate and accessible services as a base for program planning. Recognition of this fact should help to facilitate service delivery planning and implementation.

Priority goals can be suggested to overcome each of the problems in service delivery which are identified. They are as follows:

Problem	*Priority Goal*
1. Inadequate services	1. Development of additional resources
2. Inaccessible services	2. Institutional change or more effective use of available resources
3. Underutilized services	3. Increased visibility of and information about services
4. Fragmented services	4. Improvement of service system coordination
5. Discontinuous services	5. Service integration and disciplinary collaboration

Such a framework offers a starting point for problem and program analysis directed at improved health and social service linkage. Once initial decisions are made about the delivery problem and priority goal, appropriate program strategies can be developed. Such strategies will require modification based on resource availability and other feasibility considerations. Still, they provide a foundation for national intervention into a complex and multifaceted service delivery dilemma.

The chapters which follow address the service linkage issue in eight different national contexts. Each of the countries examined has approached the problem within its unique historical and environmental context. Some countries have focused on local demonstration and research projects, while others have emphasized national legislation and structural change. Still, there are many similarities in linkage efforts. Similar obstacles have been identified and similar results have been achieved. More often than not, linkage successes have been limited by organizational and professional barriers. Yet progress has resulted from these efforts, and there is much to learn from accomplishments as well as failures. The national and local efforts described and analyzed in this volume add to our knowledge about the linkage dilemma. They also provide insights into the type of planning and action required for future efforts to improve health and social service delivery systems.

REFERENCES

HOKENSTAD, M. C., R. A. RITVO, and M. ROSENBERG (1979) "International perspectives on linking health and social services." International Social Work 22, 4: 13-21.

KOHN, R. (1977) Coordinating Health and Welfare Services in Four Countries: Austria, Italy, Poland and Sweden. Copenhagen: WHO European Regional Office.

Organisation For Economic Co-operation and Development (1977) Policies for Innovation in the Service Sector: Identification and Structure of Relevant Factors. Paris: OECD.

THURSZ, D. and J. L. VIGILANTE [eds.] (1975) Meeting Human Needs: An Overview of Nine Countries. Beverly Hills, CA: Sage.

2

UNITED STATES
Health and Personal Social Services

WILLIAM J. TENHOOR

Linking health and personal social services is a complex task, if only because of its enormity. The investment of the U.S. government in health and personal social services totals almost $70 billion. Indeed, the Department of Health and Human Services (HHS), the federal agency which administers health and social services programs, has the third largest budget in the world, trailing only the budgets of the U.S. government itself and that of the Soviet Union.

The scope of public expenditures for health and social services rivals the complexity of the systems utilized for delivering services. Although they share the same administrative body at the federal level, health and personal social service funds quickly find their separate channels as they pass through a labyrinth of federal, state, and local governments; administrative structures; a multitude of public and private agencies; and practitioners on their way to individuals in need. On occasion, these separate resource streams rejoin to serve an individual's needs. However, such an occasion may have less to do with the individual's needs than it does with the needs of professionals, of service delivery organizations, of the nature of intergovern-

AUTHOR'S NOTE: *The views expressed in this chapter are my own and in no way represent the policy of the Department of Health and Human Services.*

mental and interorganizational relations, and legislative, executive, and administrative needs.

This chapter examines the relationships among the health, mental health, and personal social services systems of the United States, with special attention given to those factors which facilitate or impede service linkage. Describing the system of health and personal social services, it draws principally from two unique experiences for purposes of analysis. The first is the human services integration "movement" of the past decade. This began as a reaction to the rapid growth of federal categorical programs in the 1960s and the resulting confusion and compexity of administering and delivering such services. Based on administrative and systems theory, it was a boundary-spanning activity, which, if successful, would integrate comprehensive health and personal social services with income support, employment, food stamp, and other programs in communities across the country.

The second experience is the community mental health center (CMHC) program. One of the better-known and more ambitious categorical programs, it serves as a good example for linkage because it tends to span both sectors. Although it draws elements of theory from health and social science literature, the CMHC program belongs fully to neither.

The basic thesis of the chapter is that we are unlikely to achieve a fully integrated system of health and personal social services. Historically, these have been highly separate activities. Health services have been more universal and privately provided, while social services have been public, means-tested, and stigmatized. However, as American society has changed and our service delivery systems have grown larger, more diverse, and complex, increasing interactions occur between the two sectors, many of which have resulted in more permanent linkages. Such linkage opportunities will continue to occur.

The need for linking health and social services is compelling. There is widespread consensus about the importance of treating the "whole person," even in relation to the social environment, not merely a specialized set of organs and circulatory systems.

In medical practice, this has spawned new, more integrative medical "specialties" like family practice physicians. On a theoretical level, such concepts as holistic health go beyond traditional acute care medicine. They extend beyond health prevention into the social arena of interpersonal, group, and societal relations. In addition, the relationships among mental health, health, and social problems have long been recognized. Patients seeking relief from physical distress are sometimes not successful until they find psychiatric help. By the same token, hyperactive children referred to as social and behavioral problems in schools may not find relief until they change their diets. The case supporting the integration of health and personal social services for the chronically mentally ill and other long-term disability populations is equally compelling. The needs of such individuals clearly have profound medical and social components. Social and health linkages can modify the devastating impact of an individual's illness on the family, especially in the case of the terminal illness of a sole wage earner.

The interrelationships between health and personal social services can be examined by reviewing the federal administrative agency with responsibility in this area, the Department of Health and Human Services (HHS). HHS has a significant effect on how states and localities structure their programs. Many of the linkage problems that haunt providers and local administrators stem from this federal agency. In addition, it is important to review the basic, though overlapping, types of federal programs through which assistance is delivered: categorical grants, block grants, and entitlement programs. This chapter discusses a major program of each type; two from health (Medicaid, an entitlement program, and the CHMC program, a categorical grant) and one from human services (Title XX, a block grant). The interactive effects of varying types of assistance on one another are crucial factors affecting linkage. In addition, the framework in this chapter views linkage as a phenomenon in itself, for linkage has multiple meanings. To the health care practitioners, it is likely to mean one thing; to the social service administrator, it will mean a significantly different set of behaviors; to the federal level policymaker, it may have little to do with clinical practice.

The complex interactions of health and personal social service systems are merely elements in a larger national system of protections and benefits, including housing assistance, food stamps, income transfer programs, veterans' benefits, work and rehabilitation programs, and other human services. Each of the various elements may be viewed as a system, or all may be viewed as elements in a larger system in which they interact and are linked, sometimes causally and frequently at cross-purposes. For example, health care benefits can undermine an individual's willingness to work by eliminating the health benefit as income rises (DeJong, 1977). Thus, to view health programs and their linkage with social services without recognition of the larger environment in which they participate is to miss operating influences.

The subject of health and social service integration is especially timely and germaine to the present policy reform efforts of the Reagan administration. One of the major policies has been the consolidation of 40 categorical programs into four block grants: social services, health services, health promotion/disease prevention, and energy assistance. Entitled "new federalism," the President's policies have the same name and many features of the Nixon/Ford administration proposals which spawned the human service integration efforts of the 1970s. President Reagan's new federalism heralds a simplification of the process of federal government, a shift of power in intergovernmental relations, with the federal government and cities both ceding decision-making power to the states, and a curtailment of the growth rate of social programs. Depending on how states choose to implement these new block grants and to interweave them with remaining federal programs, there is the possibility for much closer linkage, especially with the removal of federal requirements. Many states will be threatened by the reduced federal support and, as a result, retreat into more narrow functional approaches. However, other states will seize the opportunity of reduced federal presence to institutionalize those areas of linkage with demonstrated cost-effectiveness. This chapter attempts to define the parameters involved in accomplishing the latter course.

BACKGROUND

The backbone of federal health and personal social service legislation in the United States is the Social Security Act. The act was passed in the 1930s to provide social insurance against the risks of unemployment, disability, old age, widowhood, and being orphaned. It currently contains 20 titles and is typically amended significantly in each session of Congress. It contains the major entitlements in health and social services. However, the Social Security Act is only one piece, albeit a very significant one, of federal health and personal social services legislation. A host of other laws and programs, primarily categorical programs, abound. Though they represent fewer dollars than the Social Security Act programs, they have an impact far beyond their dollar level. Almost all are administered by the Department of Health and Human Services.

This section places the health and social services programs in perspective by describing briefly the structure of HHS and its legislation and comparable state and local structures. It illustrates the three basic types of federal programs: categorical, block, and entitlement. Finally, it explores the fundamental aspects of these programs which contribute to integration or separation of the two sectors.

The Federal Level

From its inception in the 1950s until 1979, the agency which administered most federal health and social service programs was the Department of Health, Education and Welfare (HEW). However, the "E" was removed in 1979 to become a separate department. The fact that health and welfare remained together, though retitled, suggests an ongoing commitment to their integration.

The Department of Health and Human Services has four operating divisions. Two have health-related missions: the Health Care Financing Administration (HCFA) and the Public Health Service (PHS). HCFA administers the two Social Security Act health entitlements, Medicare (Title XVIII) and Medicaid (Title XIX). Both programs were enacted in the 1960s as a first step toward national health insurance. Medicare is a program of health insurance for the aged, and Medicaid funds the purchase of health services for the poor. The fiscal year 1981 budgets for the two programs (in outlays) are $41 billion for Medicare and $16 billion for Medicaid.

In contrast to HCFA, the Public Health Service administers over 50 separately legislated categorical health programs, totalling almost $8 billion. PHS contains six major components, including the Alcohol, Drug Abuse, and Mental Health Administration (ADAMHA), which funds specialized services, research, and training; the Centers for Disease Control, which include occupational safety and health as well as traditional disease control activity; the Food and Drug Administration, which assures the quality of food and drugs consumed by Americans; the Health Resources Administration, the health manpower and training area; the Health Services Administration, which provides primary, secondary, and tertiary health care programs; and the National Institutes of Health, which conduct biomedical and behavioral health research. Among the larger service programs administered by PHS are the Maternal and Child Health program (approximately $400 million in 1981); the Community Health Centers program (approximately $325 million); the Indian Health Service program (approximately $600 million); and the Alcohol, Drug Abuse and Mental Health programs (approximately $1 billion).

Just as the health side of HHS contains a health reimbursement and a health services division, so the human services side of HHS contains a social reimbursement (or income transfer) and a social services division. Social reimbursement programs operate within the Social Security Administration (SSA), the giant of the department in dollar terms. Its 1981 budget of $150 billion was consumed almost entirely by individual income transfer payments. SSA operates the Old Age, Survivors and Disability Insurance programs (OASDI), commonly thought of as social security; the Supplemental Security Income (SSI) program for those aged, blind, or disabled persons not eligible for other income support programs; the Aid to Families with Dependent Children program (AFDC), commonly called the "welfare" program; the Child Support Enforcement program; and the Low Income Energy program.

The Office of Human Development Services (OHDS) is the social service division of HHS. Approximately half of its 1981 budget of $6.5 billion is consumed by the Social Security Act Title XX program, the social services entitlement. OHDS contains four operating components: the Administration for Children, Youth and Families, the largest in budget and programs, including the Head Start program ($820 million in 1981); the foster care, adoption assistance, and child welfare services programs ($520 million); the Administration for Older Americans, which administers a program of food, social services, research, and advocacy for older Americans ($680 million); the Administration for Developmental Disabilities ($61 million); and the Administration for Native Americans ($34 million). The Title XX program transfers dollars directly to states for social services; its 1981 budget is $2.9 billion.

The State Level

The 50 states (and 7 territories) tend to structure their health and social services systems along the same lines as the federal government. However, while this is a general rule, there are as many exceptions. States have initiated different systems for different purposes. Prior to federal involvement in mental health and corrections, the states developed and operated their own institutions. They also operated their own health and

welfare programs. Although they have adjusted their administrative bureaucracies to meet federal requirements, each state
structure is unique in its human service institutions. One of the
more notable distinctions between federal and state structures is
that the typical welfare agency at the state level is responsible
for programs from three of HHS's four operating divisions: the
Title XX program and most other programs from OHDS, the
Medicaid program for HCFA, and the AFDC program from
SSA.

Although many federal programs pass directly to local
entities, increasing federal health and human service dollars pass
through states first. The Reagan administration block grants
accentuate this trend. The reason states were bypassed initially
was the suspicion of states' ability to solve human service
problems. In the mental health area, federal dollars were originally targeted to local community mental health organizations.
The concern was that if states gained control over federal
dollars, they would simply put these funds into their state
psychiatric hospital system rather than develop community-
based care systems. Though they may have been appropriate for
the time, such strategies failed to acknowledge the tremendous
budgets states controlled in the mental health area. For example, the New York Department of Mental Hygiene has an annual
mental health budget larger than the entire federal alcohol, drug
abuse and mental health appropriation. Another salient characteristic of state governments is a movement away from providing services directly. Instead, like their federal counterparts,
the states are increasing their planning, funding, and monitoring
of services rather than providing them directly. This trend is
continuing to the local level as well.

The Local Level

The shape of services at the local level is determined largely
by the relationship of cities and counties to the state. In strong
state-controlled (as opposed to county-controlled) states, it is
the state that provides most services, often directly. Where

counties are strong, they tend to operate directly or to supervise the operation of local services. In most counties it is possible to find a mix of locally controlled but federally funded services. Whether a service is state or locally operated, all three levels of government may provide funding.

PROGRAM FUNDING OPTIONS

Categorical Programs

Of the three basic federal mechanisms for operating programs—categorical, block, and entitlement—categorical programs are the greatest in number. They proliferated significantly during the "great society" era under President Johnson. During his tenure, Congress enacted approximately 240 such programs. The Community Mental Health Center program (CMHC) was among them. Categorical programs continued to grow, even through the consolidations of "new federalism" under Presidents Nixon and Ford. During that period, another 120 new categorical programs were enacted. As of 1980, approximately 500 categorical programs existed.

These programs assume the necessity for federal government intervention on behalf of special groups (the mentally retarded) or to provide special services (mental health) where existing efforts have been insufficient. Categorical programs guarantee that the needs of special populations will be addressed through federal presence and resources. Categorical programs have a special stimulus impact, not only through the dollars and activities they directly provide but also by their impact on other resources, particularly entitlement programs such as Title XIX or XX. Frequently, categorical programs for the underserved contain legal and other advocacy services directed toward fundamental structural reform on behalf of its interest group.

Categorical programs focus on nationally identified needs and have an impact on all the states. These programs tend to create stable administrative structures and powerful constituencies, both of which can become resistant to change over time. Categorical programs tend to have strong accountability and program quality demands to document the achievement of federal goals. When carried to extreme, these features became extremely grating to state and local officials and provide ammunition for those arguing for simplification, effectiveness, and efficiency. Often noted for its conservatism, Virginia recently withdrew from the federal Developmental Disability program, noting that costs exceeded the federal grant allocation for implementing just one provision of the grant, the requirement for a comprehensive evaluation system.

The Community Mental Health Center (CHMC) program is an excellent example of categorical funding. It was enacted in the early 1960s as a federal-local partnership, with only a minimal role for state governments which were perceived as the cause of many difficulties. It was the states which operated the custodial state psychiatric hospitals and which appeared to be committed to long-term care institutions. CMHC reformers argued that treatment in such facilities was more profoundly disabling than the factors which brought persons into treatment in the first place. The program was boldly conceived as the means to eradicate mental illness by locating new mental health service delivery organizations in communities across the country and ultimately closing the state psychiatric hospitals. Since its inception, the CMHC program has initiated almost half the 1500 CMHCs originally thought necessary to cover the country. Federal support has totalled almost $1.8 billion since 1977 (National Institute of Mental Health, 1977).

CMHCs received federal dollars over eight years, typically starting at 90 percent and declining to 10 or 20 percent. It was assumed at the start that national health insurance would be enacted, making mental health services universally available to all citizens. However, national health insurance was not enacted, although it was approached with Medicare and Medicaid, both of which set severe benefit limits on mental health coverage. Title XX failed to fill the coffers of CHMCs as federal funds declined. Ironically, the state mental health agencies which were almost totally bypassed in the design of the program have picked up the costs of CMHC services for public clients.

The CHMC program is funded from the health side of HHS and is administered by a "health institute," the National Institute of Mental Health, the directors of which have always been drawn from the ranks of psychiatry. Its original goal to eradicate mental illness is couched in epidemiological terms, and five of its core services are defined in medical terms (inpatient, outpatient, partial hospitalization, screening, and emergency services). Though health-oriented in these respects, it has a strong community focus, requiring a local citizen board and links to other provider groups within the community. It also has a strong social science, social change emphasis, resulting in the community being perceived as the legitimate subject of intervention or of mental health treatment.

The CMHC program has all the hallmarks of a categorical program. It provides a specialized service to a special group of persons. It has a national constituency, including the National Council of Community Mental Health Centers, which is a vocal and effective advocate on Capitol Hill. It has had a stable administrative structure at the federal level, and contains strong accountability provisions supplementing the numerous rules and regulations regarding the administration of CMHCs. Although at the organizational level there has been coordination and collaboration between CHMCs and other local providers, the CMHC program has remained largely insular.

Block Grants

Block grants are the antithesis of categorical programs. They tend to be the response of Republican administrations to the profusion of categorical programs inaugurated by prior Democratic administrations. Block grants consolidate categorical programs, combine and broaden their purposes, reduce their accountability demands, and transfer large amounts of federal funds directly to state and local government. They assume less need for federal oversight and allow the translation of federal dollars into programs by state and local officials within a broad framework of goals and purposes. Block grant advocates argue that state and local governments are closer to people in need and therefore know better how and where to target resources. The consolidation and simplification of the block grant approach is usually provided as a basis for reducing overall budgets.

Title XX is the section most recently passed of the Social Security Act (1974) and the major social services title. Its enactment separated social service functions from income transfer functions. The federal government first provided matching funds for social service activities in the 1950s. In the 1960s, the matching rate was increased to 75 percent to stimulate states to develop rehabilitation programs to help welfare recipients become reemployed. In 1968, the federal government attempted to refocus the program toward employment-specific purposes rather than the broader purposes of self-sufficiency and self-support. The attempt was unsuccessful in curtailing the purpose or scope of the program.

Social Security welfare programs allowed for open-ended funding. Realizing the benefit of transferring their previously unmatched social service dollars into dollars matched three for one by the federal government, the states' claims for federal matching grew 500 percent between 1967 and 1972. This phenomenal growth led Congress to place an authorization ceiling, or cap, of $2.5 billion on the program in 1972. The Title XX program has been capped since its inception, although the ceiling increased from $2.7 in 1979 to $2.9 in 1980. Thus, the impact of inflation on the program has been severe. Estimates are that if Title XX grew at the rate of inflation since 1974, it would purchase $4.7 billion in 1980 instead of the $2.9 billion authorized (U.S. Department of Health, Education and Welfare, 1980).

An attempt was made in the early 1970s to regulate the program to keep social services focused on the poor. However, because of political pressure from many constituencies, these regulations were never implemented. Instead, the administration decided to separate income transfer from service functions, making the service funds available to the states as a block grant, distributed according to population.

As a block grant, Title XX is a flexible program, especially when compared to the categorical approach. Its flexibility is reflected by its purposes. By law, states can direct federal resources to any social services which meet five broad goals:

— achieving or maintaining economic self-support;

— achieving or maintaining personal and social self-sufficiency;

— reducing inappropriate institutional care by providing alternative community or home care;

— preventing or reducing abuse, neglect, or exploitation of children or adults and strengthening families; and

— securing admission for institutional care when other alternatives are inappropriate, or providing services in institutions.

Under this goal structure of Title XX, each state has the flexibility to deliver whatever services it believes are appropriate. The national Title XX office compiles a list of over 1100 reported services, arranged in 39 broad categories (U.S. Department of Health, Education and Welfare, 1979). In addition, states have the flexibility to deliver some services in one county and other services in another county.

The Title XX program has only a few restrictions. Like Medicaid, it is targeted to categorically needy persons. At least 50 percent of Title XX funds must go to AFDC or SSI recipients and to persons eligible for Medicaid, the so-called medically needy. This is the major provision to keep the program targeted to the poor. Title XX legislation specifically excludes funding for medical or remedial care. An exception to this restriction is provided for cases where such care is an "integral but subordinate" part of a funded service. Also, Title XX funds may be used only if Medicaid and Medicare are not available to the individual.

Although Title XX does not fund medical care directly, except as noted above, it provides the means for linking health and social services. One of the essential elements in service integration efforts is case management. This service allows for comprehensive assessment of need, the capacity to link a person to needed services, and to follow the case, especially when more than one provider is involved. Case management provides a crucial linkage function, and Title XX pays for case management services. In fact, case management is the fifteenth largest service funded under Title XX, totaling approximately $60 million in 1978. Some of the larger and better-developed states funding case management services include Florida, Illinois, Massachusetts, New Jersey, Pennsylvania, and Texas (Office of Human Development Services, 1980).

Entitlement Programs

Entitlement programs differ from categorical or block grants. They are based on the concept of citizens' entitlements to certain services, such as health care for the poor or the elderly. The Food Stamp, Unemployment Compensation, Old Age, Survivors and Disability Insurance, AFDC, Medicare, and Medicaid programs exemplify the entitlement approach. They tend to be permanent in nature, large in terms of the number of persons covered, and expensive. Their growth is difficult to control because they are often appropriated on an open-ended basis, which means that annual costs vary according to utilization.

Medicaid was enacted in the mid-1960s as a way of providing basic health services for the poor. Its passage was heralded as an initial step toward universal national health insurance. Medicaid has its roots in the welfare sector and automatically makes AFDC and SSI recipients eligible for services as categorically needy persons. States must cover a basic range of health services for the categorically needy, including physician services, hospital inpatient and outpatient services, skilled nursing home care

for adults, health screening and treatment for children, labora-
tory and x-ray services, home health care for those entitled to
skilled nursing home care, nurse-midwife services, family planning, and rural health clinic services. A number of additional
services may be covered at the states' option.

Medicaid programs are designed and administered by the
states in accordance with federal requirements. The federal
government shares the costs of the program by matching state
expenditures at rates varying from 50 to 78 percent. By formula, higher matching rates are provided for states with low per
capita income. Overall, the federal share of Medicaid benefits is
about 56 percent. Forty-nine states (all but Arizona) and five
territories have Medicaid programs. States vary the amount,
duration, and scope of services offered; they may limit the days
of hospital care or number of physician visits covered. States
must meet specific federal requirements for hospitals and skilled
and intermediate care nursing homes, but may determine the
reimbursement rates for other services.

The fact that state welfare agencies administer Title XIX
programs has great appeal from a linkage perspective. However,
state welfare agencies typically determine eligibility for the
program, while state health departments establish payment
mechanisms and reimbursement rates and handle quality control aspects of the program. In doing so, health departments
utilize medical yardsticks and concepts, not social service ones,
and generally tend to maintain traditional autonomy and separation from the social services sector.

The growth of the Medicaid program has outstripped inflation by doubling in cost over the past five years. This rapid
growth may be explained partially by the increasing use of high
technology in routine health care practice. Another factor is the
institutional bias of the program. It reimburses care in an
institution but has strict limits on less costly home care and
office care procedures and treatments. This has been especially
troubling to many social care providers, who argue they can
provide similar results at less cost. A final factor in this growth
is that Medicaid is beginning to cover the costs of services that

traditionally have been social service costs. A 1981 General Accounting Office (GAO) survey found services normally funded under Title XX being transferred to Medicaid in amounts totaling $20 million annually.

Because Medicaid is a reimbursement program based on a fee-for-service model of medical practice, it does not actively encourage linkage. It merely buys certain types of services. There is no incentive to provide preventive services (which are not reimbursed) or to refer a client for treatment. In addition, many physicians point out that Medicaid reimbursements are inadequate and untimely. On the other extreme are physicians who treat only Medicaid-eligible patients. Referred to as "medicaid mills," such practices respond to the fiscal incentive to provide most of those services which are reimbursable to every patient.

LINKAGE THEORY AND THE
HUMAN SERVICE INTEGRATION MOVEMENT

Theory of Interorganizational Linkages

Linkages are generated by organizations' need to change, survive, and grow in response to the environment. Warren (1967) and Emery and Trist (1965) developed a field theory of organizations and typologies of environments in which organizations find themselves. When their environment is complex, turbulent, and rapidly changing, the potential for developing linkage diminishes because of the risk and difficulty in developing and maintaining the linkage. By the same token, when the environment is too predictable or too stagnant, there is little incentive for reestablishing or modifying one's interorganizational boundaries.

Linkages are also affected by the properties of organizations. Organizations with similar goals, values, size, and functions are likely to form linkages. In addition, positive prior experiences, support from a higher auspice, and a voluntary basis for entering into agreement facilitate linkage (Litwak, 1970). Organizations which have great resources and control over those resources are the least likely to form linkages with organizations with limited resources and control.

Four additional factors of organizations affect linkage: interdependence, awareness of that interdependence, standardized expressions of that interdependence (such as written rules of organizational behavior), and the number of organizations involved. A state of interdependence is a minimum condition for any linkage: The greater the degree of recognition of the interdependence, the stronger the linkage. The latter two characteristics—standardization and numbers—have to do with the linkage itself. Litwak argues that little standardization leads to no coordination, while too much standardization produces rules and coercion. As the number of organizations involved in linkage grows, so do the rules, until at some point coordination falls apart (Litwak, 1970).

Linkages between organizations are stronger when there is reciprocity and cooperation, when there is a mutual exchange of feedback and when benefits to the participants are relatively equal. Well-organized and coordinated organizations with great capacity for information-processing and distribution are better candidates for linkage. In addition, successful linkages tend to be implemented gradually, through a bargaining strategy, rather than a highly managed and authoritarian approach. Frequent and regular exchanges of information over short distances produce more successful linkages. When applied to human service settings, this suggests that linkage is difficult, since most human service programs are funded on an annual basis and exist in a political environment where leadership changes regularly.

Human Services Integration

The theory on interorganizational linkages was utilized by human service integration advocates as part of the technology to achieve their goals. The human services integration "movement" is a broad phenomenon. It spans the political philosophy of "new federalism," several federal demonstrations (including the Comprehensive Services Delivery project and the Services Integration Target of Opportunity [SITO] projects), and state and local government efforts to rationalize and manage an increasingly complex array of federal programs in the health and human services arena.

Human service integration has as its state level manifestation "umbrella" organizations, often known as departments of human services. These human service umbrellas cover many separate "categorical" programs. Their primary goal is more rational and effective policy and programmatic integration in the human services. As a local service delivery entity, human services integration typically refers to multiservice centers in which a variety of health, personal social service, welfare, and sometimes educational services are located together. At the level of local government, human service integration is typically a process of administration which involves developing service system characteristics, including

- common service areas,
- co-located services,
- joint core services,
- case planning,
- case management,
- joint management services, and
- common eligibility.

Service integration as a federal human service intervention strategy is the foil to categorization. It is the attempt to fold categorical programs into block grants. The proponents of integration cite management deficiencies in categorical programs: strong accountability demands, overlapping jurisdictions, lengthy applications, auditing requirements and procedures, and the difficulty of meeting increasing coordination requirements. They point to the efficiencies and cost-saving potential of consolidation and integration. They argue that the need for targeted (categorical) approaches have outlived their usefulness and that guarantees for special populations can be provided by the state government as well as by the federal government.

Service integration tends to be associated with a political philosophy that state control should replace federal control. Its appeal to state officials lies partly in the recognition that federal dollars in a specific program area may represent only a small portion of the total funds—sometimes almost exclusively state funds—expended on behalf of a population. Integration also tends to be associated with budget reductions, decentralization of authority, and reorganization of government bureaucracies. Agranoff (1979) views human services integration as a process to organize, make relevant, and rationalize the complexities of administering human services. Human service integration involves structuring and maximizing individual organizational linkages into an integrated system which redefines every health and social service as having a human services dimension. Human services integration is a sustained effort to break down rigid organizational boundaries and maximize the relationships among human service organizations.

Proponents of service integration were often welfare administrators concerned with income payments and work requirements. They formulated arguments from administrative science rather than medical or social science. Their experiences are important because they enlighten the structural and administrative dimensions of linkage between service networks. If the rationale for the linkage between health and personal social services is to match needs more fully with a more comprehensive range of services, then the argument for service integration has potentially greater merit, for its goal is to match need with the most complete range of services.

LINKAGES BETWEEN SYSTEMS: OBSTACLES AND OPPORTUNITIES

This section describes some of the major obstacles to and opportunities for linkage to occur in the present system of health and personal social services. The discussion is organized by level of government. In addition to defining the executive and administrative issues, it also treats legislative issues affecting health, mental health, and social service linkage. Finally, it draws principles from human services integration and CMHC experiences at each level of government.

Discussing only the CMHC and human services integration experiences in linking health and social services does not suggest the lack of other experiences and models of linkage. One could argue that the pervasiveness of social service units within general hospitals is the oldest and perhaps most nearly paradigmatic linkage between health and social services (Falck, 1978).

In the private sector, the joint practice of physicians and social workers appears to be rising. Often such physicians stress family practice, while the social workers may specialize in children's diseases, such as learning disabilities, or in family-centered practice and therapy. This type of linkage appears to occur only in the most favorable climate, where there are large numbers of persons who have private insurance programs with broad coverage. However, this linkage suggests potential future directions. Other examples of linkage may be found in industrial settings, schools, drug programs, and alcohol treatment settings where medical and social workers practice in concert.

Federal-Level Linkages

Legislative, executive, and administrative actions at the federal level may have a considerable impact on the linkage of health and human services. Such actions are not well described in the literature on linkage and integration, which generally focuses on linkages between local-level organizations and has meaning at the federal level only by implication. This holds true for much of the literature on human service integration, which focuses primarily on state and local situations. This section describes the effect and contribution of various federal activities related to health and social service linkages.

Legislative Factors

The federal legislative process can either hinder or facilitate service integration and linkage. This fact is recognized clearly by the Reagan administration, which has the consolidation of federal categorical assistance programs as one of its major agenda items. The White House Office of Management and Budget originally proposed consolidating over 40 categorical programs in the health and social services into one block grant whose funding level would be reduced by 25 percent. However, because of the many congressional committees with jurisdiction over these 40 programs and the likelihood that these committees would be unwilling to give up the power associated with authorizing 40 separate programs (totaling several billion dollars), the single block grant strategy was rejected. Instead, the administration proposed four separate block grants, each of which contained programs within the jurisdictions of separate committees. It was believed that the smaller blocks could be achieved legislatively, while one separate block had little chance for enactment.

The arguments for block grants generally stressed budget, control, and efficiency issues. It had little to do with whether health and social services should be more closely integrated at the delivery level. However, had the Office of Management and Budget proposal been successful, the impact across health and human service structures would have been profound. Currently, health and social services are in separate block grants. This experience suggests that the committee structure in Congress and the federal legislative process generally do not lend themselves to integrating health and social services.

Executive/Administrative Factors

The potential for facilitating or impeding linkage at the administrative level is not as dramatic or far-reaching as in the legislative arena. However, the potential of a cabinet officer and a federal department to promote linkage and greater policy integration is considerable.

The Secretary of Health and Human Services has eight staff divisions, in addition to the four operating divisions, which manage the 140,000-employee department. Though the staff divisions tend to be small when compared to the relative baronies of the four operating divisions described earlier, they do include several thousand staff. The potential for policy integration must be implemented through the staff divisions, for each operating division has its own separate agenda and priorities. Although assistant secretaries are appointed by and serve the secretary, they rapidly become captives of their staff and the interests of their constituencies. Turf struggles among the operating divisions are legion.

Another difficulty in achieving intradepartmental integration is that the structure of many of the staff divisions parallels that of the operating divisions. Staff offices tend to have health analysts and social service analysts, income transfer experts and health care financing experts. Clearly, the complexity of the issues contributes to such specialization. Only at the level immediately below the assistant secretaries do these separate areas of substance generally merge. Occasionally, cross-cutting initiatives are generated by operating divisions. More often, they come from the staff divisions, primarily the Office of the Assistant Secretary for Planning and Evaluation. These cross-cutting initiatives require forceful executive leadership, and their fate is notoriously poor. By the time the results of a demonstration are received, executive leadership has changed and compelling interest in these policy issues has waned.

Another impediment to health and social service linkage is the fact that the social services are organized around target groups, while the Public Health Service programs are organized around health providers. This structure sets up a competitive situation and maintains a latent tension between various program components for legitimacy and funding.

Functional Versus Targeted Services

A number of basic human service program design considerations fundamentally affect the structure of services and the ability to link services. One of these is the decision to structure services by function or to target to need. The human service integration approach is a functional approach to system design, while categorical programs represent the targeted approach. This chapter has described some of the arguments for and tensions in either approach. However, several observations illustrate the considerations federal planners and legislators may take into account in making basic program design decisions.

Structuring on a functional basis is likely to result when resource constraints are severe, for such a structure does not make various groups compete for resources. However, functional structures do not always provide services equally for all groups. They are likely to be challenged over time by the less well-served, to the degree that such groups can organize successfully to make their needs and demands felt. Differing components of the service delivery system perceive structural strategies in different ways. To the consumer of services, a functional structure appears fragmented. A consumer must seek health services from one provider, social services from another, and income support from still another. On the other hand, the targeted structure appears fragmented to the provider. For example, the 1978 federal amendments required a CMHC to provide services for the special needs of children, minorities, and the chronically mentally ill, in addition to already mandated services.

From the federal perspective, a flexible response to a problem is affected greatly by how state and local governments and the private sector have responded to the problem in the past. To the extent that they have demonstrated success and sophistication, a more flexible response is appropriate. To the extent the traditional delivery system and its existing institutions have been unsuccessful or have not dealt with the problem, a more targeted approach may be appropriate.

Another federal concern relates to options for solutions to problems. It is logical to restrict programs to a proven technology or approach when it is clear that such technology is effective. When it is not clear what works, flexibility in the delivery response is more appropriate. As a case in point, there is greater knowledge about what works in helping the handicapped return to work than is known about the ways to prevent child abuse.

Clearly, the health and personal social service system in the United States gives the appearance of being a highly fragmented system. Theories of public administration view this as an evil to be ameliorated because of the potential gaps or duplication in service and perceived waste. The human services integration efforts stem from such notions. However, there are arguments for a fragmented service delivery system. One argument is the potentially greater choice offered to individuals through such a system. A fragmented system allows consumers to select those services or practitioners which are most suitable to or effective for their specific needs. Since health and personal social services, such as child care or psychotherapy, are intensely personal experiences, the freedom to choose may be among the key factors in successful outcome.

Another argument is that fragmentation provides greater financial flexibility for state and local government to select the various programs required to provide comprehensive services. A powerful financial incentive exists for planners to shift social services into the health care sector (with its open-ended Medicaid funding) when the state reaches its Title XX ceiling. A final argument for fragmentation is that there has been relatively greater political success in initiating new federal programs targeted at specific populations and problems than in seeking general increases in overall social services funding. The Title XX ceiling, which only recently was authorized to increase beyond $2.5 billion, is a case in point. Thus, a more rationalized and integrated system may result in fewer services or service options for those in need.

Federal-Level Linkage Concerns for
Community Mental Health Centers

The CMHC program does not have the full set of organizational linkages anticipated by its supporters. The background section of this chapter described how the CMHC funding formula for eight years of declining federal support was predicated on passage of a national health insurance. However, only the Medicaid and Medicare programs were enacted, neither of which covers the majority of the adult population. Even more problematic is the fact that both Medicare and Medicaid have severe limitations on their mental health benefits. Over the years, the National Institute of Mental Health has conducted numerous studies to convince their counterparts in the Health Care Financing Administration that mental health programs should be covered more generously. These efforts have been unsuccessful.

There has been greater potential for linkage between mental health and primary health care providers. From a federal perspective, the public primary care system is financed by the Health Services Administration. The organizational proximity of ADAMHA which administers the CHMC programs out of its National Institute of Mental Health to HSA, which administers primary care programs out of its Bureau of Community Health Services, may enhance this particular linkage. Other factors suggested by the literature on interorganizational relations are the fact that these two groups are both oriented toward provider groups, are in the nonprofit or public sector, support comprehensive service delivery models, and utilize multidisciplinary team models to deliver services.

The CMHC program has not linked its efforts as a whole with efforts in the social services sector. This may be explained in part by its organization within the health side of HHS, the fact that it has health in its title, and because of the relative dominance of psychiatrists within NIMH. It also may be explained by the fact that social service programs are structured around populations, as opposed to organizations, as well as the fact that OHDS is distant organizationally from NIMH. In addition, it has its roots in the welfare sector. Typically, poor persons have stigmatized enough for being poor without the additional stigma of having emotional problems. The double stigma is exacerbated further by the extensive use of verbal therapies in the mental health field. Although these have been effective with middle-class persons, they tend to have less relevance and effectiveness with poor persons.

Some state mental health agencies have been successful in negotiating agreements with the Title XX agency to use resources for the mental health needs of their clients. This may be explained by the proximity of state Title XX and state mental health agencies. However, it is not clear that many federally funded CHMCs have tapped these resources, even though the government has published a resource handbook on Title XX for use by alcohol, drug abuse and mental health agencies (Alcohol, Drug Abuse and Mental Health Administration, 1979).

Federal-Level Human Service Integration

Human service integration efforts at the federal level were inaugurated primarily through the Services Integration Targets of Opportunity (SITO) projects in the early 1970s (Agranoff, 1979). Like most federal demonstration efforts, SITO projects provided resources to states and localities to integrate services without a comparable federal effort to accomplish similar objectives jointly among the many parts of the federal bureaucracy. Other integrative federal demonstration efforts, among them the Community Support Program demonstrations launched by the National Institute of Mental Health, theorized that similar risk-taking by the federal government is necessary to achieve better outcomes in these reform efforts (TenHoor, 1980). Both horizontal and vertical integration at all levels of government is necessary for health and mental health programs to produce meaningful change for clients. Thus, when hidden federal policy or procedural difficulties impede achievement of project objectives at the state or local level, there is a mechanism in place to resolve such difficulties. It is a design failure when a more active federal role in human service integration efforts is precluded. This is especially valid since much of what generated human service integration was the problems created by federal programs in the first place. Such a mechanism was not in place in the SITO demonstrations. Providing federal funds within a conceptual framework was not sufficient to resolve the problem (Turner and TenHoor, 1978).

The major federal-level question to be asked of human service integration as a service delivery strategy is, "Did it work?" Many observers raise questions, but a thorough and adequate evaluation is not available. Hugebock (1979) notes the need for rigorous research of ongoing experiences. Agranoff (1979) views human services integration as a process which will continue as long as service delivery systems are complex and managers remain committed to making them more effective. Ross (1981) views human service integration as advantageous for some, such as governors, heads of general purpose government and generalist administrators, and as undesirable for special populations, consumers, and professionals.

State-Level Legislative Issues

In almost any state, the governor is the key person to make decisions regarding service linkage and the organization and flow of federal funds. However, increasingly legislators are challenging gubernatorial authority in these areas, making organizational change and linkage more difficult by involving more power brokers. Just as the federal legislature plays a crucial role in determining the degree of linkage or integration of health and social services, so the state legislature also plays a key role. It would probably be impossible to undertake any fundamental reorganization within a state without legislative cooperation, even though reorganization of administrative bureaucracies is clearly an executive prerogative.

However, the budget formulation process gives state legislators the opportunity to challenge the power of governors.

Historically, legislators have given a rubber stamp to governors and their cabinet officials in accepting federal funds. But since federal funds play such a key role in state budgets, state legislatures are increasingly demanding approval of the acceptance of federal funds and requiring closer accounting of their use. The concern of legislators stems from such classic examples as the CMHC program, in which federal funds declined over an eight-year period. The federal CMHC grants induced states to operate new, community-based mental health centers to serve populations never before served. But after eight years, this program left states with the bill for ongoing operations.

Even more dramatic than the case of cutbacks through declining federal grants are the administration's proposed block grants, a program supported by many governors. The block grant concept shifts power that previously resided with the federal government to the states. However, it will cut by 25 percent the federal funding for those services. Although efficiencies can be realized through reduced regulation and requirements, such efficiencies are no doubt less than 15 percent. Considering both inflation and real funding reductions, the states may receive considerable pressure from those constituencies whose services must ultimately be cut. In many cases, the programs included in the block grants are programs that few states would have initiated without a federal partnership.

The changing nature of intergovernmental relations between the state and federal level, and the relatively bigger stakes involved in state-level politics, suggests that legislators will be playing a larger role in policymaking. Their views will determine whether more categorical or more integrated service systems result from the shifts taking place.

State-Level Human Services Integration Experience

Human service integration as a strategy has great significance at the state level. It is typically at this level that the contradictions of a complex and fragmented delivery system are first apparent. State agencies become aware of differential payments for comparable service, such as a $25 payment for a home health service visit under Medicaid as compared to an $8 per visit reimbursement for a comparable homemaker service under Title XX.

Ross (1981) indicates that 28 states have created umbrella organizations comprising 10 or more federal programs in the past decade. Four states which invested heavily in service integration are Florida, Washington, Minnesota, and Georgia. Among these states, Minnesota has been the most successful. It is a state with strong county government and a correspondingly weak state government. Welfare functions are state supervised and county administered. In addition, heavy county financing is involved. The Minnesota experience was based initially on SITO project funding. It also was built on the passage of enabling legislation at the state level in 1973. This permitted the creation of a county human services board to manage and coordinate public health, mental health, welfare, and corrections functions. Categorical interests were diffused by allowing program categories to remain relatively intact. With recognized success in several counties, the basic philosophy of the Minnesota experience builds on the local experience and recognizes that integration is a process which must achieve consensus among local officials, providers, service workers, and other interest groups. Once consensus is established, the integrative links, such as case management systems, can be established.

The state of Washington made a similar investment in human service integration with the creation of its Department of Social and Health Services. Certain management functions were centralized in the department with positive results, including overall planning, budgeting, and purchase of service functions. In addition, Washington attempted to regionalize the supervision of services and to integrate field operations. However, its local service integration demonstrations, particularly in Seattle and Bremerton, when compared to the control site in Bellingham, had no better success in terms of appropriateness, accessibility, cost, or effectiveness of services. The lack of success resulted in the cessation of the statewide integration attempt. The Bremerton multiservice center closed. Although the umbrella agency at the state level remains, service integration attempts have ceased (Washington State Department of Social and Health Services, 1975).

The state of Georgia had a similar experience. It found that central administrative consolidation was far easier to achieve than changing the delivery of services in the field. Although its efforts to achieve decentralization and integration went farther and lasted longer than those in Washington, the results seem to have been the same.

Local-Level Linkages and Service Issues

It is as difficult to define the impact of human service integration at the local level as it is at the state level. Its major contribution appears to be in systems improvement and administrative areas, rather than in client impact. A large number of local-level experiences are summarized in "Multi-Service Centers, Co-Location and Service Integration" (U.S. Department of Health, Education and Welfare, 1977). These descriptions contain examples of increased linkages, improved coordination between agencies, and greater system clarity; but without additional evaluative research, it is difficult to substantiate contributions.

Henton (1975) reviewed 35 integration projects to determine the factors facilitating linkage among service providers. He found that linkage was more readily achieved in small, rural environments than in large, urban ones, a factor seemingly explained by greater field complexity in urban environments. He also found that projects involving state human service agencies operating at the local level were more successful than projects which mandated linkage from the state level to local governments. This finding reinforces the concept that voluntary linkage tends to be achieved more readily than mandated linkage. Local general purpose governments with a similar "top down" management approach were not successful in establishing linkages. Finally, Henton found that projects employing technical planning strategies were less successful in achieving linkages than those which employ political bargaining strategies.

There are professional, educational, and consumer dimensions to human service integration. The impact on professionals is significant, since service integration sets up a tension and competition between generalists and specialists. Human services integration problems are primarily administrative and management problems which specialists and clinicians are not trained to solve. Systems theory and management provide the knowledge base needed for services integration. Specialists are perceived as committed to maintenance and growth not only in the services they administer but also in their professional bureaucracies. They are concerned with client outcomes and improved technology. Human service advocates seek to replace specialists with generalist managers who are committed primarily to management rather than service values. A layer of generalist suppervision of specialist operating units is a desired outcome.

The dimension of education is also crucial. To facilitate integration projects, many types of training efforts have been launched. Roessler and Mach (1975) reviewed the literature on strategies for effecting interagency linkages. They identified three mechanisms for improving attitudes toward coordination: (a) the development of domain consensus among participating organizations, or agreement regarding the appropriate role and scope of an organization's activities; (b) ideological consensus, or agreement regarding the nature of tasks and appropriate approaches to those tasks; (c) interorganizational evaluation consensus, or the agreement among staff in one organization of the value of the contribution of staff in another organization.

Service integration also has a special impact on consumers, who, like professionals, experience a loss of power and influence in an integrated system. It is largely the force of special interest groups that sustains categorical programs, encouraging their passage and reauthorization by Congress. In an integrated system, consumer groups must compete with one another for generic services, such as health care. They have no unique set of providers, bureaucrats, and legislators to lobby for special consideration or increased appropriations.

Local CMHC and Primary Health Care Relationships

The relationships of health and mental health have been somewhat limited historically. The stigma associated with mental health contributed to its relative isolation from other fields. Lefkowitz and Andrulis (1981) refer to the problem of stigma in recommending policy directions for primary care providers serving women and children. They note that stigma may account for the infrequency of referrals from the primary care sector to mental health providers. They point out that physicians, because of their training, may feel competent to deal with mild mental health problems without other support, though they are unlikely to have had training to enable effective treatment.

Just as referrals to the mental health sector from the primary care sector are infrequent, referrals from the mental health sector to the primary health care sector also are infrequent. Mental health practitioners typically focus on remedial treatment, often avoiding issues of primary health and prevention. They tend to practice in specialty settings so that the opportunities for interaction with other health practitioners is limited. Another significant factor is that much of the training of both mental health professionals and primary health care providers does not stress the interactions between psychosocial factors and the disease process.

Lefkowitz and Andrulus point out the relatively greater capability of health maintenance organizations (HMOs) to form linkages with mental health providers. HMOs are oriented to the cost efficiencies of prevention. Incorporating mental health and other psychosocial services (such as drug and alcohol abuse services) within the HMO may reduce health care utilization. Like HMOs, public primary health care providers have a greater propensity for linkage with CMHCs because the public health providers are oriented to comprehensive services and are staffed with multidisciplinary teams.

CONCLUSION

It is clear from the many dimensions and manifestations of linkage that we are unlikely to achieve a fully integrated system of health and personal social service care in America. Both historically and presently, the health field is dominated by the private sector while the public sector dominates the social service delivery. This distinction, more than any other, tends to separate the systems in a fundamental way. However, under Title XX, more and more social services are being provided by nonprofit, private-sector providers. The growth of private, nonprofit organizations in the social service sector, particularly in the voluntary sector, increases the possibilities for social and medical practices to be integrated within a single organization, since there is a structure of private organizations through which to achieve collaboration. The trend toward the growth of nonprofit, private organizations is likely to continue because of provisions in the Title XX program which allow states to purchase services from them.

The turbulence that the new administration's block grant concept will cause in the human services environment is likely to inhibit organizational linkage efforts for the short term. However, if it interprets new federalism as the Nixon administration did, the Reagan administration will seek ways to advance integrated service systems. In addition, it is committed to bringing the public and private sectors into closer collaboration. These factors suggest an environment in which health and social service providers will be in closer contact, and one in which the possibilities for linkage efforts are very real indeed. It is a time in which states will have the opportunity to link their health and social services systems more closely, if they so choose.

REFERENCES

AGRANOFF, R. (1979) Dimensions of Services Integration. DHEW Publication No. 13. Rockville, Maryland, April.
Alcohol, Drug Abuse and Mental Health Administration (1978) Title XX Handbook for Alcohol, Drug Abuse and Mental Health Programs. Rockville, Maryland.

AMADIO, J. B. (1976) Integrating Human Services: An Evaluation of the Jackson County Integrated Human Services Delivery Project. Murphysboro, IL: Jackson County Health Department, September.

BROSKOWSKI, A. (1980) Evaluation of the Primary Health Care Project—Community Mental Health Center Linkage Initiative. Executive Summary, September.

DeJONG, G. (1977) "Interfacing national health insurance and income maintenance: why health and welfare reform go together." Journal of Health Politics Policy and the Law 1, 4: 405-432.

EMERY, S. E. and E. L. TRIST (1965) "The causal texture of organizational environments." Human Relations 18 (February).

FALCK, H. S. (1978) "Social work in health settings." Social Work in Health Care 3, 4.

HENTON, D. (1975) Feasibility of Services Integration. Washington, DC: Office of the Assistant Secretary for Planning and Evaluation, May.

HUGEBOK, B. R. (1979) "Local human service delivery: the integration imperative." Public Administration Review (November): 575-582.

Inspector General of the Department of Health and Human Services (1981) Title XX Service Delivery Assessment. Washington, D.C.

JONES, K. and T. VISCHI (1979) "Impact of alcohol, drug abuse and mental health treatment on medical care utilization: a review of the research literature." Medical Care 17.

KEARNEY, C. P. and E. A. VANDER PUTTERN [eds.] (1979) Grants Consolidation: A New Balance in Federal Aid to Schools. Washington, DC: Institute for Educational Leadership, George Washington University, August.

LEFKOWITZ, B. and D. ANDRULIS (1981) The Organization of Primary Health and Health-Related Preventive Psychosocial and Support Services for Children and Pregnant Women. Background Paper for the Select Panel for the Promotion of Child Health. Washington, DC: Assistant Secretary for Planning and Evaluation for the Department of Health and Human Services.

LITWAK, E. (1970) "Towards the theory and practice of coordination between formal organizations," in W. R. Rosengren and M. Lefton (eds.) Organizations and Clients. Columbus, OH: Charles E. Merrill.

LOVETT, J. B. (1973) New Patterns for the Administration of Health and Social Services in Rockland County. New York: Rockland County Department of General and Fiscal Services, September.

National Institute of Mental Health (1977) Directory of Federally Funded Community Mental Health Centers. Rockville, Maryland.

Office of Human Development Services (1980) Title XX Secretarial Program Review. Washington, D.C.

ROESSLER, R. and G. MACK (1975) Strategies for Inter-Agency Linkages: A Literature Review. Fayetteville: Arkansas Rehabilitation and Research and Training Center, November.

ROSS, E. C. (1981) "Preparing for federal grant consolidation: a reexamination and search for affiliate guidance." Word From Washington 10, 2 (February).

San Jose State University Joint Center for Human Services Development (1976) Integration of Services is a Process, Not a Product. San Francisco, California.

TENHOOR, W. J. (1980) "National developments in rehabilitation: a National Institute of Mental Health perspective." Rehabilitation Counseling Bulletin 24, 1.

TURNER, J. C. and W. J. TENHOOR (1978) "The NIMH Community Support Program: pilot approach to a needed social reform." Schizophrenia Bulletin 4: 319-349.

U.S. Department of Health, Education and Welfare (1980) Implementation of the Title XX Social Services Programs: A Report to Congress. Washington, D.C.

——— (1979) Annual Report to Congress on the Title XX Social Services Program. Washington, D.C.

——— (1977) Project Share. Human Services Bibliography Series. Multi-Service Centers. Co-Location and Services Integration. Rockville, Maryland, December.

U.S. General Accounting Office (1981) Intertitle Transfers—A Way for States to Increase Federal Funding for Social Services (HRD-81-166). Washington, D.C., July 10.

U.S. Senate Committee on Government Affairs (1980) Report to Accompany S. 878, The Federal Assistance Reform Act of 1980. Washington, DC: Government Printing Office, September 19.

Washington State Department of Social and Health Services (1975) Integrated Service Delivery Report. Olympia, Washington.

WARREN, R. L. (1967) "The interorganizational field as a focus for investigation." Administrative Science Quarterly 12 (December).

3

DENMARK

ERIC HOLST and HIROBUMI ITO

This chapter discusses the development of and interaction between health and social services in Denmark. Initially, there will be a review of the history and organizational structure of the Danish system. In later sections, emphasis is given to the role of the social worker and the medical profession, whose interaction is critical to linkages in the provision of services.

HISTORICAL TRENDS AND FINANCING PATTERNS

Public participation in health and social services is rooted in Danish traditions. Hospitals were the earliest public service. The Royal Decree of 1806 ordered counties and cities to establish hospitals using their own financial resources. This system basically remained until 1973, when the 14 counties and the metropolitan municipalities of Copenhagen and Frederiksberg took over the entire hospital system in Denmark. The single exception was the State University Hospital in Copenhagen, a research and teaching institution administered by the Ministry of Education.

In Denmark, primary health care has always been separate from hospital care. Primary health care includes the services of

AUTHORS' NOTE: *We would like to thank Thomas Kennedy for his English-language editorial advice.*

TABLE 3.1   Source of Financing of Health and Social Expenditure
             Denmark, 1969 and 1978 (percentages)

Year	Public	Employer	Employee	Total
1969	88.6	4.1	7.3	100.0
1978	92.5	6.0	1.5	100.0

SOURCE: Danmarks Statistik (1980: 78)

general practitioners and nonhospital specialists, and pharmaceutical and dental care. This system derives from the long
Danish history of well-organized sickness funds set up by private organizations (Ito, 1979). The Voluntary Health Insurance
Law (or Sickness Funds Law) first appeared in Denmark in
1892. Thirty percent of the expenditure was provided by the
state until 1973, when the entire system became publicly
financed. The 1898 Occupational Accident Insurance Law stipulated that premiums be paid entirely by employers. A voluntary Unemployment Insurance Law enacted in 1907 produced a system similar to the voluntary health insurance. Financing was largely from the insured, with some state subsidies.
Today, almost 90 percent of unemployment insurance expenditures are financed by state subsidies, although in principle the
system is still a voluntary one.

The social service system in Denmark started its development
in the 1890s. The Poor Law, which ultimately developed into
the current Social Assistance Law, was enacted in 1891. The
same year saw the enactment of the Old Age Assistance Act,
which, by 1922, evolved into the comprehensive Old Age Pension Law. These expenditures were financed by public means
and were administered by the local government.

In 1978, the total health and social expenditures in Denmark
reached 77,996 million crowns (approximately $13 billion),
approximately 25 percent of the GNP. There was a considerable
expansion of health and social expenditure during the 1970s. In
1969, this section comprised only 16 percent of the GNP. Table
3.1 documents this growth.

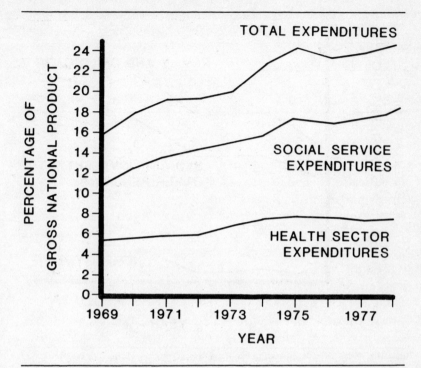

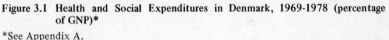

Figure 3.1 Health and Social Expenditures in Denmark, 1969-1978 (percentage
            of GNP)*

*See Appendix A.

Today, nearly all health and social services are publicly
financed, primarily through income taxes. This includes the
sickness cash benefits, occupational accident insurance, invalidity insurance, and unemployment insurance, all of which are
partly financed by employers and employees. Financing sources
are indicated in Figure 3.1.

The recent increase in public expenditures can be divided
into two periods: before and after 1973. The rapid expansion
between 1969 and 1973 was due to an increase in old age, early
retirement, and invalidity pensions as well as unemployment
benefits. After 1973, there was a major increase in sickness cash
benefits. Health expenditures also increased as the result of an

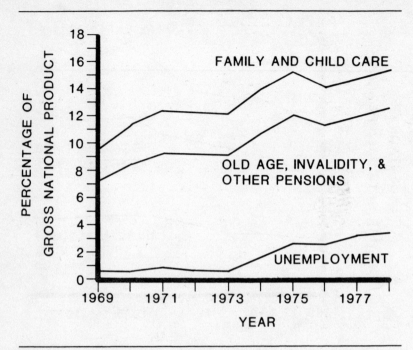

Figure 3.2   Social Expenditures in Denmark, 1969-1978 (percentage of GNP)*
*See Appendix B.

extension of public health insurance to replace the prior semi-compulsory health insurance system which financed primary health care services.

Figures 3.2 and 3.3 document the growth in Danish social services and health expenditures during this period. As can be seen, the social service sector expanded faster than the health sector. The rate of expenditure in the social sector increased from 10.3 percent in 1969 to 17.1 percent in 1979, while the rate of expenditure in the health sector increased from 5.4 percent to 7.8 percent during the same ten-year period.

ORGANIZATIONAL STRUCTURE AND DELIVERY SYSTEM

Two ministries are involved with the delivery of Danish health and social services. These are the Ministry of the Interior,

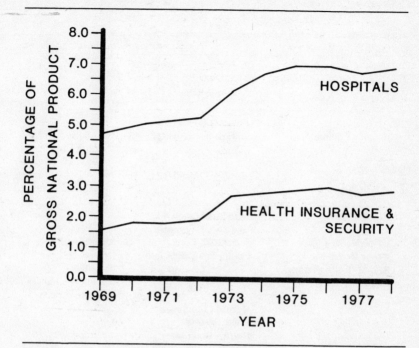

Figure 3.3   Health Expenditures in Denmark, 1969-1978 (percentage of GNP)*
*See Appendix C.

which is responsible for general health care, and the Ministry of
Social Affairs, which is responsible for primary health care as
well as social security and social services.

The National Board of Health in the Ministry of the Interior
is charged with the administration of health care resources—for
example, hospitals, physicians, dentists, nurses, medical statistics, and preventive medicine. It supervises the system of county
medical officers and public health nurses. Medical care services
are under the auspices of the Ministry of the Interior but are
mainly administered by the counties. There are 16 county
health care regions, including the municipalities of Copenhagen
and Frederiksberg, which for historical reasons have county
status. Since 1973, primary, general, and specialist medical care
as well as dental care have been financially administered by the
counties. Expenditure for these services as well as pharma-

TABLE 3.2   Organizational Structure of Health and Social Services
in Denmark

	Health Care in General	Social Services Including Public Health Security	
Central Level	*Ministry of the Interior* National Board of Health	*Ministry of Social Affairs* National Board of Social Services National Board of Social Security	
Regional Level	Hospital Committee Hospitals	*County Council* Coordinating Committee County Health and Social Services	Social and Primary Health Care Services Committee Health Security

Local Level	Home Nursing
	Public Health Nurse
	School Health Services
	Child Dental Care
		Municipal Council
		Health and Social Administration
		Social Assistance
		Family Counseling and
		  Economic Assistance
		Child Protection
		
		Medical Consultants
		Home Helpers
		Nursing Homes
		Care of the Physically
		  and Mentally Handicapped
			Cash Benefits for
			  Sickness
			Invalidity
			Family Allowances
			Old Age Pension

ceuticals accounted for 10 percent of county budgets in 1980.
Another 50 percent of county budgets were spent on hospitals.

Supervision of primary health care and rehabilitation services
is conducted by the Ministry of Social Affairs rather than the
Ministry of the Interior. The National Board of Social Security
deals with primary medical and dental services, sickness cash
benefits, rehabilitation, old age, early retirement, invalidity pensions, and occupational accident insurance. The National Board
of Social Services deals with social assistance and care for the
mentally and physically handicapped. These services are administered and delivered by the municipalities. Table 3.2 provides
an overview of the organizational structure for health and social
services in Denmark.

Such an organizational structure requires coordination of services at the local level. Before 1973, the health care financing system was based on health insurance; health care was administered and delivered by private medical professions. Since that time, the implementation of a comprehensive health system financed entirely from public funds means that the National Board of Social Security is responsible for overall supervision of a program whose goal is to provide health security to all Danish citizens. Today, funds are allocated to each county based on population, age structure, and other social variables. The primary health care service is still delivered by a private medical profession. Conflicts between a publicly administered and privately delivered health care system produce some of the difficulties in planning and coordinating health and social services at the local level.

Although both the hospitals and the primary health security are organized at the regional county level, these two sectors are governed and administered separately. Politically, the County Hospital Committee governs hospital matters and the County Social and Primary Health Care Services Committee oversees primary health security and other health and social services. Each committee has its own administrative organization. Although there is a Coordinating Committee, most policy decisions and daily administration are undertaken separately. This reflects the administrative diversity at the national level which makes it necessary for each committee to follow the regulations of, and submit plans to, different superordinate administrative bodies: The National Board of Health (Ministry of the Interior) for hospital matters and the National Board of Social Services and National Board of Social Security (Ministry of Social Affairs) for primary health security and other social services. Such organizational complexity presents obstacles, making the coordination of health and social services difficult (Gannik et al., 1976).

Professional linkages do occur despite these obstacles. "Medical consultants" serve to bridge the gap between the social and health sectors across municipal and county levels. These consultants are normally general practitioners; in some cases, they are sociomedical specialists who work primarily for the municipal Health and Social Administration in the social services sector. They investigate and give advice to municipal and county authorities in cases of disability and early retirement pension, alternative rehabilitation care, and child abuse and family problems (Holm, 1978; Pallesen, 1978). Although their function is to coordinate health and social services, the cases they handle are rather limited and their activity in the area of coordination is not policymaking, but purely medical.

OBSTACLES TO COORDINATION ACROSS ADMINISTRATIVE BOUNDARIES: THE CASE OF A SOCIOMEDICAL REHABILITATION CENTER FOR THE ELDERLY

Gentofte, a suburb of Copenhagen, provides a case study of the obstacles which influence the effective delivery of health and social service within the Danish system. Gentofte is a municipality in which 25 percent of the 68,000 inhabitants are over age 64. Recognizing the need for comprehensive service for the elderly, the municipality decided to establish a rehabilitation center. The organizational structure of health and social service provision accompanied by diverse laws and regulations from different ministries and national boards placed many barriers in the way of accomplishing this objective.

Struggles among the different national authorities surfaced. This was a great obstacle to the pursuit of the plan to establish the Tranehaven Rehabilitation Center. The concept of rehabilitation for the elderly with comprehensive health and social services was too new to be accommodated by existing regulations and the dominant mentality. Instead of creating and propagating a new concept of human needs and possible public services, the focus of the ten-year debate on this new idea was whether it should belong to the health sector or the social sector and whether superior administrative and financial responsibility should belong to the Ministry of Social Affairs or the

Ministry of the Interior. In view of the existing legal and administrative structure, this was a natural development. It exemplifies Max Weber's notion of the formal rationality of legal authority.

The controversy began at the end of the 1950s and continued until Tranehaven was built in 1969 without any change in the existing regulations or bureaucratic structure. The project was made possible by a decision of the municipal council to consider Tranehaven part of the social sector, specifically as being similar to nursing home activities, which are compulsory for the municipality. Tranehaven aspired to provide advanced and specialized medical services for the elderly as a complement to other conventional rehabilitation, health, and social services. The municipality of Gentofte decided to provide such gerontological medical service on its own rather than utilize such medical care as is under the charge of the county hospitals. Tranehaven's team practice is a unique pioneer experiment of real coordination of health and social services in Denmark. When a client needs specialist medical attention, the specialist is invited from the county hospital to the rehabilitation center instead of sending the client to the hospital. Thus, the coordination of health and social services is enhanced. The specialists often called to the center are ophthalmologists, orthopedists, neurologists, and surgeons.

This case is the exception in Denmark. So far, little empirical analysis, such as cost-benefit or clients' evaluation of the services, has been conducted. However, this model was copied by the City of Hanover, Germany, which dispatched experts to visit the center. Some other municipalities are starting to make similar attempts, but it is too early to call this a trend.

PROFESSIONAL OBSTACLES TO COORDINATING THE PROVISION OF HEALTH AND SOCIAL SERVICES

Personnel structure and professional ideology are additional obstacles to effective coordination of health and social services.

These obstacles have historical roots. While the medical profession and allied professions within the health system have a long professional and organizational history, the social service professions have existed for a relatively shorter period of time.

Physicians and pharmacists have been recognized by the state since the mid-seventeenth century. Scientific medical societies began to develop in the late eighteenth century. The physician's trade union, the Danish Medical Association, was founded in 1857; the Danish Nurses Organization in 1899. A semigovernmental health care administration, the Health College, has been in existence since the seventeenth century with physicians as members.

The profession of social work developed rather late in Denmark. The first Danish training school for social workers was established in Copenhagen in 1937. The original idea for such a school was to train personnel equipped to deal with the social problems of hospital patients. For a long time, Danish social workers worked primarily in hospitals and maternity welfare centers. Gradually, they moved into other social service areas, such as rehabilitation, child and juvenile welfare, prisons, and local government administration (Valbek, 1970). For this historical reason, social workers have been under the supervision of medical personnel in the health services. Without independent professional status, they have been viewed as an auxiliary profession.

Apart from philanthropic and voluntary activities, the development of social services started at the end of the nineteenth century. An independent Ministry of Social Affairs was first established in 1924. At that time, there was no special education for the social services and thus no social work profession. As was the case with many other sectors of public administration, the leading bureaucrats were, and still are, those with university degrees in law or economics. For a long period the social services handled primarily financial and judicial matters. Since social service administrators had little contact with clients and consumers, there was a great gulf between central administrators and local service delivery systems.

TABLE 3.3   Number of Active Members in the
             Danish Social Workers Association

Year	Number
1970	920
1975	1,516
1980	4,155

SOURCE: Danish Social Workers Association.

TABLE 3.4   Recruitment of Social Workers in Denmark:
             Selected Years 1940-1980

Year	Number of Graduates Per Year
1940	9
1950	38
1960	44
1970	143
1980	378

SOURCE: 1940-1960 in *Danmarks Sociale Hjskole 1937-1962,* p.37, 1970-1980
         Ministry of Education.

The development of the social work profession in Denmark is
shown in Tables 3.3 and 3.4. These figures show rapid professional growth during the 1970s. In 1970, there were only
920 members in the Danish Social Worker's Association. By
1980, this number had increased fourfold. The number of
newly licensed social workers increased at the rate of 500 per
year in the mid-1970s.

The dramatic increase of social workers during the 1970s
reflects the growth in the social service sector. The increase of
personnel in the social service sector also includes a growth in
the number of home helpers and administrative personnel.
Table 3.5 shows that it is considerably greater than the comparable growth of health care sector personnel during the same
period.

Curricula of social work schools reflect the expanding role of
the social work profession in Danish society. Between 1937 and
1942, 26 percent of the curriculum consisted of health-related

TABLE 3.5   Labor Forces in Health and Social Services as a Proportion
of the Total Labor Force (percentages)

	1965	1970	1978
Health Sector	3.2	3.9	4.7
Social Sector	1.7	2.9	5.6

SOURCE: Steenstrup and Madsen-Østerbye (1980: 78).

subjects, such as social medicine, hygiene, and psychiatry. This
rate decreased to 22 percent in 1962 and 16 percent in 1968.
Legal subjects are another area in which the relative rate has
decreased—46 percent in 1937-1942 to 24 percent in 1978.
These decreases partially resulted from the introduction of such
new subjects as public administration and economic planning, as
well as an increase in the amount of time devoted to independent projects and group studies. The above figures do not
include field training, which is an important part of the educational program.

Another type of education distinct from social work training,
but within the social service sector, is training as a "social
intermediary" (*socialformidler*). A professional competitor of
the social worker, the social intermediary receives education at
the Danish Public Administration College (Danmarks Social-
forvalningshøjskole). These schools are under the Ministry of
Finance, while the schools of social work are under the jurisdiction of the Ministry of Education. This education provides
increased competence to the employees of the social service
administration. The admission requirement is a minimum of
four and one-half years work within the social service sector.
Courses meet only twice a week, enabling students to continue
to perform their jobs and receive their salaries. The training is
considered a part of their work.

Although the title and organizational structure of these two
professions differ considerably, the curricula are quite similar.
They include social and civil law, economic planning, sociology,
psychology, social medicine, and psychiatry. Social intermediary training takes two and one-half years, while the dura-

tion of social work training is three years. The proportion of
hours in social medicine and psychiatry (nine percent) and
psychology (seven percent) is similar to that of social work
education.

The status of social work education is equivalent to that of
nursing. However, the size and history of the professions differ.
Nurses have a longer occupational history than social workers
and are a much larger professional group. Table 3.6 provides a
comparison of the size of different professions in the health and
social services during the past decade.

The social sector's client-oriented personnel are weakly organized in terms of size, unions, level of education, and professional history, while the health care personnel are strongly
organized. This difference poses a major obstacle when planning
of coordination between the two sectors is discussed at the
regional and central levels. The social sector's professional representatives are weak in terms of number and status, important
factors in interest group politics. While the lawyers and economists within the social sector may be strong, their knowledge of
the local level and of the social service clients is slight; their
evaluation tends to be theoretical. These are the basic organizational problems in the social sector.

THE MEDICAL PROFESSION'S PERSPECTIVE
ON HEALTH AND SOCIAL SERVICE COORDINATION

An even more important obstacle to coordinating health and
social services is the medical profession's general view on human
health, which tends to exclude social aspects of health. In
November 1979, a three-day national conference on coordination of health-related services was held. The organizing body
was the county council's Health Security Negotiation Committee. Since 1973, the county has been responsible not only
for hospitals, but also for primary health security outside the
hospitals and for specialized social services. Each county has a
social and primary health committee. Although in principle the

TABLE 3.6   Number of Health and Social Services Professions
1970, 1978 and 1978

| Year | Health Care | | Social Services | |
	Physicians	Nurses[1]	Social Workers[2]	Home Helpers[3]
1970	6,935	16,035	2,421	13,820
1975	9,397	16,806	3,500	16,180
1980	10,548	16,962	4,700	20,224

1. Full-time workers equivalent.
2. 1970 census figures of those with social work degree, 1975 and 1978 estimated
   from the annual number of graduates, based on 1970 figures.
SOURCES: "Physicians, Nurses, and Home Helpers" in *Statistical Yearbook in Denmark*, Social Workers: 1970 census data.

organizational structure is based on the coordination of health
and social services, in practice this has not been functioning
very well, as the case study of Tranehaven reveals. Participants
in the conference from the health care sector were from the
regional or national public authorities and professional organizations, while the social sector participants were all administrative personnel from regional and central government. Among
the participants from the health care sector were representatives
of the Ministry of the Interior, the National Board of Health,
the Danish Medical Association, the General Practitioners Association, the Specialists Association, the Physiotherapists Association, and the Chiropractors Association. The Social Workers
Association was not represented, and no social workers (those
whose training is particularly geared to solve their clients'
urgent social problems, which are often related to health
aspects, and to assess their needs) participated in the debate.
This seems to be a clear indication that the discussion of the
coordination of health and social services in Denmark takes
place among administrators, politicians, and the health professions, a phenomenon partially caused by professional
socialization.

Discussions of social services generally include matters relevant to health care. But the opposite is not necessarily true.

Discussions of health care often do not include matters relevant to social services. At the international level the United Nations Social Security Council seems to show an active interest in the importance of health matters (European Centre, 1976; United Nations, 1977), while, on the other hand, the UN's World Health Organization (WHO) has given little attention to social services. Health matters have long been dealt with exclusively by the medical profession. Its view of human services has often, though not always, been limited to the medical perspective. The social service area in which the medical profession is most interested—perhaps its only area of interest—is the delivery and financing of health insurance. Despite the WHO's well-known and widely quoted holistic definition of "health," in reality, little has been achieved so far. During the 1970s, increasing awareness developed that much medical treatment, but little health care, has been delivered. The holistic definition of "health" cannot be achieved by medical services alone; it requires the mobilization of other human and social services. This is the background for WHO's new primary health care policy as formulated in the Alma Ata Declaration (WHO, 1978).

Duval, who has a medical background, points out:

> Health is only marginally affected by medical care; indeed, much of contemporary, scientific medicine is almost irrelevant to good health. . . . The individual's behavior, his environment, and his living habits have a far greater impact on his health than anything medicine might do for him [Duval, 1977].

In 1977, WHO's European Regional Office published Robert Kohn's cross-national study on the coordination of health and social services in Austria, Italy, Poland, and Sweden (Kohn, 1977). This attempt should be evaluated as a positive trend within the health care sector, but so far this one thin publication seems to be the only indication of interest expressed by WHO in the issue of coordinating health and social services.

Further empirical and theoretical studies should be pursued not only by the health care sector, but together with other human service sectors.

SUMMARY AND CONCLUSION

The major obstacles to the achievement of a comprehensive coordination of health and social services are complex organizational structures and professional attitudes toward other professions and clients.

There are two problems in the current organizational structure. First, the administrative functions are divided between the health and social sectors and the Ministries of Interior and Social Affairs. This administrative division, coupled with the complex laws regarding development, allocation, and financing of health and social service resources through to the regional and local administrations, is a historical legacy, created over a century of development in the public administration. First and foremost, coordination of the state administration is necessary. This is quite difficult in practice because of legal and administrative traditions based on the long history of organizational fragmentation.

Second, the division of labor between the counties and municipalities presents difficulties for the continuity of services, since the county holds administrative and financing authority for major health care resources (hospitals and health security) and the municipality is responsible for social service resources (nursing homes, home helpers, home nurses, and rehabilitation services). Because of this division, the continuity of services from hospital (county) to nursing home, rehabilitation center, or home nursing care (municipality) is often not effective. Although some efforts have been made to make this continuity as smooth as possible, it cannot be done effectively with limited financial and manpower resources.

In addition to these organizational problems, there is a more basic problem for the coordination of health and social services:

interprofessional attitudes and the way clients' needs are evaluated. These problems seem to be caused by the socialization process within each profession. Professional socialization occurs both at the level of training or education and at the level of practice. Current difficulties regarding the coordination of health and social services (personal and organizational) can be traced to these two levels; thus, it is on these levels that solutions should be considered. Professional socialization through education seems to be crucial for the improvement of the existing situations.

There are two crucial factors related to the educational level of professional socialization: (a) identity formation (as a professional or semiprofessional) and (b) status internalization (or internalization of social reality). Professional identity provides the person with a view "to the society," while status internalization provides the person with a view "from the society." The professional's view "to the society" includes a view of health and other human needs (Berger and Luckman, 1966).

It has gradually been recognized that social aspects of human health and disease are of great importance for the medical profession, but courses in this subject area are still very few. It was a long struggle for the University of Copenhagen's Institute of Social Medicine, from the time of its establishment in 1970, to win full status as an intrinsic part of the medical school (Nuyens, 1978). However, courses on social medicine are still too few, and there is strong pressure from traditional medical circles to keep it that way. Implementation of well-functioning coordination for health and social services on both the organizational and personal service levels will take time and hard work. But it is a task which can and should be done.

APPENDIX A
Health and Social Expenditure in Denmark:
Percentage of GNP in Market Price

Year	Social Expenditure[1]	Health Expenditure[2]	Total Social and Health Expenditure
1969	10.3	5.4	15.8
1970	12.2	5.7	17.9
1971	13.3	5.9	19.3
1972	13.4	6.0	19.4
1973	13.2	6.9	20.1
1974	15.1	7.6	22.7
1975	16.4	7.9	24.3
1976	15.6	7.9	23.5
1977	16.4	7.6	24.0
1978	17.1	7.8	24.9

1. Includes unemployment insurance; accident insurance; old age, invalidity, and other pensions; family and child care (maternity care until 1976); and social assistance. For more detail, see Appendix B.
2. Includes hospitals, health insurance (until 1973), and health security (after 1973). For more detail, see Appendix C.
SOURCE: Danmarks Statistik (1980: 78 and 102).

APPENDIX B
Social Expenditure in Denmark: Percentage of GNP in Market Price

Year	Unemployment Insurance[1]	Old Age and Other Pensions[2]	Family and Child Care[3]	Others[4]	Total
1969	0.7	6.5	2.4	0.7	10.3
1970	0.6	7.8	2.9	0.7	12.2
1971	0.9	8.4	3.1	0.9	13.3
1972	0.7	8.4	3.1	1.2	13.4
1973	0.6	8.5	3.0	1.1	13.2
1974	1.7	9.1	3.2	1.1	15.1
1975	2.6	9.4	3.2	1.2	16.4
1976	2.6	8.7	2.9	1.4	15.6
1977	3.3	8.8	2.7	1.6	16.4
1978	3.4	9.2	2.8	1.7	17.1

1. Includes unemployment insurance, labor exchange, education and re-education of labor.
2. Includes old age; invalidity; widows' pensions; nursing homes; home care services for pensioners; care for the mentally and physically handicapped.
3. Includes maternity care until 1976; maternity cash benefits; public health nursing-care for infants, children, school pupils; child subsidy, home care services.
4. Includes subsistence aid from 1976 cash benefits under the Social Assistance Act.
SOURCE: Danmarks Statistik (1980: 78 and 102).

APPENDIX C
Health Expenditure in Denmark 1969-1978:
Percentage of GNP in Market Price

Year	Hospital	Primary Health Insurance/Security and Cash Benefits[1]	Others	Total
1969	3.2	1.6	0.6	5.4
1970	3.2	1.8	0.7	5.7
1971	3.4	1.8	0.7	5.9
1972	3.3	1.9	0.8	6.0
1973	3.4	2.7	0.8	6.9
1974	3.9	2.8	0.9	7.6
1975	4.1	2.9	0.9	7.9
1976	4.0	3.0	0.8	7.8
1977	4.0	2.8	0.8	7.6
1978	4.0	2.9	0.9	7.8

1. Includes general and specialist medical attention, cash benefits, dental care, medicine, physiotherapy, funeral expenses. Some of these, such as dental care and medicine, are not entirely covered by the public health insurance (before 1973) and security (after 1973).
SOURCE: Danmarks Statistik (1980: 78 and 102).

REFERENCES

ANDERSEN, B. R., P. MILLESEN, and J. E. STEENSTRUP (1980) Kommunerne, det offentlige og samfundsudviklingen [Local Government, the Public and Social Development]. Copenhagen: Amtskommunernes og Kommunernes Forskningsinstitut.

BERGER, P. and T. LUCKMAN (1966) The Social Construction of Reality. London: Penguin.

Danmarks Statistik (1980) Statistisk tiårsoversigt 1980. Copenhagen.

DUVAL, M. K. (1977) "The provider, the government, and the consumer." Daedalus, pp. 185-192.

European Centre for Social Welfare Training and Research (1976) Interaction of Social Welfare and Health Personnel in the Delivery of Services: Implications for Training. Vienna.

GANNIK, D., E. HOLST, and M. WAGNER (1976) The National Health System in Denmark: A Descriptive Analysis. Publication No. (NIH) 77-673. Washington, DC: U.S. Department of Health, Education and Welfare.

HOLM, O. (1978) "Laegekonsulentens opgaver i relation til pensionssager" [Consulting tasks for physicians with regard to pension cases], in Laegekonsulenten i Socialforvaltningen [Medical Consultations within Social Service Administrations]. Copenhagen: Costers Bogtrykkeri.

ITO, H. (1979) "Health insurance policy development in Denmark and Sweden 1850-1950." Social Science and Medicine 13C: 143-160.

KOCH, J. H. and C. TOFTEMARK (1976) Health Services in Denmark. Copenhagen: Amstrådsforeningen i Danmark.

KOHN, R. (1977) Coordinating Health and Welfare Services in Four Countries: Austria, Italy, Poland and Sweden. Copenhagen: WHO (World Health Organization European Regional Office).

NIELSEN, S, K. (1978) Hospital Social Work in Copenhagen: Some Practice Perspectives. Institute of Social Medicine, University of Copenhagen.

Nordiska socialstatistikkommitten (1980) Social trygghet i de nordiska landerna [Social Security in the Nordic Countries, 1978]. Stockholm: GOTAB.

NUYENS, Y. (1978) Teaching Medical Sociology: Retrospection and Prospection. London: Martinum Nijhoff.

PALLESEN, A. E. (1978) "Laegekonsulenten i socialforvaltningen: Hans funktioner, forudsaetninger, ansaettelsesvilkår og samarbejdsmaessige relationer" [Medical consultants within social service administrations: functions, conditions, and cooperative relations]. Månedskrift for Praktisk Laegegerning 56: 195-216.

STEENSTRUP, J. E. and K. MADSEN-ØSTERBYE (1981) Sundhedssektoren: Ressourcer og produktion siden 1965 [Health Sector: Resources and Production since 1965]. Copenhagen: Amtskommunernes og Kommunernes Forskingsinstitut.

United Nations (1977) Integrated Approaches to Social Service Provision at the Local Level. UN Publication No. SOA/ESDP/1976/6. New York: United Nations.

VALBEK, A. (1970) "School of social work" in Denmark: An Official Handbook. Royal Danish Ministry of Foreign Affairs. Copenhagen: KRAK.

WHO [World Health Organization] (1978) Primary Health Care. A Joint Report by the Director-General of the World Health Organization and the Executive Director of the United Nation's Children's Fund. Geneva: World Health Organization.

4

SWEDEN

KARIN TENGVALD

During the postwar period, the provision of health and social services in Sweden has gradually become a public sector responsibility. If you look closely into the matter, though, a few professionals-in private practice can still be found, especially in larger cities, and voluntary and charity organizations still provide a few welfare services. More important exceptions today are the majority of dentists (private practice) and a considerable number of employee health maintenance programs organized and funded by the companies. But the outstanding characteristic of the Swedish system for health and social services today is the absence of a complex structure of public and private, profit or nonprofit, service providers.

The nationwide system of public health and social services is an important part of the Swedish welfare state, comprising a wide array of social, educational, and labor market policy programs (von Otter, 1980). The concept of a general public service system encompassing all layers of the population dates back to the 1930s, but not until the 1960s were the economic resources available for major expansion. Between 1960 and 1975, public expenditures on health and dental services increased 500 percent in fixed prices; expenditures on social services increased 600 percent. Thus, the proportion of the GNP used for public health and social services more than doubled during the period. Between 1960 and 1970, the number of full-time positions doubled in the health sector and tripled in the social sector. During the 1970s, there was another 50 percent increase in health delivery personnel and a doubling of the social services personnel. Today, nearly a fifth of all employment in Sweden is in these two sectors (Sekretariatet för framtidsstudier, 1978). Health and social services are increasingly important parts of the public sector and of social life in general, involving a majority of the population as producer and/or consumer.

Public sector expenditures are high in Sweden (approximately 60 percent of the GNP). Comparative studies of the distribution of costs on different types of public activities have indicated another important characteristic of the Swedish system. Sweden ranks highest in terms of percentage expenditure of the GNP in the area of direct public consumption, whereas several capitalist countries exceed Sweden in the area of cash transfers (Meidner, 1979).

The conscious efforts to develop systems of public services of high quality and good accessibility have resulted in the extensive use of these services not only by low- and middle-income groups, but also by the most well-off categories of the population, and several public opinion polls indicate a continuously wide approval of the system (von Otter, 1980).

The Social Sector

The most rapid expansion has taken place in the social sector with the development of extensive services for preschool children and the elderly. The social services expenditure almost equals the expenditure on health care, which at present amounts to 70 percent of health service expenditures (the social insurance schemes are excluded from these figures). The 1960s was not only a period of rapid expansion of the social sector due to the abundance of resources; it was also a decade when new social problems became a high priority in Sweden as in many other countries. This fact might help to explain the rapidity of expansion and the leadership of the social sector in the development of new programs and new ideas.

The revitalized debate on social problems focused on the problem of social and economic inequality. Despite rising standards of living in absolute terms, leading labor union officials questioned whether there was any general tendency toward increasing equality. The government appointed a state commission to study the low income problem; it produced a scrupulous investigation of the distribution of general welfare in the Swedish population. The empirical work was carried out by economists and sociologists, and the results showed that—given a Swedish Welfare State perspective—considerable inequality still existed in terms of family income, educational levels, housing and health—these inequities dividing the population along class lines (SOU, 1970; Johansson, 1970).

Although much of the discussion about the unequal distribution of assets and resources dealt with the basic mechanisms creating inequality through the production system, the redistributive and supportive systems (i.e., the social services system) were also influenced by the ongoing debate. This is particularly true since the period of general concern and criticism of the Swedish welfare state coincided with a period of reforms, or attempts at reforming the social services system. In at least three areas new strategies became visible during this period: (a) the development of more "scientific" perspectives on social problems and new ideologies for service provision, leading to new legal frameworks more appropriate to such perspectives and ideologies; (b) the development of a more integrated social service system; and (c) attempts at reorganizing professional education.

The Health Sector

The concern about social policy and social services voiced by politicians, social scientists, and social service personnel had virtually no counterpart in the health sector (Gannik and Launsøø, 1978; Westrin, 1980). In the late 1970s, however, the development in the health sector moved along the same lines as in the social sector a decade earlier. Now there is a greater interest in social or "societal" perspectives on health problems;

the proposed legal framework for the health sector is in accordance with such perspectives. The 1970s also brought attempts to reorganize the provision of health services in terms of better-developed primary health care and better interorganizational links. Educational reforms were limited, but social medicine and social aspects of health problems were expanding parts of the curriculum for medical students.

Coordination and Linkages Between the Two Sectors

Some of the legal, organizational, and educational reforms achieved or proposed in these decades have helped to enhance coordination between the health and social services sectors as a secondary if not a primary goal. These factors, as well as economic considerations and the development of joint professional knowledge, are important determinants in the future success of service linkages. They will be considered throughout this chapter as the current situation in Sweden is reviewed and existing coordination experiments and linkage problems are examined.

In order to facilitate this discussion, there needs to be a background understanding of the coordination or integration ideology in Sweden. The idea of a better integration between the health and social services sectors was born and advocated from the health sector by a small group of socially committed doctors who were interested in the effects of social conditions on health (Inghe, 1960). The idea grew out of research studies of less privileged groups, which indicated a considerable overlap between health and social problems (Inghe, 1960; Inghe and Inghe, 1965). These studies provided an empirical rationale suggesting the need for some form of coordinated services. The early visionaries emphasized something more penetrating than organizational integration—namely, the development of an integrated theoretical framework for social medicine as opposed to the highly technical, specialized, and institutionalized development of medical knowledge at the time. Today, it seems appropriate to regard these ideas as the birth of a holistic perspective on individual health and social problems in Sweden. However, at present, the holistic perspective has not developed beyond the ideological level, functioning more as a sensitizing concept than as a theoretical perspective.

The first steps toward integration occurred at the organizational level. In the early 1960s, the national government appointed two state commissions with the directive to propose a reorganization of the governmental agencies for health and welfare. The commissions finally issued a joint report proposing the merger of the two former agencies into the new National Board of Health and Welfare. This merger occurred in 1968; the first director general was a former professor of social medicine strongly committed to the ideas of integration. In its first few years, the National Board played a major role in the development of some large-scale programs of cooperation. It also initiated specialized coordination experiments aimed at specific target groups, such as children and the handicapped.

During the last two decades, organizational integration and coordination between the sectors was supported in several ways. At the same time, politicians, government officials, and some professionals recognized that organizational coordination of the health and social sectors needed to be complemented by reforms in other areas relevant to the structure and contents of service provision. For example, a Social Services Commission, appointed in 1968 with the mission of proposing a new Social Services Act, examined the issues of integration and recommended programs for coordination experiments (SOU, 1974). Later, these experiments were developed by the National Board of Health and Welfare and are an important part of the Swedish experiences about organizational coordination between the two separate sectors.

A university crisis in 1968 resulted in the appointment of a state commission for the reorganization of the university system. In 1969, one of its subcommittees issued a report proposing a joint faculty organization for the schools of medicine, nursing and social work. The report was negatively received by all relevant school and university authorities. This was the first

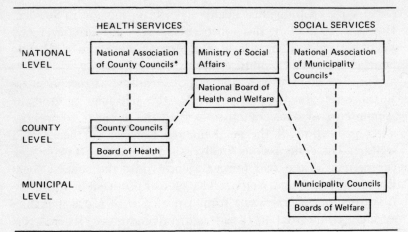

Figure 4.1 Government Bodies with Responsibility for Health and Welfare Services in Sweden

*Coordinating organization of county and municipality councils, respectively. Not subject to public law.

clear setback and a sign that the idea of integration was not accepted by all groups (Gadd, 1979).

ORGANIZATIONAL STRUCTURE OF THE SWEDISH HEALTH AND WELFARE SYSTEMS

Organizational bodies dealing with public sector health and welfare exist at three levels—the national level and two local levels, the counties and municipalities. These correspond to the three levels of national and local government in Sweden. There are only two levels involved in each sector. The health sector includes the national and county governments, and the social sector involves the national and the municipal governments (Figure 4.1).

The National Institutions

Parliament and the government, through the Ministry of Social Affairs, have the overall responsibility for health and social services through legislation, rules, regulations, and economic control. The ministry covers both health and social service issues, but there is at present a clear intraorganizational division with one minister for each sector.

The National Board of Health and Welfare is the central government agency concerned with the planning and control of the health and welfare services. Historically, the National Board had more supervisory control over the actual provision of services through directives and inspection of local authorities and personnel. During the 1970s, the role of the board shifted more toward planning and advice. It still has some direct influence over medical accountability and the distribution of doctors in the country. It also is responsible for the distribution of government grants. Other central government agencies are involved in issues of cooperation between health and social services. Most important among those are the National Board of Social Insurance—the supervisory agency for the nationwide health and social insurance programs—and the National Board of Employment—the agency dealing with employment and vocational rehabilitation issues (Westrin, 1980).

The National Association of County Councils and the National Association of Municipalities are two other important institutions at the national level. These are the interest organizations of counties and municipalities. Their aims are somewhat different from those of the National Board. For instance, they function as employers in the central wage negotiations for county and municipal employees; their main aim is to secure the "economic well-being" of their members. The National Associations today have a strong and generally increasing influence on the local governments' handling of the health and social services. In some areas they have taken over the responsibilities of the National Board by issuing recommendations covering the organizational and economic development of the health and welfare services.

This shift in the structure of influence at the national level is probably a combined result of today's economic constraints and the political ideology of defending local governmental power against the central government. A considerable amount of political autonomy at the local levels has always been highly valued in Sweden. However, what appears to be a shift in influence between the national and local levels may actually be a shift of power from the central government agency to the interest organizations of municipalities and counties. There is no doubt that the central government is loosening its grip over the organization of the health and social services systems. This is done not only by restricting the supervisory and regulatory functions of the National Board, but also through the legal frameworks for the health and social services that are now being enacted and by a long-term trend of state withdrawal from the direct provision of services in these fields.

The full impact of these changes in central government influence on the structure and content of the health and social services probably will not appear for a long time. However, even today the trend suggests risks to some of the highly valued characteristics of Sweden's nationwide system. The considerable similarity of quality and accessibility of services to the population in virtually all parts of the country may be damaged as a result of these changes. This diminishing role for central government and its agencies means a more clear-cut organizational split between the health and social services sectors.

The Local Organization of Services

Today, the provision of public health and social services is almost entirely the responsibility of the County and Municipality Councils. National government involvement is principally restricted to a few university hospitals in addition to the nationwide insurance schemes and offices for vocational rehabilitation.

The two local government levels are of major importance for the operation of the Swedish health and social services systems. The counties and municipalities also provide other types of public services, such as cultural activities and public transportation. The political importance of the local levels is increased by

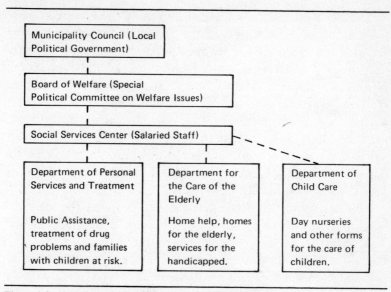

Figure 4.2 **Basic Organization of Municipality Social Services**

the fact that they have their own taxation power. Municipality taxes amount to 15-20 percent and county taxes 10 percent of all taxable incomes. Furthermore, the health and welfare services are not financed solely by local taxes. Of the health services, 25 percent are financed through state grants and another 10 percent by reimbursements from the insurance schemes and patient fees (Westrin, 1980).

Social Services Provision in the Municipalities

There are 275 municipalities in Sweden with populations varying from 5,000 to 800,000 people. This population variation contributes to the differing complexity of social services organization and delivery within the municipalities. The only institution required by law is a local Board of Welfare. Formerly, the politicians holding positions on the board functioned as welfare officers. Currently, large salaried staff with differing professional status deal with social services and treatment (see Figure 4.2).

The departments at the Social Services Centers are organized differently in each municipality. The department of personal services and treatment is always a separate department staffed with trained social workers. In larger municipalities, the geographical area is often divided into districts, each with a District Welfare Board and corresponding District Services Centers. Even within such an organization, it is not unusual for departments for the elderly and children to be centralized. In some municipalities, there are considerable intraorganizational problems demanding complex cooperation mechanisms within the local social services organization.

The development of smaller districts supports the idea of a holistic approach to social service delivery. It implies that professionals need a basic knowledge of the actual conditions of the population they are to serve, and that interprofessional collaboration is needed to meet clients' needs (Allander, 1979). However, the Social Welfare Boards seldom concern themselves with the district divisions made by other relevant service providers, such as schools or the health centers, when they divide the municipality into social service districts.

Health Services Provision in the Counties

There are 23 counties which have the direct responsibility for health and medical services. The county populations vary from 150,000 to 1,500,000 inhabitants (see Figure 4.3).

The administrative coordination for the hospitals, district doctors and district nurses varies. There is a present tendency to establish a separate primary care organization which comprises all the health and medical resources within the county. This primary care organization has its own management under the Board of Health but is separate from the management of hospitals [Westrin, 1980].

The primary care organization outside of hospital outpatient departments and emergency departments is weak in Sweden compared to some other Scandinavian countries (Gannik, 1979). In the 1970s, efforts were made to strengthen the

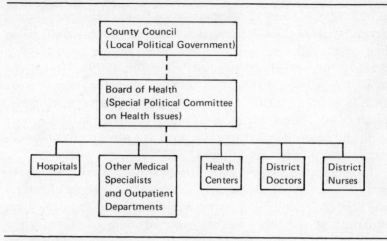

Figure 4.3 Basic Organization of County Health Services

primary care services by establishing health centers with a
catchment population of 5,000 to 50,000. However, patients
who have the choice still tend to prefer hospital outpatient
departments, probably due to their accessibility. Also, physicians prefer to work in hospitals with better technical facilities
and accessibility to specialists. In order to meet the perceived
demand for services both by users and professional providers,
the health centers currently established by most counties are
more similar to hospitals than to a district doctor's clinic. This
trend has clear disadvantages for the contact between the service providers and the population. It requires larger catchment
areas to staff the centers with specialists and to add more
technical equipment.

NEW LEGAL FRAMEWORKS AND
SERVICE IDEOLOGIES

The Social Sector

Until the 1960s, the social services provided by the municipalities to a large extent functioned as a residual system dealing

almost exclusively with a small minority of relatively poor people (3-5 percent of the population) and even fewer "social deviants." Three detailed Social Service Acts governed the handling of the clients, as often prescribing negative sanctions as positive support of the needy (Pettersson, 1979). Most social work was conducted by the politicians on the local Welfare Boards in more than 1500 municipalities. Social work was a mixture of formal social sanctions evolving from the Service Acts and informal sanctions and support resting on local knowledge about problem situations.

In the late 1950s and early 1960s, different types of organizations throughout the society underwent a process of merger and concentration. The structural changes in industry were discussed at the time, but the reorganization of other institutions like the municipalities has had far-reaching effects on "grass-roots participation" and on bureaucratization and specialization. The creation of municipalities with larger populations was a prerequisite for the expansion of public services into an institutionalized public service system with vastly expanding eligibility. The decrease in the number of municipalities from 1500 to less than 300 produced increased opportunity to give full-fledged public services in various fields. The role of the local politicians responsible for social services shifted toward policy and general program development. Professional social workers were called upon to carry out the work with clients. However, social work was still largely administrative, interpreting local political guidelines and legal prescriptions.

During the 1960s, the service agenda expanded considerably, as did the target population, which now included the elderly, children, and the handicapped. The whole orientation of municipal social services changed as eligibility expanded. Social services were no longer a residual system only for the poor and "deviants." The distribution of resources for new types of service provision was left to administrative officials who followed local political guidelines or recommendations from the National Association of Municipalities. Social workers were often in charge of the departments for child care and care of the elderly, but the actual work was conducted by personnel from other fields or unskilled personnel such as home helpers.

In the traditional social work area, covered by the Social Services Acts, there was no equivalent expansion of the service agenda or of the target population. However, there was a growing interest in group and community work. This meant a general tendency toward more preventive action, both in social planning and in individual social work. Such ideas tended to expand social workers' perspective on their target population.

The new directions of social work practice fit well into the "scientific" thinking about social problems that developed in the 1960s. One important line of thought having considerable impact maintained the view that social problems including individual problems were largely caused by "basic social and economic processes" which created unequal levels of living and generally difficult living conditions for less privileged groups. Such inequality was increased by factors such as social segregation and stigmatization. Therefore, the social services sector, together with other redistribution and supportive systems, should be concerned with this basic inequality. Thus, there was a need for more preventive social action through social planning and a genuinely service-oriented approach in traditional social work—ridding the provision of support from its negative, social control functions (Holgersson, 1980). Instead, more of a needs assessment framework should be developed covering the whole social service arena. In this way, the "holistic principle" made its way into social service thinking.

The State Commission, which developed a new legal framework for the total social service area, was clearly influenced both by the macro perspective on the causes of social problems and by the idea of a needs assessment framework as a theoretical basis for social work. At present, there is no coherent body of professional knowledge matching such demands, or any professional action programs related to this general framework. A development of the social work profession along these lines remains a challenge for the 1980s. The new Social Services Act passed in 1980 indirectly facilitates such a development by being very general; it leaves the organization and content of services to the local authorities.

The new act does not, however, secure any degree of professional autonomy in the treatment of individual cases corresponding to the autonomy provided the profession of medicine in the Health Services Act. The election of a conservative majority in the national government and a general shift in the political climate meant increasing criticism of the "liberal tendencies" in the final Commission Report (SOU, 1977). At the last minute, two special laws dealing with child neglect and teenage deviant behavior and with severe drug and alcohol addiction among adults were separated from the general act. These legal frameworks still contain very detailed prescriptions for the handling of individual cases, thus limiting local political and professional autonomy and hampering attempts to make a service-oriented attitude penetrate the whole system of provision of social services.

The Health Sector

The general notion that social and physical environmental factors have a major impact on the health status of the population is widely recognized. However, these ideas have affected the organization and delivery of health services even less than the corresponding perspective in the social sector. The new legal framework being proposed for the health sector strongly advocates more preventive action and a more comprehensive, decentralized organization of primary health care (SOU, 1979). At present, there is a rapidly increasing demand for services directed toward "the care of the healthy." These preventive services are offered to individuals interested in maintaining their health and to some extent those needing help to curb detrimental habits like smoking. Since general theoretical knowledge is well-developed in the health sector, the shifting focus toward prevention may produce better results there than in the social sector.

The proposed Health Services Act follows the lead of the Social Services Act by giving local authorities greater autonomy in deciding appropriate organizational structure and the local priorities for health services. This increases the possibilities for a more flexible organization in the future. It will not necessarily mean more similarity in organizational structure between the two sectors, since such a development would in fact demand more centralized decision-making.

The degree of professional autonomy is a key difference between the legal frameworks in the social and health sectors. Professional autonomy is given in different degrees to an increasing number of occupations within the health sector, so the development here is in fact the opposite to that of the social sector where such autonomy is legally nonexistent. While recognizing professional autonomy, the Health Services Act ranks the health professions, with physicians at the top. Thus, it maintains much of the strict hierarchy within the actual delivery of services despite much criticism of the character of professional autonomy and the structure of the power relations between different occupational groups in the health sector. Indirectly, however, these issues have been dealt with in several other recent State Commission Reports. There is recognition of the need for more teamwork and more delegation of tasks from the medical profession to other personnel groups. This is an important area of consideration in the future development of cooperation between health and social services personnel.

COORDINATION AND INTEGRATION
OF HEALTH AND SOCIAL SERVICES
IN SWEDEN TODAY

Linkages between health and social services form a diversified picture. Different forms of coordination and integration exist in three areas: (a) at different government levels (nationally and locally), (b) at different organizational levels (political-administrative and professional), and (c) for different target populations or problem areas (based on geographic districts or on problem classifications).

These varying forms and contents of linkages have not resulted in nationwide, cohesive networks between the two systems. Apart from a few traditional forms of cooperation which are spread throughout the country, coordination is generally experimental, mainly on a small scale.

Traditional Forms of Cooperation Between Health and Social Services

Some traditional forms of cooperation existed before integration became a nourished idea in the 1960s. These included informal professional cooperation, adding professional expertise pertaining to one sector into the organizational framework of the other. Within the social sector, there were "social doctors" dealing with complex social and medical problems, like drug addiction and child neglect. In the health sector, the medical social workers grew into a sizable "specialty." They were mainly concerned with practical arrangements of aftercare. Social workers also functioned as team members in rehabilitation programs and mental health programs. These professional groups worked and still work without much formal organizational links to their "own" sector. At a time when professional specialization and the diversification of services had not gone very far, the lack of organizational links was not regarded as much of a problem.

During the 1960s, when specialization increased and service programs expanded, these traditional forms of cooperation were critized for several reasons. From the political-administrative point of view, concern grew out of an anticipated development of two huge parallel organizations with considerable overlap in the provision of services. The economic concerns were evidenced in the early decision to merge the two National Boards of Health and Welfare. From a user's point of view, the traditional forms of professional cooperation no longer accomplished the goal of simplifying the combined use of services. This was because the service programs within each sector had expanded and diversified and the professionals working in an "alien" sector had no formal access to the full-fledged programs of their "own" sector.

The rational solution to the growing problem of coordination was the formation of new organizational linkages and an employment policy encouraging a more clear-cut "division of labor" between the sectors. This principle received important support at the national level in the early 1970s through an informal agreement between the National Associations of Counties and Municipalities representing the employers of health and welfare personnel. The agreement implied that social service personnel in the future should preferably not be employed in the health sector, and vice versa.

Coordinated Services:
The Experimental Projects

Strong support for the integration and coordination of services at the national level was evident in the early 1970s. On behalf of the Ministry of Social Affairs, the planning department of the National Board of Health and Welfare was involved in the development of joint District Health and Welfare Centers in several municipalities (Westrin, 1980; Eriksson and Svensson, 1975). Other board departments developed coordination projects regarding child services (SOU, 1975). The National Associations of the Municipalities and the Counties appointed a joint coordination committee and supported through local political coordination committees (the SLAKO groups) the so-called Sosam projects. These focused on coordination in primary health care and the care of the elderly (SPRI Rapport, 1977). The economic resources spent on some of the projects, especially those supported by the National Board, were abundant, allowing for more staff and considerably more research and evaluation studies than is common for experimental programs.

The following section describes the general characteristics of these projects.

The Scope of the Coordination Efforts

Primary, outpatient services have been the focus of most of the projects. Several projects have successfully combined with the recent emphasis on decentralization of outpatient medical care. Co-localization between Health and Social Services Centers has thereby been facilitated. In several projects, coordination extends beyond the health and social services sectors. Professionals from other local public sector agencies such as the insurance office, the vocational rehabilitation clinic, the school medical, and social services have also been participating. Occasionally, even police and probation officers are included (Westrin, 1980).

The Goals of the Projects

A review of the operational goals for these projects documents that coordination between the two types of services has often been a prominent goal (Westrin, 1980). The goals expressed for the Tierp project, probably the best-known, are typical: "To coordinate—on the basis of the holistic view—the work carried out in the fields of social welfare, primary health care, the school health and health and welfare services and to provide the citizens of the municipality with a more effective service" (Socialstyrelsen, 1977).

In a broader perspective, coordination is regarded as a means to achieve more basic goals of service provision: increased quality of care, improved effectiveness, or better "health and welfare in the population." One of the key questions to arise is whether these new linkage organizations are actually critical factors in the development of more effective and better services.

The Organizational Structure of the Projects

Most coordination projects were top-heavy in their organizational structure. This was partly due to the project construction of the experiments, since the lack of formal links between the systems produced the necessity of greater direct political-administrative influence than was true in routine provision of services.

Still, the heavy political-administrative superstructure was, at times, extreme. For example, a child care coordination project consisting of one social worker employed by the social sector, placed at a child health clinic, had a local political committee with representatives from the Board of Social Welfare and the Board of Health, a reference group including administrative personnel from the national level, and a group of local administrative personnel and chief professionals plus a project leader (Gurman, 1974). The larger projects could have even more complex superstructures, but they also had more complex aims, including research and coordination among several agencies. Sometimes, the political-administrative top-level influences negatively affected the professional cooperation by giving priority to the interests of individual sectors. It also played a positive role by simplifying administrative procedures and changing catchment areas (Socialstyrelsen, 1977). The organization of internal professional collaboration varied considerably with the scope and aims of the projects. Only from the longest projects is there evidence of substantial professional teamwork (Placht, 1980). In other projects, cooperation consisted of a number of professionals representing different agencies and different professional levels who met approximately once a week to exchange general information about their respective agencies and to discuss areas of common interest like prevention. Case conferences and direct collaboration in service provision were less frequent results of the cooperation.

The Results of the Cooperation Experiments

In a recent review of the evaluation material on these coordination experiments, the author concludes:

> Results as to *the clients' well-being or social function* are rather seldom reported. The only results that explicitly state that cooperation is beneficial are opinions that more cooperation implies more continuity and quicker service in the form of speedier invalidity pensions (!) and finally statements about the benefits from stronger social controls. The statements regarding stronger social control are verified by representatives for all professional groups in Tierp and are also valid in the Skara project according to the writer's opinion. To what extent this control serves the client or the environment/ community is an open question.
>
> Regarding *the personnel's working conditions* the results from several investigations point to cooperation as being support for the different professionals in their work with complicated and difficult problems, not least to help to bring a case to an end. One thing to be noted, however, is that group work is reported as an inconvenient working mode for some professionals. It is an open question to what extent this may explain the uneven participation from some groups (e.g., the district nurses)—likewise if this factor can be treated by group dynamic cooperation.
>
> The most frequent reports have concerned superficial non-specific effects as the *the quality of problem analysis and management of the cases,* increased attention on socio-medical problems or management made quicker. This is however obviously not equal with a higher quality of work in a deeper sense.
>
> Regarding *the economy of services* the reported effects are contradictory—increased as well as decreased bureaucracy, increased as well as decreased time-consumption.
>
> Some reports have dealt not only with the sort but also the degree of effects. The results indicate hitherto only marginal effects [Westrin, 1980].

COORDINATION: PROBLEMS AND PROSPECTS

There are several relatively self-evident reasons for the fairly poor and contradictory results of the Swedish demonstration projects, apart from the fact that evaluation studies seldom are precise enough to give clear directions for the future. But there are also some more basic reasons which might help to explain the difficulty of implementing the idea of a closer link between the sectors.

Organizational Problems

Most of the program evaluations have focused on problems at a "meso level"—that is, issues of program administration, management, and organization. Several of the well-known obstacles to coordination belong to this level. These problems originate from the formal organizational split between the two sectors. These include (a) no routine coordination of catchment areas and service localities (b) different organizational hierarchies and vastly different degrees of professional autonomy, and (c) different work ethics and confidentiality policies. Internal organizational problems *within each sector* as well as some general problems of large organizations are also mentioned: (a) high personnel turnover, hampering the development of common knowledge and teamwork and demanding constant introductory education; (b) large workloads, especially in the medical sector, and rigid work assignments complicating attempts to organize the work in tune with the goals of coordination; and (c) intraorganizational coordination problems between primary and secondary levels of health care and between different social service departments.

The *construction of the coordination projects* as experimental and nonroutine programs also added to the organizational problems. Among the problems noted here are a heavy political-administrative superstructure needed to deal with administrative and policy judgments and the short time period for the programs. Some programs ended after a year or two. In view of the organizational problems involved, this was too short a period for the development of well-functioning collaboration among the professional service providers.

Beyond the organizational factors are more basic questions regarding the validity of the original rationale for the attempts at service coordination. Such issues are now being raised, scrutinizing the gaps between the ideals and the reality of organizational cooperation.

The Ideology of Holism and Professional Knowledge

The ideology of holism forms the common basis for professional cooperation. Holism has been interpreted as a perspective taking physical, mental, and social aspects of a problem into consideration. Although holism is an important sensitizing concept consistent with the World Health Organization's definition of health, there is little evidence that this general idea has developed into a body of common knowledge bridging professional barriers. Professional development along these lines needs more narrow problem definitions and target populations than has generally been the case in the large-scale coordination experiments. In fact, the knowledge that is available has developed in projects outside the large-scale coordination experiments (PRU-gruppen, 1979; SPRI Rapport, 1978).

A fruitful criticism of the scope of the general holistic perspectives is now appearing (Lagerberg, 1979). There is no need to develop professional action programs on the basis of holism for the health and social service sectors at large. In several problem areas, a majority of professionals *and* patients/clients would rightly reject a holistic service program. Instead, available resources for the expansion of interdisciplinary knowledge should be used in areas where there is a common understanding of the importance of a multidisciplinary, holistic approach. Such groups include children at risk, the frail elderly, the mentally ill, drug and alcohol addicts, the handicapped, and possibly multiproblem families. Even with this more narrow goal of interdisciplinary cooperation, we can anticipate problems in reaching a consistent body of knowledge. First, the structure of knowledge within the sectors is different. Also, the differences in professional capacity, status, and autonomy of medicine and social work are highlighted in instances of cooperation. Finally, there are often quite a few cooperation situations demonstrating a gap between the professional status of the doctors and the relevance of the professional knowledge they bring to the situation (PRU-gruppen, 1979; Tengvald, 1981).

Today, there is a general need to develop research and research organizations for more personnel groups working in the health and social services sectors. Such a development has started for the profession of social work with the establishment of chairs and social work doctoral programs. A somewhat parallel development is taking place in nursing, although there are no Swedish doctoral programs in that field so far. Other personnel groups, such as preschool teachers and physical therapists, are asking for the opportunity to develop their own professional research organizations. Interdisciplinary cooperation will probably profit from this new development in the long run, although initially there may be more tension and conflict (Gadd, 1979).

Professional Cooperation or Competition?

Professional competition is reinforced by the lack of a common body of knowledge as to the explanatory value of different perspectives. This has been an evident characteristic in the coordination experiments, although it is seldom defined clearly (Socialhögskolan, 1979).

The status differentials and the general differences in command over an appropriate body of knowledge have led to uneven development for health and social service professions engaged in interdisciplinary work. The basic education for several health professions today contains more of a social perspective on health problems and general knowledge of the organization of the social sector than previously. The profession of medicine is developing specialties which emphasize social science (e.g., social pediatrics). The profession of nursing is attempting to establish a research organization combining medical and social science approaches. In summary, the health professions are clearly expanding their competence in the social services and social sciences.

In contrast to this, Swedish social work education today is more restrictive in including health-oriented content in its curriculum, at both the basic professional and doctoral levels. There is no development toward special education for medical social work, although it is a much sought-after specialty. The situation is somewhat better in the field of preschool teaching and in the very short courses for home helpers. But, on the whole, professional development within the social service professions is one of withdrawal rather than expansion of health-related knowledge.

Organizational Cooperation or Competition?

The contrasting patterns of professional education reflect the uneven development in the two sectors as a whole. In the health sector, there is a general expansionist attitude. This includes a redesigning of job tasks in some areas (e.g., child care and care of the elderly) and adding of more "social services" to the work carried out by health personnel (e.g., nurses). The increasing enrollment of social workers and psychologists adds a psychosocial perspective in health service teamwork. This development is contrary to the informal agreement between the sectors mentioned earlier. It also means that the traditional forms of professional cooperation are more easily adapted to the traditional functioning of the health sector than was true in the organizational coordination attempted during the 1970s. The inclusion of "alien" knowledge and semiprofessional groups does not disrupt the organizational hierarchy or the major professional dominance of the medical perspective.

No such development is taking place in the social sector. The "social doctors" who were once an important part of the social sector hardly exist today (Westrin, 1980). Job tasks are not redesigned toward more health-related services. Instead, contemporary discussion in the Swedish social service sector focuses more on other potential coordination partners, such as employment offices, schools, and vocational rehabilitation centers.

ISSUES FOR THE FUTURE

The period of utopian coordination visions has passed. With increasing economic constraints, more competition than cooperation between the sectors seems evident in the next few years. Still, hope for the future lies in a steady development of joint bodies of knowledge in specific problem areas. Such knowledge is necessary for both the coordination and improvement of the quality of services.

REFERENCES

ALLANDER, E. (1979) "The holistic perspective as a tool in practice. a limitation or a development?" Läkartidningen 76: 3889-3991.

ERIKSSON, T. and I. SVENSSON (1975) Collaboration Between Health and Social Services in Some Counties. Stockholm: Socialstyrelsen (National Board of Health and Welfare).

GADD, A. S. (1979) The Social Contents in Health Care. Stockholm: Socialstyrelsen (National Board of Health and Welfare).

GANNIK, D. (1979) "Primary health care: cooperation between health and welfare personnel, national report—Denmark." Wien: European Centre for Social Welfare Training and Research, R 10 (11).

——— and L. LAUNSØØ (1978) "The isolation of health services in society: development and consequences." Acta Sociologica (Supplement) 21: 209-226.

GOLDIE, N. (1977) "The division of labour among the mental health professions—a negotiated or an imposed order?" in M. Stacey et al. (eds.) Health and the Division of Labour. London: Croom Helm.

GURMAN, K. (1974) "Report from Eskilstuna—collaboration in child care." Eskilstuna: Eskilstuna Municipality.

HOLGERSSON, K. (1980) Personal and Social Services—An Issue of Human Perspectives. Stockholm: Tidens förlag.

INGHE, G. (1960) The Poor in Society. Stockholm: Stockholm Municipality.

——— and M. B. INGHE (1965) The Poor in the Welfare State. Stockholm: Tidens förlag.

JOHANSSON, S. (1970) "On the level of living survey." Draft for Chapter 1 of the State Commission Report on Levels of Living in Sweden. Stockholm: Allmänna förlaget.

LAGERBERG, D. (1979) "The holistic perspective and cooperation–contradicting concepts?" Läkartidningen. 76: 2517-2518.

MEIDNER, R. (1979) Die Expansion des Offenlichen Sektors. Einige Überlegungen auf Grundlage der Schwedischen Entwicklung. Berlin: Wissenschaftszentrum.

PETTERSSON, U. (1979) Social Control and Client Co-Determination in the Social Services. Lund: Studentlitteratur.

PRU-gruppen (1979) Lost Children in the Welfare Society. Stockholm: Liber förlag.

PLACHT, R. (1980) "Observation of teamwork." Stockholm: Socialstyrelsen (National Board of Health and Welfare–the Tierp Project). (mimeo)

Sekretariatet för framtidsstudier (Secretariat for Future Studies) (1978) Caring in Society–A Program for Future Studies on Care and Caring Needs. Stockholm: Liber förlag.

SPRI (1978) 'Psychiatry undergoing change. team functions, personnel roles and internal education." Stockholm: SPRI. Rapport 7/74, Appendix 5.

––– (1977) "Primary care, care of the elderly, cooperation." Exploratory Studies for Joint Planning by the National Association of Counties, the National Association of Municipalities and the National Board of Health and Welfare. Stockholm: SPRI. Rapport 11/77.

––– (1974) "Outpatient care, health and social services at the Tynnered health and social services center." Stockholm: SPRI. Rapport 18;74.

Socialhogskolan (1979) "Conference on cooperation between health and social services." Stockholm: Socialhögskolan (School of Social Work and Public Administration, University of Stockholm). (mimeo)

Socialstyrelsen (National Board of Health and Welfare) (1978) "The social services and the holistic perspective–social collaboration." Socialstyrelsen redovisar.

––– (1977) "Co-organization Experiments in Falun, Ljusdal and Linköping." Socialstyrelsen redovisar.

SOU (1979) "Goals and means for the health services." State Commission Report by the Health Services Commission.

––– (1977) "The Social Services Act." State Commission Report by the Social Services Commission.

––– (1975) "Collaboration in child care." State Commission Report by the Child Care Commission.

––– (1974) "The social services–goals and means." State Commission Report by the Social Services Commission.

––– (1970) "The incomes of the Swedish people." State Commission Report by the Low Income Commission.

TENGVALD, K. (1981) Professional Hierarchy and the Division of Labour in Teamwork. A Study of the Agencies for Youth Psychiatric Counseling. Stockholm: Arbetslivscentrum.

VON OTTER, C. (1980) "Swedish welfare capitalism: the role of the state," in R. Scase (ed.) The State in Western Europe. London: Croom Helm.

WESTRIN, C. G. (1980) Primary Health Care: Cooperation Between Health and Welfare Personnel in Sweden. Mariestad: Skaraborgs Läns Ländsting.

5

FINLAND

GEORG WALLS

Public services and interventions in Finland have expanded considerably in the last few decades. This growth is linked to the social structure of this country and its ability to meet the needs and everyday activities of its members. It is related to the society's goals and can be analyzed against the economic and political structures of society.

As public sector services and administration have grown, the role of special interest groups have changed. Administration has reached a certain level of autonomy. Social welfare and health care policies require contextual and functional flexibility to reach their societal goals. This, in turn, presupposes a holistic approach from the goal-setting to the supply of services and the delivery of care. An important tool in the development of this approach is cooperation both within and between these two different systems.

In order to understand the interaction of health and social services, it is necessary to distinguish between cooperation and collaboration. Cooperation refers to the degree of organizational coherence in aims and means and involves the organization's establishment of frameworks to implement the goal of interrelationships between its units and members. Collaboration refers to interpersonal interaction and concerns activities based on common goals and implemented through mutual interaction of the people involved. An analysis of functional cooperation requires an understanding of these concepts and their inter-relationship (Walls, 1981).

In Finland and other Nordic countries, social services closely reflect social security policies. However, social work has become institutionalized as a "bag" carried by social workers containing personal services provided on the basis of specific considerations. Hence, questions arise concerning connections of services, the efforts on the individual or family level, and programs on the state or municipal level. This is especially true in the allocation of resources for social security including personal services.

HISTORICAL DEVELOPMENT OF COOPERATION

The social welfare and health care systems in Finland historically differ from each other in decision-making, services, and financing. The Paupers Edict of 1879 required each town to elect a special government (later a board) to care for the poor and helpless. The state provided medical care through its network of hospitals and doctors. However, it was the municipalities' duty to care for the poor. Both of these public judicial organizations financed their operations mainly through the income tax (Walls, 1980).

There has been cooperation among municipalities since the first municipal laws were passed in the 1860s. Wider cooperation ensued in the 1920s when large municipal corporations were formed to establish and maintain tuberculosis sanatoria and district asylums. The present system of municpal corporations was established in 1932. Within the statutory municipal corporations, cooperation was obligatory (Walls, 1980). The interrelation between health and social welfare policies has long been recognized in Finland. This is apparent from the discussion of the social links between sickness and health, which has been carried on in the Finnish medical journals for nearly a hundred years. The discussion has been particularly important as an incentive to sociomedical measures (Rauhala, 1978).

Providing greater organizational stability for cooperation between the social welfare and health care systems has assumed national importance since the early 1960s. The establishment of the Ministry of Social Affairs and Health in 1968, replacing the earlier Ministry for Social Affairs, is a concrete result of this concern. Structurally, the National Board of Health in the Ministry of the Interior was transferred to the Ministry for Social Affairs and Health. Also, the National Board of Social Welfare was established as a new central office.

In the late 1960s, attention finally focused on increasing the level of cooperation on the local level in Finland. On the initiative of the new Ministry of Social Affairs and Health, a committee determined ten areas for cooperation and presented an appropriate administrative division of responsibility. It was particularly in connection with the preparation of the Public Health Law, passed in 1972, that the organization of combined social welfare and public health municipal boards was discussed (Walls, 1980),

The system of public decision-making and administration operates on three levels in Finland. On the national level, control of and authority for the social welfare and health care systems belong to the ministry, while the implementation is the task of the central boards of the ministry. On the regional level, the supervision and control of social welfare and health care belong, correspondingly, to the county government's social welfare and public health department. Its tasks are to guide, plan, and coordinate the county-level social welfare and health care, and to offer advice and assistance to local municipalities. In addition, it arranges regional training courses for the personnel in both fields. The county social welfare and health departments cooperate with the school departments, regional planning officials, employment officials, and municipal or other corporations producing social welfare and public health services.

On the local level, a reform corresponding to that on the national or county level has not yet been achieved. It must be noted, however, that some cooperation exists between the various communal administrative units and also between these units and the voluntary social welfare and health care associations and organizations. Regulations concerning the elected representatives of the local social welfare and health boards define appropriate educational and professional backgrounds. Joint memberships on the two boards promote the mutual exchange of information and cooperation between the units (Walls, 1980). Three towns in Finland have combined their social welfare and public health boards and, correspondingly, their administrative offices. A recently completed research project (SOPUKKA), initiated by the National Boards of Social Welfare and Health, documents the experiences of these mergers combining the local boards.

The accent on hospitals in Finnish health care during the 1950s and 1960s impeded the development of primary health care services. By the start of the 1970s, 90 percent of all health expenditures were for hospital treatment, with specialist medicine taking the major share. Furthermore, total health costs grew twice as fast as Finland's GNP from 1950 to 1960. In sum, the primary health system had become fragmented as a result of numerous seperate laws (*Health Services in Finland,* 1979). The primary health care legislation mandated the commune to establish a health center either on its own or jointly with one or more neighboring communes. Personal social services are provided either within the center by a social worker or in cooperation with social work agencies.

The major laws affecting social welfare and its implementation are the Social Assistance Act of 1956, the Child Welfare Act of 1936, the Act for the Mentally Disabled of 1958, the Welfare for Intoxicant Abusers Act of 1961, the Communal Home Help Act of 1956, and the Child Maintenance Security Act of 1977. The Act on Social Welfare Administration underwent some reform in 1981. This resulted in an increase of the rights of social workers to make decisions; the prior situation reserved decision-making in the clients' matters almost totally for members of the social welfare boards (*Health Services in Finland,* 1979).

The Act on Social Welfare Administration includes stipulations on the formal training of social workers. The social worker should have a vocational degree from a school of social work or a master's degree in social policy.

COLLABORATION BETWEEN HEALTH
AND SOCIAL WELFARE PERSONNEL

Multidisciplinary seminars have enhanced collaboration between social welfare and primary health care personnel in Finland. The main justifications for cooperation have been summarized as follows:

- the development of social welfare and health care organizations;
- the integration of overlapping functions and tasks; the elimination of gaps in the border areas;
- the feasible use of joint resources;
- the changing of attitudes among the different occupational groups;
- increased accessibility of services; and
- the effective performance of the alleviating, preventive, and constructive functions and tasks set to social welfare and health care [Sosiaaliturvan, 1974].

The fact that social welfare and health care share the same clients makes it necessary to integrate goals, services, and resources. It is estimated that between 80 and 90 percent of social welfare clients need health care services and are, in this respect, clients with multiple problems or multiple symptoms (Jussila, 1975).

The largest groups of clients needing both social welfare and health care services are the aged, the handicapped, the mentally disabled, and alcoholics. Even today, illness or disease accounts for one-third of the reasons why people need and receive regular social benefits. This situation exists despite the passage, in 1963, of the National Sickness Insurance Act. Additionally, thousands of others receive temporary social benefits annually in the form of hospital treatment (Sosiaaliturvan, 1974).

The SOPUKKA project was initiated by the Finnish National Boards of Social Welfare and Health in 1977 (see Kaitalo and Walls, 1978). Research examined the effects of the integration of the decision-making boards and the administrative offices of social welfare and health care in three towns in Finland— Kerava, Kotka, and Lappeenranta. Other communes considered the possibility of combining their board organizations. Instead, they searched for more informal ways of integrating some service delivery systems. To enable comparisons, eight other communes were added to the study (Kaitalo and Walls, 1978).

The survey sample included 795 social welfare and health care professionals, representing the professional groups with potential for cooperation. The list includes doctors, nurses, social workers in health centers, medical treatment personnel, home sick care nurses, psychologists, speech therapists, communal health supervisors, and government supervisors from the health care system. It also includes home help personnel, old age and child care workers, and administrative personnel from both sectors. Data were collected in directed group interviews. Seventy-one percent of the sample was selected for final analysis.

Study results indicate that satisfactory cooperation between social welfare and health care personnel does not exist in areas such as home nursing, children's day care centers, children's health center care activities, care of alcoholics and invalids, and services to the aged and the chronically ill. The social welfare system cooperated more actively than the health care sector as a rule, although the overall degree of cooperation is low. Furthermore, the attitudinal "readiness" and predisposition to cooperate is higher in the social welfare sector when measured by the opinions of social workers (Kaitalo and Walls, 1978). The combined social welfare and health care model showed a higher degree of actual cooperation between the personnel groups representing different occupations. Consequently, the need for cooperation proved to be lower on the field level in the combined system than in the separate, traditional system (Kaitalo and Walls, 1978).

Comparing different organizational frames produces some evidence supporting the hypothesis on the importance of organizational policies for behavioral modifications—specifically, actual cooperation and interprofessional collaboration. Examples of professional collaboration patterns are documented in Tables 5.1-5.4.

Most social welfare contacts with health care are horizontal—that is, administrators are in contact with their peers and fieldworkers collaborate with their colleagues in health care. Only about 10 percent of the contacts of social welfare fieldworkers are made with the heads of health care sectors (see Table 5.2; Kaitalo, 1979).

The contact network of social welfare is more complex than that of the health care sector. About one-third of all contacts by health service professionals with their social welfare counterparts are directed toward the heads of that sector. This indicates a deficiency in collaboration especially for the health care sector, which primarily contacts the social welfare sector for coordinative reasons. The distributions also indicate a greater ability to collaborate in administration than at the field level (Kaitalo, 1979).

These collaboration patterns need to be retested, as reliability problems arise when empirical measurements of collaboration are attempted. The incongruity between the actual and the ideal state of cooperation is illustrated by the figures in Table 5.3. The collaboration partners represent the municipal social welfare agency, the Alcoholic Care Clinic, the Educational Guidance Bureau, the Health Center, and the Mental Health Center, all active in Tampere, a city of 165,000 inhabitants.

These findings on the collaboration patterns come from a 1978 research study by Makinen under the auspices of the SOPUKKA project. The study sample comprised fieldworkers of the units mentioned—those professionals directly involved in the delivery of noninstitutional services. The data were collected through questionnaires in 1979. The sample comprised

TABLE 5.1 Percentage of the "Most" and the "Next Most" Important Contacts by Social Welfare Professionals to Health Care Professionals

	From					
To	Heads of Social Welfare (n=32)	Social Workers (n=42)	Home Help Workers (n=50)	Alcoholism Care (n=15)	Children's Day Care (n=29)	Institutional Care (n=34)
Heads of Health Institutions	40	6	12	15	5	12
Doctors	15	21	16	31	27	32
Home Sick Care	18	16	29	14	12	17
Health Nurse	20	33	33	26	54	29
Special Personnel	7	24	10	14	2	10
	100	100	100	100	100	100

Based on Kaitalo (1979).

TABLE 5.2   Percentage of the "Most" and "Next Most" Important
Contacts by Social Welfare Professionals to Health Care
Professionals

To	Heads of Health Care Institutions (n=48)	From Doctors (n=22)	Home Sick Care (n=13)	Health Nurse (n=31)	Special Personnel (n=22)
Heads of Social Welfare Institutions	36	30	40	18	36
Social Workers	21	21	20	39	32
Home Help Workers	26	25	35	37	24
Alcoholism Care	1	2	–	3	5
Children's Day Care	2	2	–	–	–
Institutional Care	14	20	5	3	3
Total	100	100	100	100	100

Based on Kaitalo (1979).

111 professionals; the dropout rate was 14 percent (see Table
5.3).

   Consistent with the findings of the SOPUKKA research
study, social welfare agency staff are more willing to establish
contacts with the health center than vice-versa. However, the
social welfare agency has very limited collaboration with the
small, specialized service delivery clinics, bureaus, and centers.
This is at least partly due to differences in size. Small organizations, especially the Alcoholic Care Clinic and the Educational
Guidance Bureau, maintain contacts regularly with the social
welfare agency (Mäkinen, 1980). An additional explanation
for these differences in cooperation is official sponsorship and
status. The Social Welfare Agency and the health center are
both municipally governed organizations and regulated by acts

TABLE 5.3 Frequency of Contacts in Client Matters Taken by the Social Welfare Agency to Other Service Delivery Parties and the Contacts to the Welfare Agency (percentages)

Frequency of Contact	Agency							
	Alcoholism Clinic		Educational Bureau		Health Center		Mental Health Center	
	n=10	n=30	n=12	n=30	n=34	n=30	n=9	n=30
	by	to	by	to	by	to	by	to
Often	80	3	25	–	9	13	22	–
Medium	10	7	42	7	12	37	22	15
Rarely	10	87	33	90	79	47	56	78
Lacking	–	3	–	3	–	3	–	3
Totals	100	100	100	100	100	100	100	100

Based on Mäkinen (1980: Tables 1 and 2).

TABLE 5.4   Contacts Taken by Clients to Different Service Delivery
Systems Specifically for Each System (percentages)

To	From Social Welfare Agency (n = 61)	Alcoholism Clinic (n = 43)	Educational Guidance Bureau (n = 27)	Health Center (n = 61)	Mental Health Center (n = 37)
Social Welfare Agency	–	9	4	–	–
Alcoholism Clinic	–	–	4	1	–
Educational Guidance Bureau	–	–	–	–	–
Health Center	2	12	7	–	11
Mental Health Center	–	2	–	–	–
Other Systems*	2	–	4	4	11
Several Systems (unspecified)	9	16	16	1	6
No Contacts Outside	87	61	66	94	72
Total	100	100	100	100	100

*Other systems include the court, marriage counseling, private medical services, and
kindergarten.
Based on Saarenpää (1981: Tables 5-9).

and rules, while some of the specialized service units are partly
voluntary organizations.

The contact patterns for clients of the service delivery systems were studied by Saarenpää. Clients included were chosen
by means of a stratified sample. The criteria for inclusion were
that the clients were at least 17 years of age and were able to
answer the questionnaire, and that the research did not create
treatment difficulties. The questionnaires were given to the
clients in 1979 by fieldworkers selected at random. The clients
filled out the questionnaire at home, except for the clients of
the Alcoholic Area Clinic, who answered the questionnaire on

site. The number of clients included in the study was 246; 70 percent returned the form. The movement of clients from one agency to another was studied by asking the respondents about their contacts in separate service delivery systems (see Table 5.4).

The movement of clients appears minimal according to their personal evaluations. However, it must be pointed out that respondents may have reported only those contacts necessary to solve their acute problems. Thus, the contacts to treat long-term problems may not have been considered. These results indicate the need for a more objective monitoring methodology. The "life cycle" of the problem must be considered. The fact that some of the delivery systems have parallel services is very functional for the client although questionable from the point of view of the delivery system and society.

COOPERATION FOR WHAT AND BY WHOM?

The main justifications for cooperation have been discussed earlier in this chapter. However, the SOPUKKA project and the follow-up studies focused on the reasons why the personnel thought cooperation with social welfare/health care systems is necessary in performing their jobs. Because the question is the SOPUKKA study was open-ended, there were some difficulties in specific analysis. Nevertheless, the reasons for cooperation offer a basis for outlining certain trends. Regardless of their level, employees in social welfare and health care organizations most frequently noted that general or problem-based needs were the reason for cooperation between their fields of activity. The second most numerous category of responses consisted of the general parallelism of functions and the mutual clientele. The results also noted that increased knowledge and information were benefits of linkage. The parallel organization of functions, the division of labor, and the use of resources were mentioned by both sets of employees. The obligation to cooperate did not seem to be a reason for cooperation, since it was noted by less than one percent of the sample.

The practical interaction between social welfare and health care is an indication that the need for cooperation has become recognized. Starting from individual employees' experiences, the SOPUKKA project studied how contacts were directed between the sectors. In the social welfare sector, it is those social workers working with the problems arising between social welfare and health care who play a central role in developing cooperation. Intoxicants, invalids, the mentally disabled, and problems of child care and psychic disorders fall into this middle ground (Kaitalo, 1979).

In the health care sector, the health nurse and the social worker at health centers hold key roles. Also, doctors, physiotherapists, psychologists, and speech therapists cooperate with the social welfare professionals, but only in specified functional areas (Kaitalo, 1979).

These results demonstrate that the need for cooperation grows relative to the size of the organization. On the other hand, large organizations have more cooperative programs than the smaller ones. The size of the organization seems both to increase the need for cooperation and to make it feasible.

Another study of the same organizations was based on contact diaries. It revealed that cooperation was rather immaterial. The contacts between organizations focused more on client referrals, not on actual treatment or services. The content of the contacts did not differ significantly between organizations except for the social welfare office, where the majority of the contacts concerned clients' economic circumstances. (Manninen, 1980).

The SOPUKKA project research indicates a wide range of reasons for cooperation. Only a part of the existing cooperation results from a conception of the human being as a totality. Need for cooperation is created in like manner by various malfunctions and a specific need for service or referral.

OBSTACLES TO LINKAGES BETWEEN
SOCIAL WELFARE AND HEALTH

The difficulties in linking social welfare and health care services to meet the needs of clients arise for a variety of reasons:

the location of services;

the norms and regulations affecting service delivery;

the decision-making process;

the organization of services;

the resources available (e.g., economic, personnel);

the knowledge about services;

the attitudes toward cooperation;

the readiness to collaborate.

The obstacles to linkages between the social welfare and health sectors may vary according to the organizational level in question. Social welfare administrators in Finland characterize the obstacles as well as the needs for cooperation in general terms. The obstacles cited by fieldworkers are more specified, although social welfare professionals define the obstacles in a more comprehensive way than health care professionals.

It is evident that certain professions assume special significance in developing cooperative and collaborative activities. Therefore, it is helpful to draw contact maps to reveal the linkages. The key social welfare roles in the development of cooperative and collaborative relationships with the health system are

(a) the social workers dealing with problems in the field of alcoholism, care of the disabled, the mentally disturbed, or disabled, and child care;

(b) those officials and fieldworkers treating clients with problems related in one way or another to psychic disorders; and

(c) social welfare personnel involved in home help activities.

In health care, respectively, the most important cooperation and collaboration roles seem to be held by

(a) the health nurse;

(b) social workers in hospitals and health centers, since they maintain close contacts with the social welfare agencies;

(c) specialized health personnel (e.g., psychologists and voice therapists; see Kaitalo and Walls, 1978; Kaitalo, 1979).

Since the questions regarding obstacles to cooperation and collaboration were vague in the SOPUKKA research project, it is not possible to draw conclusions about the relative importance of each. Since cooperation and collaboration are dynamic activities, including quantitative aspects and qualitative dimensions, a study may capture the "dynamics" only superficially.

CONCLUSIONS

As the decade of the 1980s begins, social welfare and health care in Finland are comprehensive systems operating within the framework of social policy. About 24 percent of all public expenditures are allocated to health care and 9 percent to social welfare. Moreover, taking care of people's health, illness, and social welfare needs requires strong, independent systems. However, these systems are at the same time weakening informal social support systems, social networks, and personal responsibility. This may be a consequence of the development of formal systems, which have created a "false imagination" that people are no longer indispensable to each other. A problem of reification of social relations and responsibility has developed (Nisbet, 1970).

Social welfare and health care services are governed by numerous official standards. These define the lines of action and the boundaries between the sectors. The problems of social welfare and health care policies are identified and defined by the operational systems, the same systems that define human needs.

Limited resources should not be allowed to misguide the pursuit of valid satisfaction of needs. The development of social welfare policy necessitates a confrontation with problems of evaluation and emphasis. Cooperation between the systems can play a part in solving these confrontations and debates. This is possible only when basic understanding of the responsibility of each sector is achieved. Thus, the importance of research, analysis, and experimentation becomes obvious. The accent on cooperation does not in itself require a negation of the specific character of either system. On the contrary, the result may be a more precise identification of areas of joint function, uniqueness, and uniformity. This identification forms a basis for operational programs.

The integration of the responsibility for care and services poses problems of control which may affect decision-making and administration. This fact becomes evident in the results of the SOPUKKA project. Appointed representatives on the boards believed that cooperation increases complexity beyond normal abilities to cope and makes it more difficult to familiarize oneself with the information needed for effective decision-making. On the other hand, they stress the need for social welfare and health care to be linked in some manner.

Thus, questions of management cause the operative problem. Governable functional units should be developed. The starting point should be a field of activity. This would constitute a need for socioecological adjustment and functional location of the responsibilities for care and services.

The governability of the social and health care of a community is closely linked with the systems of decision-making and administration of that community. The efforts to make the responsibilities for care and services more governable must become a part of the more general effort to develop functioning and responsible local communities. Business fluctuations and rootlessness of population work against these efforts. Therefore, solutions must be flexible and innovative.

REFERENCES

Health Services in Finland (1979) Helsinki: Ministry of Social Affairs and Health.

JUSSILA, A. (1975) "Sosiaalihuollon ja terveydenhuollon tehtävänjako ja yhteistyö," in J. Aer (ed.) Kansanterveystyön käsikirja. Helsinki.

KAITALO, H. (1979) Hallintoratkaisut ja työnkuvat sosiaali–ja terveydenhuollon yhteistoiminnassa. Research Reports 53. Sopukka 3. University of Tampere, Department of Social Policy (English summary).

KAITALO, H. and G. WALLS (1978) Sosiaali–ja terveydenhuollon yhteistoimintaprofiilit. Research Reports 49. Sopukka 2. University of Tampere, Department of Social Policy (English summary).

MANNINEN, P. (1980) "Eräiden sosiaali–ja terveydenhuollon organisaatioiden asiakaspalvelua koskeva yhteistoiminta Tampereella." B.A. dissertation, Department of Social Policy, University of Tampere.

MÄKINEN, P. (1980) "Asiakaspalvelun yhteistoiminta viiden sosiaalija terveydenhuollon organisaation välillä Tampereella." M.A. dissertation, Department of Social Policy, University of Tampere.

NISBET, R. (1970) Social Bond. New York.

RAUHALA, P. L. (1978) "Terveydenhoito-opista kansanterveystieteeseensuomalaisen sosiäälilaaketieteen kehittymisestä." M.A. dissertation, Institute of Social Policy, University of Jyvaskyla.

SAARENPÄÄ, M. (1981) "Eräiden sosiaali–ja terveydenhuollon organisaatioiden yhteistoiminta asiakkaiden kannalta." M.A. dissertation, Department of Social Policy, University of Tampere.

Social Welfare in Finland (1980) Helsinki: Ministry of Social Affairs and Health.

Sosiaaliturvan, Keskusliitto (1974) Raportti: Sosiaali–ja terveydenhuollon yhteistoiminta, 1973. Helsinki.

WALLS, G. (1981) "Yhteistoiminta yhteiskuntatieteiden kehikoissa," in P. Kolari (ed.) Sosiaalipolitiikkä–sosiaalityo [Cooperation Within the Frames of Social Sciences]. Acta Universitatis Tamperensis. Ser. A. Tampere.

––– (1980) "The interrelations and cooperation practices of social welfare and health care on the municipal level in Finland," in L. Simonen (ed.) Working Papers Nr. 2, Paper for the ECSW Workshop on Primary Health Care: Cooperation Between Health and Welfare Personnel. University of Tampere, Department of Social Policy.

6

CANADA

GEORGE TSALIKIS

A symbolic link between health and social services was established in Canada in 1944 by the Department of National Health and Welfare Act which extended the authority of the old Department of Pensions and Health to include "all matters relating to the promotion or preservation of the health, social security and social welfare of the people of Canada over which the Parliament of Canada has jurisdiction." This thinking was based on the Western Allies' propaganda in the war years, which promised universal prosperity through holistic planning. However, it did not agree with the constitutional claims of Canada's provinces which argued that the federal authority had no jurisdiction over these matters. In reality, the establishment of a Department of National Health and Welfare meant little more than the federal government's determination to make fiscal arrangements with the provinces in these major fields of social policy. Not surprisingly, the department became a symbol of the segregation of health and welfare services. Its two components, like a pair of cherries, were only linked at the top, where a minister supervised the actions independent of two deputies who worked in isolation from each other.

In recent years, provincial policies are moving toward linking health and personal social services. This trend draws idealistic support from the holistic approach to health care as defined by the World Health Organization (WHO). However, it is basically a reflection of government concern about the growing cost of therapeutic care. It is unrealistic to suggest that Canada is at a turning point in favor of integrating existing services or preventive care, as the popular media suggest. Traditional services are separated by constitutional, administrative, financial, ideological, and professional fetters which are hard to break. It is noteworthy that links between health and social services in Canada have not developed between the traditional forms of organization in these two areas. The links appear in the "new" personal services established under the umbrella of health care institutions. There are important historical reasons for this. Although personal social services are the focus of this chapter, it will be necessary to make occasional references to other social services as well in order to place the subject within a general social frame.

HISTORICAL DEVELOPMENT

Canada participated actively in the efforts of the League of Nations to promote social policies in the industrial world. However, Canadians were not protected by such policies on a large scale until World War II. The reasons for this related to the nation's economics, its political organizations, ideologies, and myths (Tsalikis, 1973, 1982). First, the pace of industrialization in Canada was slower and less devastating than in the crowded industrial centers of Europe. Second, this vast country provided good opportunities for agriculture and frontier development which both sustained the traditional forms of family dependency and provided some security against the ills of industrial expansion. Third, frontier opportunities and the idea of progress supported the popular philosophy that a free economy with vast untapped resources provides equal opportunity for all to prosper and to manage their own affairs without public support. Fourth, in this socioeconomic frame, the Canadian labor movement was not influenced markedly by the class-conscious spirit of European labor. It rarely exerted any effective political pressure for fundamental social reform.

The Canadian Confederation, legalized by the British North American Act (BNA), was based on what came to be known as the National Policy (Tsalikis, 1981). This was designed to serve primarily the interest of the "colonial aristocracy" of Central Canada, which was to become the industrial heartland of the nation. The other regions were to be maintained as hinterlands. The act gave the federal government unlimited power of taxation to develop the country's economic infrastructure. The provinces were granted limited jurisdiction and taxing powers. They were authorized to impose direct taxation; this was highly unpopular and had a small yield. Thus, the provinces relied on small federal subsidies to develop some public education, health and welfare programs, all of which fell under provincial jurisdiction. Since the prevailing view held that expenditures for such services should be restricted, development after Confederation was slow and subject to federal provincial controversies over public revenue. Under these circumstances, until World War I the needy received support mainly from sectarial charity or ethnic mutual aid groups. In the 1910s, the prairie provinces, particularly Manitoba, led Canada in social reforms inspired by the Progressive movement in the United States (Tishler, 1971). Massive immigration from Europe (1896-1914) and the need to assimilate ethnic groups resulted in compulsory English education, child welfare, and other custodial services. As in the United States (Tishler, 1971), the Progressives supported such services to restrict the growth of ethnic mutual aid which fostered alien lifestyles that the Anglo-Saxon majority saw as the root of poverty. In addition to the policies established to check the "foreign peril" (Mott, 1970), the provinces began to establish municipal welfare programming for the "deserving" indigent in the spirit or the letter of the English Poor Laws. Such measures were mainly concerned with widows and orphans.

In the health care field, four basic problems were influential in providing services outside the traditional private market: epidemics and severe health problems among the destitute; the inability of remote and economically unattractive communities to secure continuing medical services, the need of industrialists of remote or risky operations to secure medical services and thus attract labor; and, finally, the increasing difficulty of hospitals to secure funds for expensive technology (Tsalikis, 1982). These needs were met in various ways: by public health measures modeled on British precedents; by salaried municipal doctors; through contract practice for groups of patients; by industrial insurance plans; and through commercial insurance plans for individuals or groups against specific health risks or hospitalization.

During World War I, the Canadian government expanded its revenue policies through direct taxation to meet its war commitments. The provinces' anger against this "intrusion" into their constitutional rights was tempered by the assurance in the House of Commons (1917) that this was a provisional measure. Nevertheless, after the war the federal government continued collecting direct taxes and legitimized its new revenue through pensions, emergency aid, and public works employment for war victims and the unemployed. Between the two wars, the federal government attempted to introduce health and unemployment insurance. This resulted in constitutional deadlock when the Employment and Social Insurance Act (1935) was declared "ultra vires" by the Privy Council. The only federal insurance measure of the time accepted by the provinces was the Old Age Pension Act (1927), which protected British subjects under such rigid conditions that few people could qualify for benefits.

The Great Depression and World War II opened a new era of national social policies in the spirit of the Atlantic Charter and other "humanitarian" declarations of the Western Allies. The trend was further supported by the Rowell-Sirois Royal Commission on Federal-Provincial Relations (1940) and the 1941 Federal-Provincial Conference. In 1941, the Canadian government introduced the Wartime Tax Agreement Act and put into effect its Unemployment Insurance Act of 1940 to deal with anticipated unemployment after the war. This act was the first federal entry into areas outside its constitutional jurisdiction. Subsequently, the federal government announced a Reconstruction Plan to oil the war machine (Cassidy, 1943). A Special Committee on Social Security was appointed by the House of Commons in 1943, but it soon became apparent that little reconstruction was in store. Ian MacKenzie, Federal Minister of Health, told the committee that Reconstruction would face the "acid test" of conflicting economic interests. Finally, at the 1945 Reconstruction Conference, the provinces refused the federal proposals for national health insurance and other reforms because they entailed the loss of provincial income tax rights. Only family allowances introduced in 1944 to repair the declining population growth were accepted.

In the process of long-term negotiations since the loss of the Reconstruction, most of the provinces realized that economic circumstances doomed their claim to direct taxation. The federal government had the appropriate tax machinery which would be uneconomical for them to duplicate, and it was politically unfeasible to raise tax rates for that purpose (Moore, 1966). Thus the federal government, using interprovincial conflicts to its advantage, produced several national social policies to legitimize its paternalistic role in the economy (Tsalikis, 1982). By the mid-1950s, the provinces half-heartedly accepted national policies on a cost-sharing basis in health and welfare. Landmarks in this development were the Hospital Insurance and Diagnostic Services Act (1957), the Medical Care Act (1966), and the Canada Assistance Plan (1966).

During this period it was generally recognized that traditional forms of health care were unable to meet the nation's health needs. Public health units and other programs had limited functions and did not cover the whole nation. Private schemes were also limited. When the idea of health insurance for all began to marshal strong support, the medical profession and the insurance industry (with the consent of unions) moved rapidly to increase the number of private insurance schemes for employees. They argued that traditional private practice and private insurance could cover the whole nation if the government subsidized the medical expenses of those unable to pay. The Royal Commission on Health Services (1964) rejected this view as impracticable because it would require a means test for all Canadians who lived on low incomes (about one-third of the population).

There was never a strong political movement to detach personal social services from the tradition of the Poor Laws. As the number of those in need of such services has increased in recent decades, provincial and municipal authorities have found it increasingly difficult to provide such services on their own resources. Since the late 1960s, several groups have demanded new or better personal social services with no social stigma for certain high-risk populations, such as women, children, the aged, the handicapped, and transient youth. Such pressure on politicians came mainly from groups concerned with their own problems and from professionals eager to extend their work opportunities. The result was the development of many private social agencies, inhibiting reorganization and coordination. Some municipal or other public agencies, such as the public health units, have reviewed or enriched their programs, but they now face more competitors for the limited resources.

ORGANIZATION OF
HEALTH AND SOCIAL SERVICES

Hospital Care

Canadian hospitals confronted two major problems before the introduction of the federal Hospital Insurance Act in 1957. First, the rapid growth of medical technology exceeded their traditional resources. Second, after World War II their emergency wards became busier as an increasing number of people were unable to meet their medical expenses privately. The federal act attempted to resolve these problems by providing universal hospital insurance on a cost-sharing basis with the provinces. Its specific aims were (1) to equalize government financial support to provincial hospitals so that they could cover the whole population; (2) to include some inpatient services previously unavailable; (3) to provide a broader range of outpatient services; (4) to ensure that patients were not burdened excessively during hospitalization; and (5) to improve the standards of hospital care and administration.

These objectives were achieved to some degree (Taylor, 1973). However, federal policy created problems which persist despite later reforms and which have contributed to the trend in favor of linkages between health and social services. First, hospital expansion was stimulated in the late 1940s by Appropriations Act No. 4, which authorized federal grants for hospital construction. Thus, between 1950 and 1955 the number of hospital beds reached an all-time high of 11.3 beds per 1000 population. Second, the support of hospital expansion and insurance made the hospital the temple of health care. Hospital expenditures continued to rise at more than twice the rate of the consumer price index after adoption of the act (Soderstrom, 1978). Soaring hospital costs were due not so much to increasing population, admission rates, or labor costs (an argument often heard from hospital apologists) as to the growth of medical technology, "overspecialization" of physicians, and duplication of expensive equipment of facilities (Tsalikis, 1982).

The introduction of medical care did not restrict the use of expensive hospital services to the extent expected by the policymakers. Hospital utilization rates were seriously affected by a continuing increase in "abuse" of emergency wards. Several studies documented that in the poorer parts of the country and in the inner-city areas, the majority of emergency registrations were for "non-emergent" complaints (Robinson et al., 1969). The trend is attributed to the following: the growth of hospitals long before medical care; unjustifiable referrals of patients by doctors which shifted the burden of support services to hospitals; long waiting lists for doctors' appointments; physicians' desire for shorter working hours and longer vacations (due to their affluence under Medicare); the 50 percent reduction of house calls and telephone consultations after Medicare; the reduction of accessibility to physicians for ordinary care due to increasing specialization; and the provision of hospital-based emergency services (Frechette, 1975). The inadequacy of personal social services, the stigma attached to them, and the lack of important linkages between health and social services have also contributed to the abuse of emergency wards.

Canada has four types of hospitals: general, allied special (e.g., pediatric, maternity, rehabilitation), mental, and tuberculosis hospitals. In terms of ownership, there are public (under provincial law), private (profit-making), and federal hospitals. The public hospitals are operated by provincial authorities, municipalities, the Red Cross, and religious or lay groups. The majority of hospitals are public general hospitals; in 1974, they numbered 860, 63 percent of all hospitals and 60 percent of hospital beds. About 98 percent of all hospital beds in 1974 were operated on a nonprofit basis. Provincial governments regulate and finance most general and allied special hospitals. They operate most mental and T.B. hospitals, but few general ones. Almost 90 percent of hospital operating costs are covered by public funds, mainly drawn from hospital insurance plans.

Medical Care

The Medical Care Act (1966) provided for a 50 percent federal contribution for provincial expenditures with an equalization formula to deal with provincial disparities. To qualify for the federal share, the provincial medicare plans must meet these criteria: (a) comprehensive coverage—that is, the provision of all "medically required" services rendered by a physician or surgeon without consideration of cost or other limitations; (b) universal coverage—that is, at least 95 percent of the eligible population ought to be covered and have access to insurable services without being impeded by charges made to insured persons; (c) portability of benefits to provide coverage for those temporarily absent from a province or those moving to another one that would participate in the scheme; (d) nonprofit administration by a public authority accountable to the provincial government for its financial transaction; and (e) reasonable compensation for physicians on a method of payment agreeable to the profession.

Within four years, all provinces entered the scheme. Although the policy appeared to guarantee a uniform national approach, the plans varied markedly. In the mid-1970s, questions were raised in Parliament about the variations in application of the principles by the provinces. The federal government did not know to what extent the provincial plans violated the principles for the lack of information from the provinces. Legislation was introduced requiring the submission of such information—a requirement that has not been fulfilled so far (Tsalikis, 1982). In 1979, the federal government appointed a special commissioner to review the outcomes of the 1966 policy and make recommendations for change. The review did not make full use of its mandate and concentrated on the issue of "adequate remuneration" for physicians (Tsalikis and Manga, 1980). However, it confirmed that the principles did not work uniformly.

The principle of universality is inhibited by many factors. First, Canada is a vast country with many small communities that are not served by the medical profession. Second, the more affluent provinces financed their programs through regressive premiums which excluded many who could not pay them. Third, despite the act's firm proscription of any barriers to accessibility, some of the richer provinces introduced various user fees which reduced access to care disproportionately for the poor, the aged, and the chronically ill. Fourth, extra billing by physicians became a growing practice discriminating against lower-income groups. Fifth, increased physician specialization resulted from the hospital boom, inhibiting the distribution of services, since specialists (50 percent of all physicians) tended to concentrate in wealthier communities. Finally, as doctors became richer, after the introduction of Medicare, their working hours dropped and visits became shorter (Tsalikis, 1982).

As shown by the Special Commissioner (Hall, 1981), the principle of comprehensiveness received only lip service by both federal and provincial authorities. Whereas the Royal Commission on Health Services (1964) defined "comprehensive care" as the provision of "all health services, preventive, diagnostic, curative and rehabilitative," the act limited itself to medically required services. In fact, the act did not even have a fully therapeutic orientation; it made provisions for only part of the therapeutic process—diagnosis and prescription. Essentially, it was a fiscal measure ensuring federal payment under conditions which secured the interests of the medical profession. The fifth principle of reasonable compensation for physicians by a method of payment agreeable to them was, in fact, a provision in favor of fee for service. Moreover, the government's reluctance to control the pharmaceutical industry resulted in a tremendous burden on the economy in favor of foreign multinational corporations for which health insurance opened a golden era.

The principle of "nonprofit administration by public authority" varied in practice in the provinces, especially since intermediary agencies were allowed to carry certain functions. Provincial schemes vary in their degree of centralization within the provincial administration of health care. Most of the provincial medical care plans are administered by special commissions; this was a compromise with the medical associations. Some of the provinces have two commissions: one for hospital care and one for medical care. Generally, these two sectors are divided; their only connection is the minister to whom they are both accountable. Finally, there is an irony in this principle of "nonprofit administration by public authority," since the main function of this authority is to administer funds for the highly profitable business of doctoring people. Moreover, these funds are derived from regressive taxation and other means of revenue which discriminate against the poor, while the more affluent make more use of medical care than the poor (Tsalikis, 1982).

Under these variable fiscal arrangements medical care is provided in two basic forms of organizations: solo practice and group practice (the latter has gained ground in recent years). A third type of organization, generically called the community health center, began developing after the introduction of medical care.

Public Health Services

Public health services in Canada are heterogeneous with little information output. The annual reports of departments of health make vague references to the variety of services they provide, but these must be considered with caution. Not all the services mentioned are provided by all health units, and not all parts of the country are served; most are inadequately covered. The public health units in Canada suffer chronic personnel shortages.

The public health units provide the traditional services of environmental sanitation, communicable disease control, assessment of high-risk groups for health education or referrals of individuals to physicians, and school health programs. Due to the lack of social services in some areas or their inadequacy in most parts of the country, public health personnel have been increasingly involved in new community care programs outside their traditional roles—for example, family planning activities, free clinics for "doctor-shy" young people (mainly those with sex or drug problems), home care, lifestyle activities, poison control, or emergencies.

All levels of government are involved in public health as suppliers of funds and services. The federal government, in addition to its principal financing role, provides consultation on public health services in the Yukon and Northwest Territories. In the provinces, the typical form of organization is decentralized; most public health services are provided by regional or local health units. These are financed jointly by local and provincial governments, staffed by local government officials, and supervised by provincial authorities. Quebec represents a unique type of organization (to be discussed later), in that specific hospitals are authorized to replace the traditional public health units.

The typical regional or local health unit is headed by a physician, and its services are provided mainly by public health nurses. As needed, some units employ dentists, dental hygienists, nutritionists, and physiotherapists. The units normally cooperate with other municipal services, such as the social welfare department and other voluntary public health agencies.

In addition to these central components, Canada has a host of categorical health care programs dealing with certain diseases or providing supplementary services, such as carrier detection and treatment programs, alcoholism or drug abuse services, environmental health programs, mental health services, occupational health prevention and investigation, and home care programs.

Personal Social Services

Personal social services in Canada are provided primarily by voluntary agencies and the local government. The federal government has participated in the financing of assistance and welfare services under the conditions specified by the Canada Assistance Plan (1966). Eligibility was determined by a "needs test" established by the provincial authority—"needs test" was the euphemism for a notorious "means test" like that of Britain. The federal government believed that the provision of care to persons "is more readily achieved" by smaller regional governments than by larger, national ones (Trudeau, 1969). In fact, neither public assistance nor personal social services is all that "readily" available to those in need because of the social stigma attached to these services. In 1969, the Special Senate Committee on Poverty estimated that 25 percent of Canadians lived in poverty (Report of the Special Senate Committee, 1971). However, only 7 percent of Canadians (most of them elderly, disabled, or women with small children) received assistance and services from welfare departments. Moreover, the system allows for gross disparities among the provinces which belittle the federal government's equalization objective (Hepworth, 1975).

The provincial and municipal social welfare departments are the main government providers of personal social services to welfare recipients. They finance, on behalf of welfare recipients, health services which are not covered by the provincial health insurance programs (medicaments and prosthetics, nursing home services, and some dental services). They operate and finance programs for the mentally and physically handicapped (education, vocational training, and counseling). They provide or finance child care services and adoption services, vocational rehabilitation programs, day care centers, programs for the aged, and other services for high-risk groups. As was noted earlier, similar social services are now found in public health units independently or in cooperation with the social welfare departments in cases concerning potential welfare recipients. Personal social services are also provided in most provinces by community health centers, hospitals, and numerous voluntary organizations drawing from public funds or covered by tax shelters.

In summary, health and personal social services are provided in Canada by all levels of government and by voluntary organizations. Although there are some clear boundaries among these agencies, many health and social services are available from different providers. This is particularly true of the categorical health services and of all personal social services, most of which are categorical, for they concentrate on specific problems facing high-risk groups. Between this type of service and "universal" health care there is a fundamental difference: This duality signifies the effort of a capitalist society to reconcile its traditional principle of individual responsibility with the need to provide for social security through a type of organization based on collective responsibility. The next section stresses that this is a hard exercise hampered by the exasperating mix of old institutions trying to survive and new ones struggling to establish themselves.

LINKING HEALTH AND SOCIAL SERVICES

The Holistic Approach of the Seventies

The trend in favor of hospital care which began after World War II was the beginning of a break from home care which traditionally treated illness. Hospital growth, with federal support in the 1940s and 1950s, resulted in "catastrophic" expenses for the uninsured patient. This threat helped the introduction of hospital insurance and, therefore, the continuing growth of a technology which was gradually seen as entailing the threat of "catastrophic" expenditures for the nation. The addition of medical insurance further deteriorated the situation because the growth of hospitals had also affected Canadian physicians, who became increasingly specialized, hospital-minded, and eager to apply expensive therapies for which the fees and expenses readily came from the public purse. Concern for the growth of medical expenditures was expressed long before this became a public issue. It was the fear of such a growth which inspired the abortive proposals of the Special Committee on Social Security in the 1940s, a bill stretching far beyond therapy. But it was not until the 1960s that politicians began talking in earnest about a crisis in expenditures and the need for reorganization. More accurately, reorganization began before the process of organization was complete. Thus, in 1968 (when only two provinces had entered the scheme), a federal-provincial Task Force on the Cost of Health Services was appointed to produce a three-volume report the next year (Task Force Reports on the Cost of Health Care, 1969).

The report supported the view of some of the provinces that alternative methods of health care organization would make services available to more people in need at a lower cost. "First priority," it read, "should be given to establishing community health centres containing a full range of preventive, diagnostic and curative services. . . . Experiments in Canada have already shown that this may involve the capitalization or uniform payment per person as opposed to the traditional 'fee-for service.' " The Task Force Report marked the beginning of a new period of federal-provincial negotiations which lasted for about eight years. This was a time of unprecedented tension in federal-provincial relations (including the operation of the War Measures Act to "save the nation" from Quebec separatists), which gradually led to the present "constitutional crisis." This period of negotiations produced a new fiscal formula which was incorporated in the Established Program Financing Act (1977). The new policy was influenced, according to the prime minister, "by the growing need for spending constraint, which affected all levels of government" interacting in the field of social services (Trudeau, 1976).

Spending constraints have characterized social expenditures since the early 1970s. The aim is to reallocate resources in favor of capital accumulation in the private sector (Tsalikis, 1980). This shift at all levels of government was backed extensively by the mass media, which worked eagerly for a revival of conservatism. The pill was sugared by several government reports which made many believe (as can be seen in most of the literature of the 1970s) that a new era of social services was advancing, one emphasizing prevention but not symptomatic therapy, a trend to link health and social services for the achievement of better results at a lower cost. Before examining the various new programs emanating from this enthusiasm, it is important to comment on the "holistic" approach to health and social services which has occupied several official publications. This approach is consistent with the well-known definition of health promoted by the World Health Organization: Health is not the mere absence of disease but a state of physical and social well-being.

The earliest Canadian expression of the holistic approach was an experimental plan proposed to the government of Quebec, in 1936, by a "Montreal Group for the Security of the People's Health" comprising doctors, nurses, social workers, and others headed by the famous communist, Dr. Norman Bethune (MacLeod et al., 1978). Naturally, the proposal was rejected; Bethune went to Spain to help the revolutionaries against Franco. He returned the next year only to upset doctors by declaring: "There is no such thing as private health . . . all health is public" (Bethune, 1937). Shortly afterwards he went to China to join the Red Army. During World War II, the messenger of the Reconstruction propaganda, Leonard Marsh, wrote in his Report to the Special Committee on Social Security (1943) that it was "necessary to recognize the essential unities of social security to fit together, in other words all the branches of social insurance and social provision in such a way that they support each other, and work together as a coherent administration."

The idea of holistic health care and integrated services reappeared in public debate and reports in the early 1970s following the Task Force Reports on the Cost of Health Services. These reports were not extensive, but the sections on community health center, regionalization, and other reformist concepts were the prelude of excitement among reformers. Between 1970 and 1974, five provinces commissioned inquiries into their health services, and three of them (Quebec, Manitoba, and British Columbia) received proposals for the integration of health and social services in various degrees and forms (Soderstrom, 1978). This series of provincial reports coincided with the continuing federal-provincial negotiations which resulted in the new fiscal formula mentioned earlier. They all stressed the need for constraints. Those which spoke, directly or indirectly, in holistic terms, concentrated on structural change as if this were the key to the social and physical well-being of Canadians. This tendency to mistake the form for the essence of things was further enhanced by modern systems theory.

The provincial reports were followed by the celebrated federal document, "A New Perspective on the Health of Canadians," published under the name of the Minister of Health, Marc Lalonde. This went much further than the provincial documents, specifically regarding the analysis of existing health care institutions. However, its proposals were weak. Lalonde identified four major components of health and health care: (1) human biology (basic biology of man and the organic makeup of the individual), (2) environment (all matters external to the human body and over which the individual has little or no control), (3) lifestyle (components of health over which individuals have, more or less, control), and (4) health care organization (the existing health care system). The minister stressed that the majority of health expenditures went to the health care component (94.9 percent in 1973-1974), which was basically therapeutic. Moreover, the report noted that medicine is only the "catching net" for the many victims of new health risks produced by the "ominous forces" which inhibit "progress" (Tsalikis, 1980, 1982). Lalonde placed undue emphasis on lifestyles and individual responsibility, overlooking government and corporate "lifestyles." His list of "ominous forces" that produce the major risks to health (heart disease, accidents, and cancer) was short; it excluded many of the risks produced by economic forces over which the individual has little control. Finally, he stated that the prospect of new government policies dealing with the major risks was slim because of the huge investment in medical care.

Reform groups view the inability to reallocate resources to preventive care as a "technological bias" in favor of medicine, which must or can be controlled in the political process (Inglehart, 1977). The problem is more serious than that. Skepticism about the value of medicine has produced a variety of arguments in recent years: (a) that the great advances in health standards of Western society are largely the result of resolutions of the early social problems of industrialization, not the result of curative and preventive medicine; (b) that while this "progress" of industrial nations made modern man healthier, it has also produced its own disease burden, the so-called diseases of civilization, because the industrial way of life "is so far removed from that to which man is adapted by evolution"; and (c) that scientific medicine operating in its present bureaucratic structure produces damages which outweigh its potential benefits (Dubos, 1971; Illich, 1974). Although these criticisms concentrate on medicine, they reflect a general disenchantment with the value system of the Western industrial state and its technological rush. While some critics limit their attacks to technology and industrialization, others (Marxists in particular) see these problems as problems not of technology but of technology under capitalism (Navarro, 1976). In this view, therefore, the extravagant expenses for medical therapies are due to a "class bias," not a technological one.

Linkages and Barriers to Linkages
at the National Level

Constitutional barriers make it impossible to establish any meaningful links between health and personal social services at the national level. Although health, education, and welfare constitutionally belong to provincial jurisdiction, the federal government does act in these areas. However, its involvement relates to more general political considerations of the centralist forces in their struggle to maintain their paternalistic position. In essence, federal policy was a fiscal arrangement. Some general principles were established by the federal authority, especially in the fields of health and welfare; but these resulted from federal-provincial negotiations whose aim was to achieve some degree of consensus among the provinces. In health insurance, federal input was a necessity because such an institution was unknown at the time of Confederation and now most of the provinces wanted it. The federal government was concerned with the general economic repercussions of mass insurance and insisted on some principles that would favor labor mobility and interprovincial competitiveness in business (Special Committee on Social Security, 1943). In other words, more general economic considerations are normally the crux of all matters in federal-provincial relations; differences of opinion between the two levels of government about social services are of secondary importance (Trudeau, 1969). As one observer put it,

> This dichotomy between political and financial responsibility is a serious weakness in Canada's welfare arrangements. It means that every attempt at improvement becomes part of a complex bargain between federal and provincial governments in which, almost invariably, the needs of people are subordinated to political and administrative expediency [Morgan, 1961].

Such expediency has to do primarily with the effort of those provinces which consider themselves as the "losers" under the scheme of Confederation to break from federal economic paternalism.

As conflict over constitutional matters has increased since World War II, the tendency in social policy is for more provincial autonomy (Cameron, in Meekisson, 1977). Thus, it is in the interest of the federal government to show leniency in matters of social policy in order to maintain its paternalistic advantages in areas of greater interest to the centralist forces (i.e., the management of natural resources). On the other hand, the fiscal growth of the federal authority in wartime necessitated some kind of "national purpose" in the field of social policy. This led the federal government to a medley of contradictory policies, the outcomes of which were hardly suitable to its "Robin Hood" image (Tsalikis, 1982).

Nevertheless, the federal government has a powerful tool that should not be overlooked: a highly sophisticated network of media for its propaganda. The "national press" (a chain of centralist news agencies) and other private media contribute to federal propaganda. These means made the federal campaigns on "alternative lifestyles" the fad of the years following Lalonde's New Perspective. Across the nation, mood healers, social workers, psychologists, and "new professionals" (including gurus and their disciples) are now busy trying to modify individual behavior. They teach people how to relax, how to work, how to eat, how to love, how to think, how not to think, even how to die. These are some of the new social services often linked with community health centers, schools, hospitals, and even churches. They are also to be found in the private market for those who can afford them. In fact, the special commissioner on health suggested that the federal government should learn the marketing techniques of successful entrepreneurs (Hall, 1980). So far, the federal government has been preoccupied with behavior modification and the advertising of good lifestyles (physical exercise and abstention from drinking and smoking). It is conceivable that the provinces would accept a fiscal arrangement to include such services in health care organizations. The concept of lifestyles modification, which holds the individual primarily responsible for his or her situation, is part of the ideology of the personal social services developed by the provinces since confederation. These comments raise two questions to which we shall return later: First, for what purpose is a link between health and social services desirable? Second, are the services to be linked compatible?

Linkages and Barriers to Linkages at the Provincial Level

The bias of Canadian health care policies in favor of traditional medical institutions and the public debate about soaring medical costs brings about the concept of community health care. Although the concept is variably used in the literature, it usually means all health services provided outside the traditional medical setting (the doctor's office and the hospital). These services are not purely medical. They concentrate on the physical aspect of health, but they also take into account the nonphysical components of illness. As such, they deal with the individual's need within his or her community's socioeconomic frame. Obviously, the emphasis is on prevention to be achieved by linking health and social services. The list of such services provided in Canada can be divided into the following broad and often overlapping categories: (a) traditional public health activities; (b) new public health activities, such as lifestyle programs, home care, family planning, poison control, or emergencies; (c) community mental health, such as counseling for children and adults in stressful situations, programs for the retarded, and rehabilitation of patients discharged from mental institutions; (d) a variety of categorical programs for high risk groups—for example, free clinics for young people with drug or other problems, services to day care centers, home care and other programs for the elderly, services to battered wives and children; and (e) the traditional personal services for recipients of social assistance.

Many community services have developed recently outside the government sector. According to Schwenger (1973), a senior public health teacher, this trend, which represents the traditional distrust of government in North America, has caused anxiety among public health professionals. It explains recent moves "either to remove the word public (e.g., School of Health, Department of Health) or replace it with the word community (Community Health Nurse, Canadian Community Health Association)." Thereupon, he added that at the same time as public health organizations and personnel are attempting to dissociate themselves from the word public,

> the principles of public health have been bought by almost everyone else in the health field. All of a sudden, it seems, medical practitioners have become more community-oriented, family practitioners are now practicing "community medicine" and group practices have become "community health centers." Hospital conferences are focusing on "community outreach." Everyone is now talking about the necessity for the coordination of community health facilities [Schwenger, 1973].

This passage describes the mood of the times, the outcomes of which require analysis of two basic forms of organization of community care: regional integration of health and social services and local community health centers. As there was very little well-documented information on recent developments in this area, we addressed a mail questionnaire to the appropriate provincial departments. Two provinces did not respond. Nova Scotia has not developed any significant links between health and social services. British Columbia has a few community health centers and attempted in recent years to coordinate primary health and social services through Community Human Resource and Health Centers on the basis of the Foulkes Report of 1973. This effort was based on the same principles as those of Manitoba, which led other Western provinces in community health care in the early 1970s. Generally, regional links between health and social services have not advanced considerably anywhere in Canada. Information from Manitoba in response to the survey was poor, but some secondary sources provide a good picture of provincial efforts under the NDP government. The present Conservative government has no plans for expansion in this area.

**Regional Integration of
Health and Social Services**

As J. C. Ryant (1977), an inside observer of Manitoba's regional integration, stated:

> The imagery most appropriate to the Manitoba experience is that of two teams of bridge builders on opposite sides of a wide river, attempting to span the stream without consulting a set of plans until parts of the bridge structure extend well out over fast water from each bank. The major question is: will the two sections meet in the middle and form a single structure?

One team of bridge builders was on the side of social services. In 1971, a Single Unit Delivery System (SUDS) was created in each of the regional Offices of the Department of Health and Social Development to integrate public health and basic social services offered by the province. Personal service teams contained social workers, public health nurses, and medical officers. The team members reported to a team leader for their case loads and to a senior worker in their own discipline on professional issues. By 1978, eight regional units provided child welfare services, family counseling, community mental health services, public health nursing and education, home economics, home care, services for the aged, and other personal and community programs (Ryant, 1977). Ryant pointed out that integration began "by administrative fiat" without any definition of "teams" and "team work," with little assistance in working as a team, resolving interprofessional differences, or serving more collaboratively. However, some progress was noted in terms of converting workers who were initially opposed to integration into advocates of it.

On "the other side of the river" emerged the concept of district health centres, first described in the 1972 White Paper on Health Policy. The province was divided into seven regions. In each one a district health board was to allocate resources and decide on the degree to which health facilities should be integrated with social services. The aim was to coordinate fragmented services provided at a high cost. By 1975, several district health centers were set up in rural and urban areas providing ambulatory care and personal social services. Ryant reported that rural district health centers seemed to be more successful than urban ones, basically because the benefits from integration of health and social services were greater in the former. He cited many reasons for this, among them that (a) health care has greater public legitimacy than social services and the combination of the two in rural areas (characterized by higher value consensus) makes social services less stigmatizing; and (b) rural communities have less economic diversification and derive greater benefits by the addition of a "health and social-service industry" to their economic infrastructure. Generally speaking, it seems that although the integration of health and social services in Manitoba has achieved some degree of coordination, it has produced no profound and few tangible results in terms of reduced public expenditures for better service to the people. As Ryant put it, "in many areas and for a long time, the growing pains have been more evident than the achievements" (1977).

"Growing pains" aside, what are the expected and the actual achievements from such integration and coordination of services? The health care system has been criticized as basically therapeutic; the social service system has been similarly criticized as symptomatic or crisis-oriented and stigmatizing. Other generally recognized "endemic" problems in both systems are fragmentation, noncoordination, duplication, and nonaccountability. "The advocates of integration," Ryant correctly stated, "assert that the structural alteration implied in the integration process offers direct leverage on, and a reasonable solution to these difficulties." Here lies the illusionary expectation of the advocates of integration: that alterations in the *structure* of services alone can result in change in the *essence* of the services provided—that is, change their predominantly symptomatic nature. Basically, social work education and practice in Canada are therapeutic, as is most health care. The expectation that the mixing of these two can produce "physical and social well-being" is tantamount to a belief in alchemy. The White Paper on Health Policy (1972) saw the structural changes mentioned earlier as "solutions" to the problems of *waste* and *inequality* in health care. "The solutions," it stated, "would *of course* be evolutionary . . . would *of course* be pluralistic in kind" (the government's emphasis). Another government paper, *Guidelines for the Seventies* (1973), explained that the White Paper did not suggest any rigid formula but that its "special strategy" was "still a proposal" to the providers of services and to the community as a whole. Therefore, there was not much of a strategy involved here, simply the government's intention not to rock the boat. This was made clear in a special "Declaration re Manitoba Government Health Policy" (1973), which assured the medical profession that their traditional rights were not in jeopardy.

Regional integration can be viewed in a wider social perspective. In the words of a critic of such efforts in Canada, Brian Wharf: "A preoccupation with the structural arrangements of the social services, which exclude employment income and housing programs, might be compared to rearranging the deck chairs on the Titanic. It is an exercise in frivolity" (Wharf, 1978). Drawing from the works of several writers in the field, Wharf identified four basic myths about integration: (1) it makes services more readily available; (2) it results in more effective and efficient services; (3) it is necessary because what exists is a chaotic situation; and (4) integration enhances innovation. Subsequently, he concluded that "integrated services have a real potential for increasing levels of bureaucratization, for centralizing authority, for decreasing opportunities for participation by staff and consumers, for reducing choice and increasing expense." Wharf worried about increasing control of human services by both federal and provincial government at the time of fiscal constraints discriminating against social services.

The seemingly disorganized child welfare system in Ontario allowed the staff and board members of many of Ontario's 51 Children's Aid Societies to picket Queen's Park to protest budget cuts. I am not aware of any such possibility in a regionalized integrated child welfare system such as exists in British Columbia [Wharf, 1978].

Local Integration of Health and Social Services

The most important effort at local integration is the community health center (CHC), a generic term for a variety of organizations developed since the 1960s. At that time, the West began increasingly to look to the socialist world for alternatives in health care. This type of community organization combined preventive and curative services (Roemer, 1972). In Canada, the movement to create CHCs began in the era of the Medical Care Act (1967). In 1969, the Task Force on the Cost of Health Services recommended that first priority be given to the establishment of CHCs to reduce the high demand on hospitals. Such centers, providing a full range of preventive, diagnostic, and curative services, were envisaged as branches or satellites of hospitals. By that time, a few CHCs had been established in some provinces by unions or other groups. There also were several clinics (in Alberta and British Columbia) established by medical students. The Canadian Association of Medical Students, at its 1969 convention, supported community clinics providing both medical and social services, but the idea did not spread.

In the early 1970s, two types of CHCs began to develop. One was part of provincial policy to create such organizations linking health and social services at the local level (e.g., in Quebec, Manitoba, and British Columbia); the other appeared as a result of provincial policy to support such organizations established by community groups (e.g., in Ontario). The *ideal* type of a CHC can be defined by its principles, services, and finances. The principles are administration by a mixed board including laypeople and teamwork; the services are primary health care and social services; and financing is based on global budgeting (e.g., Medicare payments, government grants, and private donations). Closest to this ideal type are the organizations set up in Quebec; most remote are some urban clinics simply bearing the name of a CHC and little of its essence.

Quebec was the first province to support the idea of CHCs combining health and social services. Since World War II, Quebec has resisted most federal proposals on social policy except those which gave the province special fiscal advantages or allowed it to develop local policies. The standard policy of Quebec has emphasized its own priorities due to cultural differences and culture-specific needs. However, it is argued that this emphasis did not reflect a genuine intent to improve services, but was simply an expression of the interests of provincial elites and politicians (Renaud, 1976). In 1966, the government of Quebec resisted the deferral plans for Medicare "for self-serving political reasons" (Renaud, 1976). To delay "federal reform" the province appointed the Castonguay-Nepveu Commission to examine both the implications of the act for Quebec and the province's social security and social services. The extensive scope of the review was largely due to pressure from unions and other reformist groups availing themselves of political instability in the province. Ironically, whereas the government of Quebec had been emphasizing cultural uniqueness for decades, these groups lobbied for a system of health and social services such as the British one. Moreover, a survey showed that a higher proportion of people in Quebec than elsewhere in Canada wanted a federal plan (Taylor, 1978). Presumably, this facilitated Quebec's entry.

The Commission's Report (1970) was based on the belief that ill-health is rooted in social conditions. Therefore, treatment must occur in a comprehensive system linking health and social services and making them accessible to all who needed them. Thus, the Health and Social Services Act (1971) grandly declared: "Every person has the right to receive adequate continuous and personal health services and social services from a scientific, human and social standpoint." However, the fulfillment of this right was subject to "the organization and resources of the establishments providing such services" (Article 4). The reform was based on three principles: regionalization, consumer participation, and reorganization. Regionalization was not concerned with linking health and social services as in

British Columbia and Manitoba. In each regional capital, a regional board and a specified general hospital were to undertake the preventive services of the traditional public health unit. The second fundamental reform in Quebec incorporated two principles of the act, reorganization and consumer participation. These Local Community Service Centers (Centre local de services communautaires, CLSC) were designed to be the backbone of the primary health care system, linking preventive and curative services and providing continual patient care. Financing was based on global budgeting; personnel were salaried. The CLSC stressed the team approach. All members of the team (doctors, nurses, dentists, psychologists, and social workers) were considered equal in treating the patient. The CLSC was intended to be the screening agency for referring patients to more specialized centers for secondary and tertiary care or to social service centers dealing with other aspects of social security.

The CLSC concept drew opposition from general practitioners, who believed the new organization posed a threat to their professional autonomy (Hamel, 1974). Whereas the legal representative of the profession was the medical association, the new organization made contract and salary negotiation a matter of agreement between the doctor and the government. General practitioners felt that the creation of these services in areas already served by general practitioners would result in duplication of services and higher costs. They suggested that, before creating a new bureaucracy, the government should establish CLSCs on an experimental basis. While these arguments did not avert government action (for reorganization was related to more general political considerations), the medical profession won other battles. Learning from similar professional reactions in the United States, the doctors competed with government in the spirit of the traditional conviction that the private sector can do better. "Instead of bleating about the government development of community health centres... why not set some up ourselves," advised a doctor in 1972 (Wallace, 1972). The idea was particularly successful in Quebec, where the threat was greatest. The doctors began establishing private polyclinics at about the same time the first CLSCs opened. This race was won by the hare, not by the turtle. Today, there are about 450 such polyclinics in Quebec, but only 100 CLSCs of the 210 the government intended to set up (Rheault, 1980). The polyclinics provide almost all the services of traditional care, from plastic surgery to emergency services, on a continual basis. Family care is their token approach to holistic medicine, and group practice their substitutes for team work. Doctors in these polyclinics "by nature or by formation . . . remain soloists," said a senior medical consultant and administrator of these groups (Rheault, 1980).

Quebec was not the pioneer of the CHC development, but the government fully committed itself to the concept in its effort to emphasize the uniqueness of Quebec. Other provinces experimented in CHCs and encountered strenuous opposition from doctors. An expression of professional reaction to the concept occurred at the First International Congress on Group Medicine in 1971 (Tsalikis, 1972b). Economists at the conference disagreed over whether economies could be achieved through a group practice. There were similar disagreements about the CHC. Although the Economic Council of Canada saw "a considerable scope for the development of more economical 'team approaches' . . . including various 'mixes' " of health and social service professionals, some politicians and administrators were cautious (Economic Council of Canada, 1970). For example, in 1969, the federal minister of health stated to the Canadian Labour Congress:

> Although I don't think a full understanding of the long-range impact of the community health centre is completely clear . . . some advantages are immediately foreseeable. The very fact that the consumer has a real role in the planning, development and operation of these centres . . . represents a substantial step forward [Munro, 1969].

The "advantage" foreseen by the minister was not all that "real"; but it was something the Labour Congress was pleased to hear because consumer control of health care had been one of its principal objectives for decades (Tsalikis, 1982).

Under the pressure of heavy health costs, coupled with a growing belief that CHCs could reduce them, the federal minister, acting on behalf of the Conference of Health Ministers of Canada, set up a Community Health Care Project to look into the prospects of the concept. In 1972, a report was submitted by Dr. J.E.F. Hastings, chairman of the project. It added to existing ambiguities and had few concrete predictions about the long-term effects of the CHC. For example, it noted that "the community health centre can only be effective if it is a mutually acceptable partnership of the members of the community and the members of the health care team" (Hastings, 1972). The report recommended a "partnership" between government and professionals, and made three principal recommendations: (1) "the development by the provinces, in mutual agreement with public and professional groups, of a significant number of CHCs"; (2) the reorganization and integration of all health services to ensure accessibility and economy; and (3) the initiation by provincial governments of "dialogue" with the health profession and services to plan, budget, implement, coordinate, and evaluate this system. What resulted from the report? "Neither sweet nor sour," wrote Hastings in 1978. Besides Quebec's and Manitoba's CHC plans (which had been conceived before the Hastings Report) and some sporadic efforts elsewhere, the concept failed to attract widespread support or government interest. The present Conservative government in Manitoba discontinued the NDP plans in this area (Manpower Health Services Commission, 1980). Generally, "mutual agreements" or "dialogues" with the medical profession proved impossible or fruitless. On the contrary, the profession fought the concept with passion everywhere in Canada where governments expressed interest or wished to experiment.

In 1981, there were 172 CHCs in Canada, of which 100 were in Quebec. Most of these (105) served rural areas. The population in the catchment areas of all centers was roughly 3.5 million, about 16 percent of the Canadian population. Most of these centers provide primary health care, primary social services, and home care for high-risk groups. Only three provinces (Saskatchewan, Ontario, and Quebec) had initiated some evaluation of these organizations. As we understand from all sources of information, the evaluations had a limited scope.

The survey of the centers in the three provinces mentioned above revealed several problems in service delivery. While no comprehensive study of the outcomes of these Canadian programs has been published, there is a growing body of plausible critical literature which is supported by the diminishing enthusiasm about the prospects of CHCs across Canada (Renaud, 1976). Naturally, most of the critical literature comes from Quebec, where the promise of reform was unsurpassed.

First, a diversity of developments has fueled confusion over terminology. Even in Quebec, where the CLSCs seemed to be developing under a systematic government plan, there were few specific guidelines. The process of community action was largely open to interpretation by the participating professionals. Thus, there were as many conflicting ideas as there were different workers and divisions within disciplines. The situation did not improve after the Parti Quebecois came to power in 1976. The new government was not impressed with the CLSCs because of their inability to define their role; but it did not provide guidelines. Freezing their budgets and halting their expansion, the new government favored the growth of private polyclinics. Outside Quebec, CHCs developed variably in areas where there was a lobby group. Politicians encouraged such developments under the pretense that community groups know community needs better. Although this is true in some cases, it is questionable in most, especially since no CHC was established after a study of community needs. An additional difficulty arises from the nature of most Canadian communities which lack economic diversity and host a highly mobile population inhibiting the development of a sense of community. Confusion over terminology resulted from diversity of development and from persisting characteristics of traditional care in the new types of organization.

Second, a basic aim of the CHC movement was to make services accessible to underserved groups. Accessibility to social services improved marginally in rural areas where such services were linked with the nonstigmatizing health care system. But there are strong indications that CHCs are unpopular elsewhere. One province attributed this to the "failure of the public" to recognize the need for alternatives to institutional care. Before blaming the public, however, one must take into account (a) the long-standing support of institutional care by government, (b) the stigma traditionally attached to social services and social work in Canada, and (c) the CHCs' tendency to concentrate on the poor. These reasons explain why hospital emergency departments and polyclinics are more popular even in Quebec, where the government developed CLSCs on a broader social basis (Drouin and Paquin, 1978). Three additional problems identified by the provinces relate to accessibility: difficulties of integration, coordination of services, and the lack of a comprehensive patient information system. If such aims were achieved, a shortage of services would result. Most services, especially the popular ones, have long waiting lists and "successful" programs of integration and information made such lists longer. There are many in the position of that lady in Washington who said, "I used to go to ten different agencies to find out there was no help available. Now I can go to one" (Kahn, 1976).

Third, opposition from the medical profession to any form of payment other than fee for service created manpower problems. Family physicians and general practitioners were reluctant to enter these schemes because of the stigma attached to them by the profession as a whole and the reported failures of the team approach. Additional repelling factors were the lack of security for career advancement, low pay, and the unattractive location of the CHCs. Even in Quebec, where the new form of organization was more promising, only 3 percent of family physicians worked in CLSCs in 1978 (Desrosiers, 1978). The vast majority of general practitioners showed preference for solo practice or for polyclinics (Rheault, 1980).

Fourth, negative reports about the outcomes of the team approach correspond to the growing international literature on the topic. As a provincial official stated, "doctors are reluctant to accept responsibility . . . for holistic rather than episodic care." This makes them the "bad" members of the team. However, the problem is more general. All professions compete for status; professional antagonisms perpetuate the vagueness of professional roles and differences of opinion about team work even within disciplines. Thus, pediatricians and family physicians find it hard to work together, as do specialists in social work, administration, and other professions (Kong-Ning, 1968). This is one of the inescapable effects of increasing specialization and professionalism in modern society. As Hokenstad, Ritvo and Rosenberg (1979) pointed out, professional ideologies and organizational rigidity "obscure the view that health and social services are complementary." These barriers exist even in countries with a longer and stronger government commitment to holistic care. However, successful teams can be found in areas where CHCs emerged out of local group action and attracted workers of a more or less similar ideological outlook (Ryant, 1977). Such teams are difficult to form on a large scale in extensive programs, such as that of Quebec, where the "forced marriage" of health and social services resulted in organizations whose common denominator is interprofessional conflict.

Fifth, one of the most dubious aims of the CHC movement was citizen or consumer participation. Invariably, at a time of increasing disenchantment with the political process, government tokenism of citizen *representation* was mistaken for or misrepresented as *consumer participation* (Canadian Council on Social Development, 1979). The concept perpetuated traditional illusions about the democratic process and about the degree of choice consumers can enjoy in relation to professionals (Tsalikis, 1972a).

Sixth, it would be impossible to assess if the CHCs contributed to a reduction in health expenditures. In response to our questionnaire, Quebec reported as one of the problems facing the new system "the agony of preventing duplication of services." However, there is a more fundamental problem in that province as elsewhere in Canada: the continuing bias in favor of curative services. As Villedieu pointed out recently, "Today (and tomorrow) as in the past it is curative services which corner almost all expenditures" (1976). Despite medical advances, soaring expenditures, and reorganization of structures, the health status of Quebec remains the same, if not deteriorating (Villedieu, 1976). The main factor of increasing expenditures in Quebec (from $282 million in 1971-1972 to $770 million in 1979-1980) seems to be a shift toward more expensive cures (Rheault, 1980). The same is true of all Canada.

Seventh, the provinces reported organizational and fiscal problems arising from departmental division and federal-provincial arrangements, difficulties with integration of services, and coordination with other elements of the system. It is hard to conceive any considerable prospect of inducing or forcing a marriage between the heterogeneous systems of health and social services insofar as efforts to do so in each of these two components separately have not shown a remarkable record. Each sector comprises fragmented and often competitive organizations. The pressure of a large number of voluntary organizations in both these sectors makes holistic care even more difficult, especially at a time of emphasis on "less government," a phrase that could mean reduced public expenditures and less integration and coordination.

In recent years, there have been other small-scale efforts to link health and personal social services. Two noteworthy approaches are the social service departments of hospitals and some voluntary organizations specializing in linking other organizations. The latter are a relatively new type of service, operating in large cities. They are few in number, and there is little information about their current output. We surveyed one in Ottawa (a patient orientation agency) to find that social service workers did not think highly of it because of its health care orientation. As far as "underserved" patients were concerned, this organization's output was, in many cases, their addition to existing waiting lists.

Few data exist regarding hospital social work departments to indicate whether they are doing better or worse than the organizations discussed earlier in terms of the barriers to linkage. Such

departments have been established in most big hospitals across
the country and vary remarkably in many respects. They have
not been systematically researched or evaluated. The "community care" services they provide are more or less those
provided by the "extended" public health unit or the CHC
(from family or parent counseling to lifestyle and stress coping).
They also present many of the same problems discussed earlier
and are primarily faced with confusion and lack of direction. A
recent study concluded:

> If the trustees, administration, medical and other professional staff
> do not have a common understanding and agreement as to how their
> hospitals should provide primary, ambulatory and community
> care . . . development of a consistent and logical policy is impossible
> [Ontario Hospital Association, 1980].

Obviously, the trend developed primarily as hospitals' response
to widespread criticisms of their role in the community due to
their rising expenditures. Thus, it is not surprising that their
community departments are primarily a window-dressing operation for institutional legitimization. As a social worker stated in
one of our interviews, "many of these departments were set up
mainly to meet an accreditation requirement."

THE UNCERTAIN FUTURE

Canadian efforts to link health and social services have one
major purpose: to reduce the utilization of expensive medical
and institutional care by preventing illness which increases
demand for such services. The effort has been inhibited by six
factors inherent in the socioeconomic and political system of
the country: (1) the fragmentation of such services, some of
which are provided in the private and others in the public
sector; (2) the involvement of different governments in the
funding and provision of such services and the resulting jurisdictional or ideological conflicts which relate to interprovincial
economic antagonism; (3) the incompatibility of the services to

be linked, some of which are provided on a universal basis and others selectively in a stigmatizing manner; (4) the inability to reconcile the pluralistic idealism of the political process with the need to integrate and coordinate the conflicting components of the health and welfare industry; (5) the inability to reallocate resources in view of the new health risks due to the vested interests in traditional forms of care and organization; and (6) the unprecedented growth of the helping professions and their increasing specialization, which limit their chances of communication in the "Babel Tower" of community care.

It is doubtful that the government of Canada will be able, in the foreseeable future, to produce an integrated picture of health and social services (to the extent that there are important and compatible services to be linked). Even if the many fragments of the mirror are put together, they will reflect a distorted image, not that desired by the enthusiasts of integration. A complete reorganization is equally problematic due to an uncertain economic future and the growing federal-provincial jurisdictional conflicts. The resolution of the present constitutional crisis requires more concessions to provincial governments to run their own affairs. The concessions most likely will inhibit further reorganization at the national level. As few provinces show continuing interest in linking health and social services (a trend which lacked strength and continuity), the prospect of such reorganization at the provincial level decreases. However, one may expect that the establishment of links at the local level will continue to the extent that reformist groups manage to secure resources. Nevertheless, such efforts will be limited and may contribute to additional expenditures because of the emergency of new helping occupations and their drive for professional status.

REFERENCES

BETHUNE, N. (1937) "Take private profit out of medicine." Canadian Doctor 3, 1: 14-15.

Canadian Council on Social Development (1979) Roundtable discussion: "Citizen participation in health care delivery: What are the prospects?" Ottawa, April 20.

CASSIDY, H. M. (1943) Social Security and Reconstruction in Canada. Toronto: Ryerson.

DUBOS, R. (1971) "The biology of civilization–with emphasis on perinatal influences," in S. V. Boyden (ed.) The Impact of Civilization on the Biology of Man. Toronto: University of Toronto Press.

Economic Council of Canada (1970) Patterns of Growth. Seventh Annual Review. Ottawa: Queen's Printer.

FRECHETTE, G. (1975) "Emergency care and hospital centers: a new system in Montreal." Dimensions of Health Services 52: 45-47.

HALL, E. M. (1980) Canada's National–Provincial Health Programme for the 1980s: A Commitment for Renewal. Ottawa.

HAMEL, G. (1974) "Une mise au point des omnipracticiens." Le Devoir (14 Mars).

HASTINGS, J.E.F. (1978) Community Health Centres. "What Happened Since the Hastings' Report? Neither Sweet nor Sour." University of Toronto Faculty of Medicine, Division of Community Health.

––– et al. (1972) Community Health Centre Projects. Report to the Minister of National Health and Welfare, July 21.

HEPWORTH, H. P. (1975) Personal Social Services in Canada, Vol. 1.

HOKENSTAD, M. et al. (1979) "International perspectives on linking health and social services." International Social Work XXII, 7.

ILLICH, I. (1974) Medical Nemesis: The Expropriation of Health.

INGLEHART, J. K. (1977) "The cost and regulation of medical technology: future policy directions." Milbank Memorial Fund Quarterly 55: 25-29.

KAHN, A. (1976) "Service delivery at the neighbourhood level: experience, theory and fad." Social Service Review 50, 1.

MacLEOD, J. W. et al. (1978) Bethune, The Montreal Years: An Informal Portrait. Toronto: Lorimer.

Manpower Health Services Commission (1980) Letter to the author by T. R. Edwards, December 5.

MARSH, L. (1943) Report on Social Security for Canada, 1943. Submitted to the Special Committee on Social Security, House of Commons.

MEEKISSON, P. I. (1977) Canadian Federalism: Myth or Reality. Toronto: Methuen.

MOORE, A. M. et al. (1966) The Financing of Canadian Federation. Toronto: Canadian Tax Foundation.

MORGAN, S. D. (1961) "Social welfare services in Canada," in M. Oliver (ed.) Social Purpose for Canada. Toronto: University of Toronto Press.

MOTT, M. (1970) "The foreign peril." M.A. thesis, University of Manitoba.

MUNRO, J. (1969) "Medicare in relation to organized labor." Speech delivered on behalf of the Minister by Dr. S. Haidasz, Sault Ste. Marie, December.

Ontario Hospital Association (1980) Hospitals Inside Out. A Position Paper (October).

RENAUD, M. (1976) "Reforme ou illusion?" Sociologie et Societes IX.

RHEAULT, G. (1980) "Une affaire qui roule." Quebec Science (October): 24-29.

ROBINSON, G. C. et al. (1969) "Use of hospital emergency services for children and adolescents." Canadian Medical Association Journal 101: 69-73.

ROEMER, M. I. (1972) Evaluation of Community Health Centres. Publication H, Series 48. Geneva: World Health Organization.

RYANT, J. C. (1977) "The integration of services in rural and urban communities." Canadian Journal of Social Work Education 2, 3.

SCHWENGER, C. W. (1973) "The future of the local health department." Canadian Medical Association Journal 108: 966-971.

SODERSTROM, L. (1978) The Canadian Health System. London: Croom-Helm.

Special Committee on Social Security (1943) House of Commons.

Special Senate Committee Report (1971) Poverty in Canada. Ottawa.

STEINMETZ, N. et al. (1978) "Hospital emergency utilization in Montreal before and after medicare." Medical Care 16: 133-139.

Task Force Reports on the Cost of Health Care, Vol. I-III (1969) Ottawa.

TAYLOR, M. G. (1978) Health Insurance and Canadian Public Policy. Toronto: University of Toronto Press.

——— (1973) "The Canadian health insurance programme." Public Administration Review (January-February).

TISHLER, H. S. (1971) Self-Reliance and Social Security, 1870-1970. New York: National University.

TRUDEAU, P. E. (1976) "Established program financing." Statement tabled at the Conference of Federal and Provincial First Ministers, Ottawa, June 14-15.

——— (1969) Income Security and Social Services. Working Paper on the Constitution. Ottawa: Queen's Printer.

TSALIKIS, G. (1982) "The consequences of Canadian health care policy," in Canadian Council on Social Development, Issues in Canadian Social Policy, Vol. II.

——— (1980) "Remodelling the staff of Aesculapius." Social Science and Medicine 14A: 97-106.

——— (1973) "The community approach to education: linking health education and welfare," in T. Morrison and T. Burton, Options: Reforms and Alternatives in Canadian Education. Toronto: Holt, Rinehart & Winston.

——— (1972a) Consumer Choice and the C.H.C. Commissioned Paper, CHC Project. Ottawa: C.P.H.A.

——— (1972b) "Doctors in confusion. Impression from the First International Congress on Group Medicine." Social Science and Medicine 6: 269-273.

——— and P. MANGA (1980) "The Hall review: a commitment for renewal?" Canadian Journal of Public Health 71 (November-December): 385-389.

VILLEDIEU, Y. (1976) Demain la sante. Le Dossiers de Quebec Science. Quebec.

WALLACE, J. D. (1972) "Don't just sit there." Canadian Medical Association Journal 106 (Jan. 22).

WHARF, B. (1978) "Integrated services: myths and realities." Canadian Journal of Social Work Education 3, 3.

7

FRANCE

JACQUES FOURNIER and
NICOLE QUESTIAUX

Any analysis of the delivery of health and social services in France must include the range of public interventions. Public authorities intervene in three ways: They set the regulations and standards for private enterprise to provide services; they allot resources for health or social services; and they deliver services directly. Every five years, French social planners give public authorities a global view of their different fields of intervention. While some hope this process would assist the understanding of the organization of, and links between, health and social services, this is not the case. It is useful to refer to the documentation of the Commissariat au Plan, but these plans often reinforce the distinctions between health and *action sociale* (the field of social services) sectors.

In France, the share of both health and social services in total consumption of goods or services is noticeably high. Demand depends on public financing. It is heavily subsidized (80 percent) by budgetary funds and wage contributions. However, public authorities are not in a position of power because of the importance of the private practitioners. Both the public and private sectors are developing rapidly because of the increasing need and demand for such services and because of national involvement in financing. The growth of expenditures for such services is considered one of the main causes of the pressure on the economy due to the extension of socialized commitments. This is a growing source of controversy in France, as in other industrial countries, which try to combine the rules of economic liberalism with forms of collective intervention. When health or social services are discussed, it is often with a financial bias. Relations between the two sectors center on the problems of rationalization and economy.

The historical development of these two service sectors did not stress rationalization and planning. This may explain why linkage between health and social services encounters barriers and resistance. Zones of conjoint action are restricted, and achievements do not become comprehensive policy. However, costs and contradiction may stimulate a different evolution. This is where social planning may provide some direction. Certainly, if France has some contribution to make, it will be in the development of social indicators designed to evaluate needs.

HISTORICAL BACKGROUND

From its origin, French social intervention was directed toward poverty and illness. In fact, it was initially repressive. For a long time society was confronted by vast cohorts of beggars. One of the first legislative attempts in 1701 defined as vagabonds and *gens sans aveu* those who had no profession or trade, no fixed abode or household, and those who could not provide witnesses of good faith and morality. Something had to be done for them. From naive attempts to put them to work or keep them out of mischief, authorities discovered that the *gens sans aveu* included many ill, invalid, or aged individuals.

In the Middle Ages, a number of establishments were open to the poor, often for one night. Some provided for expectant mothers, the blind or the mentally ill, all to the pious glory of their founders. In the sixteenth century, the official Bureau of the Poor began to distribute alms. In the seventeenth century, after the destruction of the celebrated ghetto, *cour des miracles,* the poor were forcibly housed in the "general hospitals." These became simultaneously the beggars' depots, the prisons, the lunatic asylums, and the old people's homes.

On the eve of the Revolution, such measures led to a fierce conflict between the Church and lay authorities. They resulted in total failure. An official report at the time, authored by La Rochefoucauld Liancourt, noted the "charity mascarade." The revolutionaries envisioned a comprehensive system of public assistance. They mentioned the objective of government respon- sibility for the poor. Assistance was seen as a duty incumbent on the public authorities. The right to assistance included the complementary duty for the beneficiary to work for a living. These ideas suggested a network of institutions, the list of which could inspire our contemporaries: assistance to children, creches, homes for the mentally ill, public works projects, hospitals, retirement homes, and even mutual assistance soci- eties. It also included the provision for free medical care.

The "Convention," by law of March 1793, proposed nation- alization of all forms of aid to the poor. Each department would have a maison de secours (home for help) as a base for its interventions. Able people would be required to work. Home help could be provided to the invalid and the aged. The religious communities' properties were to be handed over to the state. Private charitable enterprise was outlawed. These were the pre- mises of a coordinated policy, but it was not yet the time for realization.

The Revolution left its mark on the administration of health and social services. Assistance became the duty of local author- ities. But it was a subsidiary duty. And if it remained true that townships, departments, and local hospital boards had a role in delivering such services, the geographical unit never became the proper framework for organization. France preferred com- pulsory insurance but through professional structures.

The hospital became the refuge for the poor, the miserable, and the sick. This population was ready prey for epidemics. The staff were often from religious orders and could barely face the task of nourishing and controlling the hospital "inmates." How- ever, the involvement of the faculty was a factor of change, the same faculty which now controls medical examinations and professional standards to deliver the title doctor of medicine. By the mid-nineteenth century, medicine and hospital practice became symbiotic partners in health delivery. The number of patients actually treated grew spectacularly. The wealthy slowly overcame their distrust of the hospital. However, the legislature and the courts waited until the 1940s to recognize officially that a hospital is meant to deal with illness and gave access to paying patients after World War II.

The more important medical discoveries were not made in the hospitals, but rather in outside structures. Pasteur was not a doctor of medicine. It was progress in bacteriology and vaccination which gave a scientific base to a large-scale intervention. Medical progress was translated into several important laws for prevention of diseases. In the early years of the twentieth century, insalubrity in lodging conditions gave local mayors a general jurisdiction to ensure a healthy environment and prevent epidemics. The public hygiene code, passed in 1902, mandated the communes to enforce health regulations approved by the *préfet*. The purpose was clearly public health with a public financing provision. It could be enforced through specific penalties. This was also the time for legislation dealing with the prevention of tuberculosis, VD, and mental illness. The protection of maternity and childhood justified a national network of services. *Dispensaires* and the centralization of information, and supervision were staffed by civil service doctors and budgeted with public funds, drawn from state and local authorities.

All of the actors of the health and social services were in place by the end of the nineteenth century, but the Revolution involving the health services was postponed until the middle of the twentieth. Scientific progress, involving the use of pharmaceuticals, had by then made medicine efficient and effective on a wide scale. The private practitioner was in a position to provide real service using the technical facilities of the hospital. The pharmaceutical industry had become prosperous. But as the hospital had delayed its intervention as a key element of the health services, the field was taken over by the private practitioner. This form of medicine, as opposed to hospital medicine, became relatively predominant in France. The private sector had its clinics and profit-making establishments. Charities and mutual assistance societies lagged in the provision of health services, and their role remains limited.

Private enterprise became dominant in health service with compulsory medical insurance. In 1930, it was enforced for wage earners, and in 1945, medical insurance became part of the national social security plan. It was extended to independent workers in the 1960s. Today, 98 percent of the population is insured. A "right to health" is included in the French Bill of Rights amending the 1946 Constitution. In 1978, medical expenses represented 7.1 percent of the gross national product.

Currently, the French system includes social transfer schemes in which the beneficiaries are entitled to reimbursement for health and medical care. They may select the private practitioners or the public or private hospital.

Solidarity through the social transfer scheme was simultaneously extended to the retired population and, with a particular accent in France, to families. Financing relies on the same mode of contribution based on the active workers' income. Transfers ensure a surplus income to be spent freely by the beneficiaries. But the French social security system provides for some forms of service delivery. This explains why a small percentage of all social security contributions goes to those forms of collective action which the boards of the *caisses de securite sociale* may initiate.

Social services are particularly supported by the family allowance system and are directed toward the needs of the family. In France, this includes all families, not just the poor. This approach stimulated similar interventions for other sectors of the population in need.

When the legislature did intervene in the social services delivery system, it was to put things in order. The only important legislation in the field was a 1950 law to coordinate services. In the same way, a 1975 law based on the hospital law attempted to give a rational status to those establishments which provided social services without being entitled to deliver medical service. Despite such developments, some sectors of the population remained without coverage. In the 1970s, administrative research and programs investigated the needs of the aged and the handicapped. It seemed that there was room for provision of special services, rather than relying only on income transfers. The 1975 law for the handicapped extended the tradition set at the beginning of the century through a comprehensive approach to all aspects of health and social care, including invalids.

HEALTH AND SOCIAL SERVICES

Over the past two centuries, France was developed ambitious aims for its human services. Many health programs support the definition of the World Health Organization of seeking the total physical, mental, and social well-being, going beyond the elimination of sickness or invalidity. A comparable philosophy inspires the social services. Their mission may be defined not only as compensation for the human consequences of maladjustment but also as a factor of social change enabling all individuals or groups to become autonomous and to make full use of their capacities. It includes prevention and individual and collective action. Individuals should be considered with all their potentials, biological, psychological, and affective. Global social action means considering each person's status and that status in society. It is designed to allow this person to live in conditions respectful of personal integrity, permitting choice which benefits both the individual and society.

The Health Services

The health services delivery system is in a dominant position. It functions essentially as provider of medical care and interventions. Preventive services receive only 0.4 percent of the total expenditure on health. Medical insurance is financed by a contribution on wages. (We have limited our description here to the system applicable to salary earners in industry and commerce, who represent two-thirds of insured persons.) This allows for partial compensation of wages lost through inability to work and for reimbursement of medical expenses, whether dispensed at home or in a hospital.

Reimbursement is based on the tariff of medical intervention or medicine as guaranteed by the insurance system, a small share being paid for by the beneficiary (25 percent for a consultation with the doctor). All wage earners and families are entitled to this, and formulas cover the needs of public service workers or independent workers. It is noteworthy that the organization of the delivery of these funds is based on the professional framework, involving separate structures for salary earners, independent workers, and agricultural workers, a characteristic of French social security. Professional organizations, alias trade unions and employer unions, are represented in the administration of the funds, although government policy dictates the level of benefits and the applicable rules.

The population's requirements for health care are financed as a part of the indirect wage scheme. This share is determined through the worker-employer relationship in the economy under the firm arbitration of the government. But since the right to medical insurance is guaranteed by law, the system covers all expenses engaged by the beneficiaries, except the share legally accruing to the individual.

Currently, the insured population chooses the form of medical service it requires. The key to the functioning of the whole system is the way medical goods and services are defined and the form of rate-setting. Medical services are produced as the activity of a largely liberal profession. More than 75 percent of the 100,000 active doctors in France are in private practice. But no matter how liberal, the profession is subject to strict regulation. Access to the profession, since the nineteenth century, is subject to the award of the diploma of Doctor of Medicine after seven years of study. Professional practice is protected against illegal competition; this leads to the definition of medical care as an activity which may be exercised only by the profession.

Moreover, these rules define the scope of the specialist practice. In France, specialists may not practice outside their specialty. Doctors are not supposed to associate in their activity with nonmedical personnel, and the standards enforcing personal exercise of the profession have only recently allowed for group practice. Paramedical professions may practice within a strict definition of the service which they are allowed to offer.

All these professions become closed professions, with their codes of conduct supervised by a professional body called Ordre. Since the number concerned has increased rapidly in recent years, access to the medical profession has been limited by selection of a maximum of 9,000 students yearly. Thus, the medical profession has managed to preserve its privileged status on the income scale.

A medical act is what the doctor is authorized to do, and a parallel ruling for social security defines the acts and the medical specialties which are entitled to reimbursement. This consolidates the idea that the medical practitioner defines medical activity and controls health goods and services.

Some constraints have been established on the liberty of doctors to fix the terms of payment and to determine the liability of the social security system. This occurs through collective agreements negotiated between the social security boards and the doctors' unions. They determine the price of each medical service, which then becomes both the price demanded from the patient by the doctor and the basis of the patient's compensation. The agreement also includes matters of common interest; for instance, it contains clauses by which the social security board will develop clinics or other forms of salaried medicine. These contracts may establish procedures to increase self-discipline within the profession. For example, practitioners are invited to compare their frequency of prescription and frequency of intervention to model situations. Nearly 90 percent of all private practitioners adhere to the agreement.

In such a system, it is easy to see how the producer of health care determines and controls the level of expenditures. Capacity to limit demand for medical services is limited. Physicians have been exhorted to discourage consumption by moderating their intervention on a voluntary basis.

Within the framework of a general law of 1970, "hospital public service" is divided into public and private sectors. The public sector includes 2,100 facilities (out of these 2,100 public hospitals 1,000 establishments are really the old-fashioned homes for the aged, alias hospices). The private sector consists of 2,500 hospitals (765 are nonprofit). These sectors include 800,000 beds. Figures reveal how diverse the service may be in size and variety of potentialities. These facilities work on a system of day costs, which determine the level of reimbursement by the medical insurance system. This day cost is set for public and nonprofit organizations by the *préfet*, a public official. Private hospitals and clinics contract with the social boards. In all cases, the prospective tariff is based on a provision for the following year based on an estimated number of days of service in each specialized ward. Financial equilibrium depends on occupany level and length of stay.

Physicians may receive a full-time salary. This is characteristic of the more prestigious public hospital centers where the elite of the medical profession divide time between hospital and teaching activities for a salary in the highest rank of the civil service.

The current medical system weighs toward increasing the involvement in health care expenses. The growing medical profession is inclined to increase its services, and the pharmaceutical industry encourages use of new forms of medicine. Despite many efforts to reduce drug utilization, consumption remains high in France. Until recently, this characteristic was overshadowed by a relatively efficient price control system, a system of controls which may change according to the general economic policies of the present French government (1981). Also, hospital expenditures are rapidly rising. Now hospitals are well-equipped and personnel expenses and interest on loans must be paid. While length of stay has been decreasing, the day cost mechanism does not induce reorganization. Although most hospitals are conducting a thorough review of their expenses, they have no reason to move out of the traditional definition of medical activity. The goal is to deliver the proper number of days of care and services to a sufficient body of properly insured patients. There is no reason to innovate on the fringe of these traditional activities. The social security focus is on reimbursing traditional medicine, and it is loathe to extend liability to any new form of service. These conflicts reinforce the traditional definition of medical services.

Social Services

Social services are organized largely on different lines. Of course, parallelism and imitation of the medical profession's status do exist. The most ancient profession in the field of social work, the *assistante sociale* (assistant social worker), also must earn a state-delivered diploma. The same type of conditions are attached to the exercise of professions such as specialized educators, counselors in domestic economics, and technical supervisors. In each case, this means activity needs to be defined with reference to qualifications. However, two serious differences appear here: training for social worker careers is not based on the high-prestige, selective medical curriculum in the universities. There are many high-quality training institutions, each with its own particular status. Second, definition of the professional activity may be extremely vague. An assistant social worker acts as an intermediary between individuals, families, and institutions of a medical or medico-social nature, giving individuals and families the help and training which enable them to cope without an intermediary. On other occasions, the function of the social worker is strictly defined by an institution, whether it be the agency responsible for specialized education, aid to abandoned children, or family assistance.

Functional specificity is where a substantial difference appears between these two human service systems. While health care is well-defined and recognized, social action needs justification. It does not receive full support from its clients, who do not necessarily use services on their own initiative and have no preconceived idea of what they expect from it. This irritates the social worker who would appreciate a relationship parallel to that of patient with doctor. But when social services are efficient and effective, they encourage continuous intervention by individuals or groups who are concerned with their activity. A successful social worker leaves with responsibility assured by the worker's representatives in the workplace, by parents of handicapped children, by retired wage earners dealing with their own services, or by families active in their neighborhood. It can then be argued that voluntary action may assume the role of the social worker, leaving social work professionals to plead the cause of their professionalism.

Social workers receive salaries according to the regulatory statutes or to the collective agreements negotiated with their employers. Most of them are employed by a variety of institutions which serve specific population groups. As specialists, social workers are usually organized around a specific technology or a specified clientele. Social services are located in hospitals, prisons, industries, and agriculture. Social workers also practice in preventive health services, migrant workers' social services, and services provided by the social security and family allowance systems. In each of these cases, financing is dependent on the funds of the institution—either a voluntary contribution of the firms, the percentage leveled on contributions in the social security system, or public subsidies. In all cases, the activity of the service is budgeted in the ordinary manner: a specified sum per year for salaries with the necessary office space and support services. This system bears little resemblance to its counterpart in the health sector. The only exception is found in the social centers and juvenile prevention clubs. A 1971 law instituted a day cost system called the "service grant." If the beneficiary is so entitled, financing is automatic.

Coordination has led to instituting a form of geographic organization. Since 1965, the territory is divided into units of up to 50,000 inhabitants. Coordination of existing social services at this level occurs in many instances. The aim is to place a generic social worker to serve from 3,000 to 5,000 people. In the better-equipped localities, this jurisdiction is given to the social centers; that is, neighborhood units which offer the local population a wide range of services, such as prevention clubs, aid to children, and citizens clubs. However, this structure remains a rarity.

Social services rely on "social establishments" to assist or educate groups in need of care. These "social establishments" include institutions such as an orphanage or an infant home, a creche, a maternity care center, a retirement home, or sheltered housing for the aged. This category also includes sites for medical therapy or sheltered workplaces. Analogous to the hospital law of 1970, a "social" law in 1975 attempted to give these establishments increased status. They may not open without authorization and are subject to sanitary and technical control from the Ministry of Health (and from the social security bodies when they are subsidized by them). This legislation is founded on a strict separation of social and health services, and, in general, medical insurance will not pay for these services. They may be paid for by individuals or families, or financed by the administration (e.g., aid to abandoned children or the penal system). Otherwise, they receive compensation from the social assistance funds for the destitute or by the special assistance for the handicapped. These financing mechanisms are more dependent on fixation and changes of policy by the authorities concerns than are the medical insurance funds. Social services are not reimbursed on the same scale as health services. They are increasing mainly because salaries are increasing and services are provided to wider sections of the population. They do not pose financial concerns comparable to health services.

The preceding discussion illustrates how health and social services are organized to function in parallel. Central authorities are not in a position to link the development of both sectors. The ministry has extensive powers of authorization. But while the authorities develop a health service map, they have few resources to work on more than the medical aspects. Private practitioners settle where they choose. By deciding what hospital equipment is necessary, the ministry has to account for the influence and perspectives of local doctors. These decisions constrain future policy decisions. Other problems relate to the respective roles of different specialties and the hospital versus the town doctor. Also, the minister arbitrates between the competing development of public and private hospitals.

Coherence between health and social services is not an administrative necessity in France. However, there are zones of action where, either by the whims of history or through conscious evaluation of objectives, these services work together and reinforce each other.

LINKAGES BETWEEN HEALTH AND SOCIAL SERVICES

Health and social service linkages occur in two directions: Social action supports health action to facilitate access to health services, and health care is seen as a component of global social action.

Social Action in Support of the Health Services

This first aspect should not be important in a developed country. Theoretically, universal health insurance places the health services within reach of all those in need. With one doctor for 550 inhabitants and one hospital bed for 700, French citizens should find the service at their doorstep. However, medical density creates visible differences between regions, and studies on medical utilization reveal noticeable inequalities for individuals with low income and little education.

Even with generalized medical insurance, it is still necessary for local authorities to dispense public assistance to the sick who are without resources. Free medical assistance is available to the impoverished. This share represents a major expenditure in cases of hospitalization, and here public assistance intervenes. Local authorities assess the patient's income; they may request an evaluation of the case by the social worker. Social workers must assume initiative to obtain access to the health services for their ill clients. This is the constant role of social workers in the social security and hospital organization, a necessary function because the system may appear very complex to the poor client. It is not possible to evaluate the number or cost of these services.

Social workers intervene when the users of the health service are not inclined to contact the service. This happens often in the field of preventive medicine, where the tracing of illness, vaccination, and regular supervision require the population to consult health authorities. It may easily be done at specific stages: prenatal visits, entrance to school, or conscription. But this is not sufficient to draw the entire population into health services.

Such roles were created by the archaic and elaborate legislation enacted to combat the so-called social evils. It provides for networks of dispensaries and medical consulting services to work in association with social workers. This model proved efficient in fighting tuberculosis and venereal disease. Medical treatment was supported and followed up by advice on hygiene and preventive attitudes. The antituberculosis network has now lost most of its utility, but the model proved satisfactory with its systematic provision of services on a geographic basis financed by public funds. Originally, there was one physiologist per department with numerous clinics. Now, with the decrease in tuberculosis morbidity (down to 37 per 10,000 in 1976 from 76 cases per 10,000 in the 1960s), the service has returned to the hospital and its staff. Dispensaries are now hospital clinics; many are closing. But this form of organization can be applied to venereal disease treatment. There are 380 services staffed by part-time physicians with specialized social workers attached to the more general services. The social worker's role is to signal a case to the health service.

These actions must prove their worth, both as forms of therapy and by the number of successes. But dealing in the complexities of such actions, one always finds social workers.

They serve to relay information and provide drug training programs. On the other hand, as liaison with psychiatric services, social workers participate in a variety of new programs related to drug addiction: night hostels, sheltered lodgings, work placements, and community centers.

In the same way, social workers support psychiatric services for alcoholics. General hospitals are organized to deal with problems related to alcoholism as a whole through their social workers. A law of 1954 allows forcible hospitalization of dangerous alcoholics. Such cases are referred to the health authorities, who can order an inquiry before a special commission. If the patient refuses treatment, the case may be referred by a court order. In most cases, the social worker initiates reeducation procedures.

Social workers are the best providers of public health education. The means developed here are most parsimonious. Social work training programs include basic concepts of medicine and hygiene, and many *assistantes sociales* have a nursing degree. They are likely to organize training programs on hygiene for their clients, such as socially handicapped families or migrant workers.

However, the social worker only supports the medical services and refers patients. The health service is not expected to adopt social work methods in order to cooperate with social services. The medical professions' conception of its role remains unchanged.

**Delivery of Health Services
as Part of Global Welfare Programs**

The definition of service appears in a new light when the intervention shifts away from actions directly related to curing or preventing illness to programs designed to maintain the well-being of the population.

Welfare Programs Directed Toward
Specific Situations or Population Groups

This is the case whenever the collectivity recognizes the need
to provide for the well-being of a specific population. In France,
this appears in actions concerned with family and childhood,
the workplace, the aged, and the handicapped. If the first two
forms of action are traditional, they remain politically important. The latter two programs surprisingly made a late appearance as forms of social protection.

Maternal and child welfare. Since 1945, maternal and child
welfare has been organized systematically for all of France.
Financed by public funds, it relies on two measures: preventive
medical supervision and medical social supervision in the home.
It covers all children up to school age, as well as expectant
mothers who live in normal family surroundings or outside of
their families. Services combine clinics open to the entire population and technical supervision of all establishments entitled
to receive children. Such supervised health and social conditions
are found in 1,100 *crèches,* 380 day care centers, 1,030 temporary care centers, 450 family *crèches* where young children
are cared for, and 100 infant homes. This is an elaborate
structure with each departmental office or decentralized consulting service staffed by well-trained teams of physicians, social
workers, and nurses. They are referred by the professionals
directly in charge of the children, such as nurses and maternal
assistants.

Despite the importance of these activities, the number of
personnel involved remains low. In 1978, the cohort included
342 full-time and 5,600 part-time doctors, about 60 midwives,
120 specialized *assistantes sociales,* and 1,280 nurses. But general social services contribute significantly to the program. The
paucity of resources for personnel is apparent in the figures
referring to the care possibilities with 80,000 places in the
crèches.

This situation reflects insufficient financial support from the
public authorities. They still recognize the value of the program.

In fact, existing facilities and programs explain the effectiveness of the effort to reduce infant mortality. To avoid natal accidents or the birth of handicapped babies, seven different programs were launched in 1970, coordinated during the planning period of five years. These included training, research, vaccination against German measles, prenatal medical supervision, reinforced supervision on private maternity wards, new baby units, and intensive care units in the hospitals. Resources were directed at the objective of reducing the number of deaths by 180,000 and the number of babies born with handicaps by 235,000 over a 15-year period. This action certainly had a part to play in the noticeable drop of the infant mortality rate in France. It is even more important to note that this result came about by linking new, advanced techniques with the preventive health programs which had been established for 30 years. Financial studies on effectiveness and efficiency of these programs documented the value of systematic prevention programs at a time when the population could have questioned their utility.

School health services date from 1945. Financed by the state, they initially relied on the education system, but responsibilities were transferred to coordinating them with the general preventive programs offered by local administrators of the health and social services. Tutorship of the program is now exercised by the Minister of Health. While general preventive medicine is funded by the department, the personnel of the school health service receive monies from the state budget.

As noted previously, the same type of team structure draws together full- and part-time doctors and social workers. At each departmental level a liaison doctor and a head social worker coordinate services. In each sector, the team includes a doctor, one or two social workers, two or three nurses, aides, and secretaries. Here again, there are insufficient personnel. Ideally, each sector should cover up to 6,000 children, but often a team has to serve 10,000 children. A group of 1,000 full-time doctors, 1,300 social workers, and as many nurses is supplemented with about 1,000 part-time professionals. It is not surprising that nearly half the children are not regularly checked.

Health and social services at the workplace. Health and social interventions in the workplace are funded by the employer. There is a legal obligation to provide both medical supervision of working conditions and social intervention as required by the employees.

Medical supervision in the workplace is well-established. Created in 1913, it protects the workers' health through a series of rules applying to the employer. These concern the hazards of technology, dangerous products, and the factory environment. Lighting must be sufficient to ensure security, and noise must be held within limits compatible with the workers' health. This requires some monitoring and expert assistance. Doctors monitor the employees' state of health and advise the employer and the workers on industrial hygiene. The workers' committee on hygiene and security assumes a more important role than the social worker.

Once again, the failings of the system relate to lack of sufficient personnel. Of the 5,000 doctors only 2,000 work full-time. They must function in 2,370 clinics covering 2,000,000 workers. In addition, 576 service clinics attempt to screen 8,000,000 additional workers. A 1976 reform reinforced the standards of security in the workplace and control of work inspectors in the plant. Inspectors may intervene to suppress immediate dangers and are entitled to apply penalties for noncompliance.

These reforms are not fully responsive to the claim made by the workers' unions that their committee should exercise such powers to stop dangerous activities. But it is clear that the physician acts as expert and is not expected to prolong intervention through social work. On the contrary, health and safety in the workplace rely on the employees' participation far more than on social workers' assistance or intervention.

Services for the aged. Social legislation initially did not specify services for the aged. Recent efforts have been made to provide the aged living at home with a variety of neighborhood services combining health and social interventions. This resulted from demonstration in 1972 which convinced the planners that these models should be expanded. They recognized the fact that many of the elderly prefer to remain in their own homes and are ready to do so if they have accessible support services. To spend resources on these programs meets the needs of the elderly and is less costly than institutional care.

The policy stated that the elderly should have access to local health and social services near their homes, meeting places, and clubs. Examples of the minimum services include nursing, personal hygiene care, home help services, and meals on wheels. Day centers are be available to receive those who can sleep at home. A team comprising the doctor, the nurse, and the home help aide deliver treatment and support in the home. State funds have been spent to develop these programs. In addition to professional services, over 20,000 clubs have been established enabling the elderly to participate in their own welfare. These clubs provide such practical supports as telephone, washing, repair, and transport.

This policy created an increased consciousness of how health and social services relate to a specific population. It worked better on the social service side, where services were more easily provided and could utilize assistance from the elderly themselves. But difficulties remain. The program was perceived as temporary. State funds were designed to initiate programs which would be turned over to local authorities or social security organizations. Since these are labor-intensive services, their cost remains once the service becomes permanent. Medical insurance refuses to reimburse, except on an experimental basis, services which cannot be categorized as medical. The few experiences which are permitted remain precarious. Home help and reassurance are not included in the regular financing plans. Local authorities rely on supplementary funds from the social security organizations, and programs are often limited to persons without resources.

One can conclude that this is an interesting analysis of social needs, but not yet a full-scale program which could be assessed according to its results and efficiency.

Services for the handicapped. Delivery services to the elderly compete with another long-delayed task, comprehensive programs to meet the needs of the handicapped. The two categories overlap. But since 1975, the French legislature has intervened to give new status to all handicapped persons. Thirty years after the institution of social security, protection remained patchy. It relied on public assistance and did not consider the invalid's life from childhood to adult status as a continuum. Nothing would have happened if the families had not organized themselves. The first organizations and social services were built through private initiative. These associations include over 1,300 homes. Such pressure contributed to legislation to provide for the needs of the handicapped. The idea is to follow these problems through the person's lifetime and deal with the combined problems of health care, education, and income.

Children or younger handicapped individuals are entitled to special education if they do not fit into the normal education system. This education is free and combines special techniques of pedagogy with medical intervention. It can continue beyond school age and is designed to meet the special needs of each individual, including orientation programs. A commission of administrators meets with private associations to select services which may be adapted to the case, and, if the parents agree, the organization must take the child. The Ministries of Health and Education have created 380,000 places for special education. In these cases, upkeep and treatment are reimbursed by medical insurance.

This is an example of diagnosis based on both medical considerations and the capacity of the person to find a proper place in society. The interested public criticizes the fact that protection occurs only when the handicap is judged sufficiently severe. Parents are encouraged to have their child diagnosed as handicapped even though this may contradict the changeable nature of the young person's relation with society. In the same way, the child who makes the effort necessary to follow common education is financially in a less favorable situation than the beneficiary of special education.

At adult age, the same orientation reappears to determine the handicapped person's right to a financial allowance. Once again, 20 member commissions including doctors, administrators, local elected officials, social security personnel, and trade union representatives refer cases for rehabilitation, training, and work in normal or sheltered conditions. Employment is facilitated by the obligation of employers to offer a percentage of jobs to the handicapped. The commission also allots the financial aid.

Any employed handicapped person is entitled to a minimum wage; the state subsidizes the difference between this minimum and the norms applicable to the job. This subsidy may not exceed 20 percent of the official minimum wage, and the total wage may not exceed 130 percent of the official minimum wage. If unable to work, these individuals receive an allowance equal to the pension minimum—about half the minimum wage.

This program represents one of the more modern approaches to linking health and social services. The services offered deal with all aspects of daily existence, including work. Action has moved away from the original strict therapeutic attitude to cope with chronic situations. In these situations, medical insurance can be utilized. In addition, income support is available, although no rights have been acquired through work. The program is launched on the basis of principles which could be disturbing for the existing structures if they were to be generalized. But it is too soon to evaluate the program's possibilities and society's reaction.

One can see that from category to category, these forms of the combination of health and social services reach many citizens. They still do not pertain to the population as a whole.

Programs Concerning the Entire Population

Mental health services. The basic structure of mental health services combines prevention and cure. The structure is simultaneously ancient and modern in its conception. By 1938, the departments were under obligation to receive the mentally ill. These establishments were staffed by salaried practitioners.

Mental health care is reimbursed by social security as one of the few illnesses where the patient is not required to pay part of the costs. This is, in fact, free medicine. If hospital beds are added to the private establishments and the psychiatric wards in the general hospitals, approximately 150,000 beds are available for inpatient mental health services.

Since the 1960s, geographic divisions have resulted in units of up to 70,000 people for general psychiatry and 200,000 for child psychiatry. At the local level, a medical-social worker team ensures prevention, early diagnosis, hospital and community treatments, and aftercare. This team approach allows treatment and discharge of many patients to their daily activity without hospitalization. A head psychiatrist, assistant and part-time psychiatrists, social workers, full-time psychologists, and nurses constitute a typical team. They work in relation not only to the hospital but to outpatient clinics, day or night care units, aftercare centers, and sheltered lodgings. Twelve hundred catchment areas have been created; local hospital services have recently developed in proximity to other mental health services. The consulting activity has grown fourfold between 1962 and 1976, while the population in mental hospitals has fallen from 120,000 to 100,000. The state supports 80 percent of the budget of the consulting services.

General health maintenance services. The same type of organization has not applied to the general needs of the population so far, although the social security organization would be pleased if the prevention dispensaries evolved into health centers. But agreements with the medical profession have not found a compromise to allow the development of these model programs. The medical profession's control of contracts signed by its members is strong enough to discourage such initiatives. Integrated health centers are being proposed in the political arena; some towns have, in fact, initiated over 10 of these demonstrations. A few centers are functioning successfully.

The idea is to provide a global service through a team structure. Prevention and cure must be coordinated with medical, paramedical, and social welfare activities. Practitioners should not be paid by the service; rather, the center should function on a team basis. This implies salaried status for the doctors. The town, the social security organizations, and the state should help in the financing, with the client contributing in some limited form. The centers would function under collective direction, where local authorities, personnel, and beneficiaries would be represented. In those proposals, maternal and child welfare and school medicine would be integrated into the activities of the center. These proposals have not received sufficient support to become reality. They illustrate that French thinking is influenced by the Canadian reform of health services.

CONCLUSION

Social protection in France currently faces the problem of rising costs. At the same time, growing needs, equalization of attitudes, and demographic trends all seem to demand greater expenditures. It has become quite clear that the consumer is not in a position to control collective expenses. The population holds health care as a right and is accustomed to a situation which will only increase free services. The same population has never considered the social workers' intervention as requiring payment.

If this evolution is to be controlled and rationalized, it is through the coordination of services. Increasing costs have stimulated additional research and evaluation. It may be common sense that payments to support the elderly in their own homes are less costly than placements in expensive hospital structures. It may be more scientific to document different interventions for maximum effectiveness for lowest cost. This research has developed a series of social indicators, many of which relate to health and social services. Although some technical criteria receive criticism, it is now more frequent to denounce the definition of professional roles, the excessive "medicalization" of some situations, the medical service concept, the present hierarchy in income and status between doctors in practice or engaged in prevention, and the distinctions between doctors and social workers, as too rigid. It would seem, if one were to listen to what is said, that some traditional barriers are ready to come down.

Public authorities are not in a position to steer this evolution exactly as they may desire. They are able to plan the development of the hospital service, an area where they intend to act in the near future. These authorities now give priority to a stronger rationale for hospital care. They require better information on the reasons patients enter the hospital and prolong their stay. It is expected that a more rigorous system of financial assessment through tighter audit procedures may provide new standards. The law allows alternative financing. Some hospitals or wards receive an annual budget of social security and state funds as an option to the day cost method. This prospective reimbursement system may reduce unnecessary hospitalization.

Problems remain in the ambulatory medical services. Here, change comes from the profession itself. Employment perspectives are more difficult, with increasing numbers of new physicians vying for jobs. The new generation of practitioners may be more willing than their predecessors to accept team or group work. They are not as strongly opposed to salaried status as an infringement on proper relations with the patient. Many of the new doctors are women and may have a different attitude toward their own status when compared to that of the social worker or the nurse. It is significant that in the latest collective agreement with the private doctors, their contributions to preventive medicine were mentioned. The gap may be closing between the professions. It might close further if training and university programs allowed for greater interaction between these different professions.

With the growth of environmental consciousness, prevention was rediscovered and the public may be ready to pay the price for increased services. It is interesting to note that the consumer movement has sometimes focused on delivery of acute health and social services. Now, prevention requires the public to relate medical and social techniques. This is a major shift in attitudes.

Change will occur, but it is difficult to predict when the current system will be considered outdated. As recently as the 1970s, legislation reaffirmed the traditional principles of private medicine. Evolution is closely linked to how ideas and plans may be viewed by financial intermediaries. It may be necessary to budget additional funds for a transition period in order to initiate a new relationship between services. This is very difficult when cuts in public services are being proposed. The paradox comes from the fact that public spending is the lever of change in France, and public spending is under fire.

A final important issue is decentralization. A different relationship between medical and social services results from the active intervention of the public. With the exception of trade union and family associations, representatives on the social security boards, and a few local counselors on the hospital and social service boards, participation is not well-organized at a local level. This is probably the most important step to change in the well-intentioned, technocratic approach which characterizes most recent innovations in the field of human services.

8

UNITED KINGDOM

ERIC SAINSBURY

In principle, health and social services are freely available to everyone in the United Kingdom as a right. Relatively small payments are required for some services; contributions defray the costs of pharmaceutical prescriptions, some dental and ophthalmic work, the provision of "home helps," and residential care. But payments fall well below the actual costs of these services, and exemptions are granted to those who are unable to afford such care because of inadequate income, unemployment, youth, or retirement from work. Thus, these services continue to be provided in general accordance with the two basic principles of social legislation in the postwar period: that services should be universally available and "free at the point of delivery." Although no precise research data are available, it is virtually certain that few citizens are deterred from seeking medical or social help on grounds of cost. Access to general medical practitioners and to social workers is free.

The National Health Service receives funds principally from the central government exchequer. Only ten percent of the cost is met by that part of the weekly "national insurance contribution" allocated to this service. Statutory social work services are funded by the local authority system of "rates," an annual levy on homeowners based on the size and amenities of their accommodation. This is supplemented by the central government exchequer through an annual rate support grant to local authorities.

Thus, the provision of health and social services has no price mechanism to act as a regulator between people's experiences and definitions of needs and the demands they actually make (Hill, 1980). In operational terms, a major issue arises because of the almost unlimited nature of medical and social needs. Professional criteria cannot define the limits of improving standards of health or the quality of health care. Thus, decisions to limit the total flow of resources into these services become political rather than professional. They are made in recognition of the fact that the more accessible, acceptable, and effective the services, the greater their utilization. As services improve, overt expression of need increases. Political decisions regarding the allocation of resources are highly complex, because they are made in a context of increasing demand with economic and social consequences. For example, timely and effective medical treatment or social support may lead to increased life expectancy, to the survival of the chronically ill and handicapped, to the maintenance of families, and thus to future demand for services from the same patients/clients. On the other hand, untreated illness and the breakdown of unassisted families, while permitting a financial saving for both services in the present (and possibly in the future), may give rise to an increasing burden of social and economic costs in other aspects of public life. For example, such policies may prolong a person's incapacity for productive employment and may contribute various forms of deviant behavior.

These political and economic uncertainties mold public attitudes toward services. As Hill suggested (1980), the easy availability of services increases public satisfaction in Britain; at least until recently, political consensus stressed the desirability of these publicly funded services. Yet, there is inevitably a continuing expression of frustration and dissatisfaction among the public and the professional workers, that the outcomes of services would be more effective with additional resources.

Within the political process, administrators and professionals are confronted with similar dilemmas of resource allocation and the setting of relative priorities of particular groups, problems, and conditions. Another concern is how much to invest in preventive and curative services. Recently, in response to national economic difficulties, debate has focused on the extent to which the demand for statutory services can be regulated (a) by greater use of voluntary help, (b) by greater expectation of self-reliance, and (c) in respect of health services by encouraging the use of private insurance. The impact of these strategies on the quality of statutory services has become the central issue. The outcome of debate cannot be forecast; a stronger economy, higher productivity, or a change in government and its policies would have major effects on those decisions.

Political consensus still stresses the importance of ensuring that available resources by efficiently deployed. Efficiency should be defined in terms of the needs of service users and not simply by the preferences of administrators and professionals. Thus, emphasis is placed on the need for close collaboration between the health and social services and on the appropriate sharing of their resources in promoting community-based (rather than service-based) help to people in need.

ORGANIZATION OF HEALTH AND SOCIAL SERVICES

Before World War II, public financing for health and welfare services was administered within the framework of the Poor Law and, from 1929, by local government. Since the National Health Service Act of 1946, a tripartite administrative structure has effectively removed the major aspects of health care from local government control (Willcocks, 1967; Brown, 1978). Hospitals and specialist medical services previously provided by local government control (Willcocks, 1967). Hospitals and specialist medical services previously provided by local authorities and charitable foundations were brought within the financial responsibility of central government. They were administered by 14 regional hospital boards which delegated day-to-day responsibilities to local hospital management committees. The 35 hospitals attached to university medical schools were similarly financed but administered by boards of governors. Second, 120 executive councils, wholly financed and partly appointed by the central government, provided for the work and fees of general practitioners, dentists, opticians, and pharmacists. Each of these professionals remained independent contractors within the health service. Third, local authorities retained responsibility for environmental health services, home nursing, and supportive domiciliary provisions. Social workers in hospitals and clinics were employed within the health service structure.

The subsequent development of health service focused on internal administrative unification. Following a major restructuring in 1974, the service is organized as depicted in Figure 8.1.

The 14 Regional Health Authorities are responsible for planning and managing capital expenditures for the hospitals and for the appointment of specialist medical staff (except in university medical schools). Area Health Authorities, which are roughly coterminuous geographically with local government counties, are responsible for planning a comprehensive program of local health services. An essential aspect of their planning function is to act as liaison with the Family Practitioner Committees, whose work is broadly that of the former executive councils. Health Districts often relate to the geographical catchment areas of specific hospitals and are responsible for the day-to-day functioning of a hospital and its community health services. The reorganization of 1974 also created Community Health Councils, which lie outside the "line-management" structure of the health service and represent user interests. This structure is modified in parts of the United Kingdom. Wales and Scotland have no tier of management equivalent to the regional health authority. In Scotland, area health authorities are entitled Health Boards; in Northern Ireland, four Health and Social Services Boards undertake responsibilities which elsewhere are

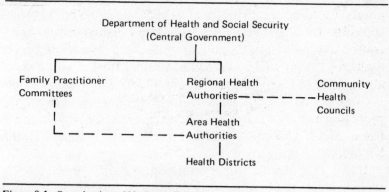

Figure 8.1 **Organization of National Health Service**

allocated to area health authorities. Since 1974, social workers within the British health service have been employed by local authority social services, not by the health authorities.

Publicly provided social work services, like the national health service, have also undergone major administrative reorganizations during the last ten years (Sainsbury, 1977). Before 1971, local authorities provided a range of service structures based on social work specializations, the special needs of particular clients, and the piecemeal accumulation of social legislation. Local education authorities, responsible primarily for the provision of schools and colleges, employed welfare officers to deal with truancy and with ad hoc requests for educational grants. Local housing departments employed welfare officers to assist public housing tenants who were in difficulties with rent payments or the adequate maintenance of their accommodation. Public health departments were responsible for the hospitalization and aftercare of the mentally ill, domiciliary and day-care services for the handicapped, home helps, home nursing, meals on wheels, and school clinics. Children's departments held a general responsibility for the well-being of all children, and particularly for the care of those who were unable to live in their own homes or were at risk of removal from home. Welfare departments assumed responsibility for elderly housing and, in some areas, homeless families. In addition, local probation and aftercare services, administered by specially appointed committees outside local government but financed jointly by local authorities and central government, were responsible for social services attached to criminal and domestic courts and penal establishments, for the aftercare of people discharged from these establishments, and for the provision of alternatives to custodial care. Responsibility for juvenile offenders was shared, on the basis of local agreements, between the probation and children's departments. As stated earlier, hospital-based social workers were employed by the National Health Service.

Under this organizational arrangement, social work services to individuals and families were difficult to coordinate. Families whose needs spanned the specialist interests of several services were likely to be overvisited, while those difficulties outside the administrative and legal definitions of service functions encountered problems in obtaining help, except from the voluntary services. Responsibility for the coordination of services to families and for preventive work was left to the cooperative initiative of chief officers, who, by the structuring of their independent services, found themselves competing for local authority resources. Furthermore, service structures created difficulties in providing services based on the needs of a whole family rather than of its individual members.

Following the report of the Seebohm Committee on Local Authority and Allied Personal Social Services (1968), the Local Authority Social Services Act of 1970 established in each local authority a Social Services Committee and Department responsible for all these various functions, except probation services. In Scotland, 1968 legislation achieved a similar unification, which included the probation service. Education and housing welfare officers were not included in the statutory implementation of the 1970 Act, but there have been moves within several local authorities to incorporate these workers within the new departments.

The Seebohm Committee's report was based on certain principles which have guided the organization of social services departments and which are directly relevant to the achievement of effective collaboration with the health service. First, the department's work should be oriented to the needs of families. Second, it should respond to these needs without regard to administrative or legal definitions and categorizations. Third, it should be community-based. As resources have become available, there has been a decentralization of service staffs into local communities, usually divided into population units of 50,000-100,000. In some areas further experimental decentralization has led to the formation of small groups of social workers operating in "patch systems." Fourth, area teams should harness the self-help potential of local citizens in order to achieve collaboration in the promotion of community well-being rather than simply the rescue of social casualties. This will "blur the distinction between the givers and receivers of help." Fifth, social workers should be competent to respond to the range of clients' needs. Thus, the generic basis of social work education should be matched by a generalist approach to social work practice. This does not deny the value of additional specialist assistance for those clients with very difficult problems.

Following the reorganization of local authority boundaries in 1974, social services departments served entire counties, except in the five "metropolitan counties" and London, where services are provided by district councils and boroughs, respectively.

The present organization of health and social services has three main preoccupations. First, both have moved toward greater internal unification, though at the risk of increasing their operational separation. The National Health Service no longer directly employs any social workers, but relies on their "attachment" from local authority social services departments. Local authority social services no longer provide direct medical or paramedical services to individuals and families. Second, both services have devised procedures for collaborative work within different systems of organization, public accountability, and finance. Third, both have expressed a growing concern with the problem of implementing the concept of "community care." In part, this concern represents a movement away from institutional care because of rising costs. More positively, it reflects a growing awareness that the causes of malfunctioning, whether medical or social, are partly found in the social environment, that medical and social needs and services interact, and that help based on the felt needs of citizens should be provided in a familiar social context. The definition of "community care" is elusive. As Bayley suggested (1973), it can be defined in two ways with different consequences for professional practices. Care *in* the community can be achieved simply by outposting professional personnel and establishing small service units. It does not necessitate closer collaboration between professionals, desirable as this may be. It may be based on multidisciplinary activity in which professionals maintain separate roles, and achieve a consensus, but have an incomplete understanding of the factors which lead an individual to seek help. In contrast to this, care *by* the community implies sufficient professional and organizational flexibility to blend formal and informal service systems. It implies interdisciplinary work, in which professional roles and tasks are more loosely defined and emphasis is placed on reciprocity within a coherent pattern of help.

Both services have been preoccupied with administrative rationalization. In the local authority, since 1974 this has led to the creation of large hospitals and the development of a monolithic administrative structure. Both services have become more centralized in administrative terms; this process includes the risk that programs may lose their focus on "community care." For example, the assumption that increased size is cost-efficient and effective in service may not hold. Additional assumptions are that hierarchical management ensures effective pursuit of socially desirable goals and that *all* services are best provided by professionally qualified staff. In the period from 1959 to 1975, the number of hospital nurses increased by 50 percent and hospital-based doctors by 75 percent. Since the 1971 reorganization, the number of local authority social workers has more than doubled. These expansions are desirable, unless they lead to less public participation in defining and meeting needs, to reduced accountability, and to a less sensitive

response to the social context in which the services are
provided.

LINKAGES BETWEEN THE SERVICES

Formal consideration of the need to relate health and social
services was mooted in two central government papers published in 1962 and 1963. These were concerned with planning
the hospital services and the development of community care
(Ministry of Health, 1962, 1963). Since then the need has been
recognized, first, that policy decisions made by one service
affect the caring capacities of the other, and, second, that
organizational structures sometimes reinforce fragmented and
inequitable service delivery. During the 1970s, an accumulation
of policies (reinforced by but not ascribable to an adverse
economic climate) shifted the location of care for certain client
groups from the health sector to the social services sector. These
policies helped achieve common agreement about priorities of
intervention in both services. The need for this agreement was
particularly apparent in respect to the care of the frail elderly
and the handicapped, whose needs are self-evidently related to
the interest of both services. Similarly, if the old and the
handicapped can be helped to continue living in their own
homes, a rational system of support must combine the day care
and domiciliary services of local authorities with the activities
of "primary health care teams" of general practitioners, health
visitors, and community nurses. In cases of child abuse, a
complex partnership is essential among the primary health care
teams who are the most frequent detectors of the problem, the
social workers who hold responsibilities for legal action and for
the prevention of further abuse, and hospital-based pediatricians
who provide consultant services for both professions.

Effective collaboration between services has been a growing
concern to central government since 1972, when the Secretary
of State for Health and Social Services established a task force
to examine the issues involved and to make recommendations
(Department of Health and Social Services and Welsh Office,

1973). The opportunity for this initiative had been increased by a reorganization of central government responsibilities following the Seebohm Committee's report. The newly established Department of Health and Social Security absorbed the responsibilities of the former Ministry of Health and some work of other central departments (notably the Home Office) concerned with the provision of local authority social services. Since then, a succession of circulars have discussed various aspects of the collaborative process. A major discussion paper was published in 1978 by the Central Health Services Council and the Personal Social Services Council (both bodies advisory to the Secretary of State) on collaboration in community care.

In addition, the Department of Health and Social Security (DHSS) issued a series of reports and guidelines on the needs of particular client groups, stressing the importance of interservice and interprofessional collaboration, for the mentally handicapped (1971), the mentally ill (1975), the care of children injured by their parents (1974), and the elderly (1978). Regarding the elderly the components of collaboration were extended beyond the medical and social work professions to include policies related to housing and pensions. Similarly, a committee chaired by Professor Donald Court in 1977 identified the need for an integrated child health service to create effective links within the health service among general practitioners, school health services, and consultant (hospital-based) pediatricians.

To date, achievements can best be considered under two headings: (1) strategies for the planning of services and allocation of resources, and (2) procedures for coordination.

Strategies for Planning and Finance

The DHSS Consultative Document on the Reorganization of the National Health Service (1971) recognized that administrative unification of services would not be feasible because of political, financial, professional, and administrative constraints. Therefore, in 1973 the Working Party on Collaboration recommended that the health service and local authorities should establish Joint Consultative Committees at the county level. These committees are responsible for developing general strategies governing the priorities of collaborative work within the two services. They receive advice from Joint Care Planning Teams set up in response to the DHSS Circulars published in 1976 and 1977. The teams are made up of officers drawn from Area Health Authorities and coterminous local authorities. Area Health Authorities have a major responsibility for facilitating joint planning with local authorities; to this end, one-third of their members are nominated by local government.

The same DHSS Circulars provided for a system of joint financing, currently at the level of about £40 million per annum, as an incentive to pursue the strategy of community care in preference to institutional care, particularly for the elderly and mentally handicapped. Joint financing may be used for both capital and revenue expenditures as an alternative to the use of hospital beds or other hospital-based accommodation (Sargeant, 1979).

Coordination in Day-to-Day Practice

Irrespective of these measures to improve strategic planning, the perceived quality of service depends on the attitudes of the professionals involved. As suggested earlier, a qualitative distinction must be drawn between multidisciplinary and interdisciplinary approaches to service delivery. The first acknowledges the potential value of discussions between professionals to achieve a coherent pattern of care, while the second acknowledges varieties of professional expertise and seeks to adopt a more flexible approach to the allocation and sharing of tasks. Of course, it is easier to begin discussions than to implement a model of collaborative work (Central Health Services Council and Personal Social Services Council, 1978).

Teamwork has been a characteristic of hospital services for nearly a century, initially through the appointment of medical and psychiatric social workers attached to wards or to individual consultants. Reorganization of the National Health Service in 1974 changed the employment status of these workers, but not their roles. Social workers continue to act as members of medical teams attending inpatients, outpatients, and users of community-based clinics and "day hospitals." More recently, some general practitioners have welcomed the full-time or occasional "attachments" of local authority social workers to primary health care teams. In some instances, a fruitful sharing of tasks has been achieved with health visitors, community nurses, and community psychiatric nurses. Particularly in work with the elderly, the chronically sick, and the handicapped living in their own homes, regular monitoring of progress and the maintenance of domiciliary support systems constitute essential functions of primary health care. In these cases, it is not unusual to find a flexible allocation of tasks. Similarly, in the development of day care services by local authorities (e.g., clubs, training and recreational centers), medical and paramedical practitioners may give advice and provide ad hoc minor treatments. At a more general level of cooperation, area teams of social workers may consult with doctors regarding neurotic behavior, drug dependency, or disease.

Some aspects of teamwork are required by legislation. In the Mental Health Act of 1959, certain procedures leading to compulsory hospital admission require that the social worker (designated for this purpose as "mental welfare officer") recommend and negotiate admission to hospital, acting on medical advice. Although it is not essential for the doctor and mental welfare officer to make a joint visit to the client, this is frequently the basis for these decisions.

Although teamwork between the professions is not demanded by law in child abuse cases, a DHSS Circular in 1974 recommended the establishment of interprofessional Area Review Committees based on the geographical boundaries of social services departments to develop and monitor service procedures and to establish a family "case register." This recommendation has been implemented; case conferences on individual children are strongly urged within the wider framework of this strategic review (Department of Health and Social Security, 1974).

Informal interprofessional case conferences on specific situations have been a regular aspect of professional work for many years and are regarded, both in medicine and social services, as "good practice." On the whole, these are more often initiated by social workers than by doctors. A study by the National Society for the Prevention of Cruelty to Children in 1976 showed that the usefulness of case conferences increased with advanced planning, including the setting of time limits, flexibility of location, and opportunities to contribute ideas in writing (Castle, 1976).

Considerable use is made of *referral* between services. A study by Jeffreys (1965) showed that in general medical practice, about one-third of the patients who seek medical help are in some kind of social or psychological difficulty. It is no doubt true that many patients regard their family doctors as the most suitable persons with whom to raise personal problems. However, the major reorganization of social services has inhibited referrals from doctors because of uncertainty about the functions and structures of the new unified departments, and because of the lack of face-to-face knowledge of the social workers available. Increasing use of attachments might overcome this difficulty and encourage greater use of social workers in more complex and sustained forms of casework help. Certainly, effective liaison and referral are more readily achieved in hospitals than in community-based work.

OBSTACLES TO EFFECTIVE LINKAGE

Despite the advances made in strategic and local collaboration between services, difficulties remain in respect of structures, professional attitudes, and the availability of resources

(Hill, 1980; Sargeant, 1979). Effective liaison is difficult to achieve, partly because of the structural difference between services, partly because professions hold different perspectives on the cause and treatment of problems, and partly because of difficulties in achieving a mutual understanding of each other's tasks.

In structural terms, the services are managed by different authorities, occupy different premises, and are not geographically related. Reorganizations have been carried out independently of each other. Generally, the "district" level of the health service is not equivalent to any geographical entity within social services. Thus it is easier to achieve formal collaboration at the area health authority/county level than at a more local level. Furthermore, despite the development of joint financing for certain user groups, in most work with patients/ clients professional responsibilities remain financially divided. For example, both the health service and the local authority services provide some hostel accommodation, yet the criteria of need by which people are admitted to hostels are seldom adequately differentiated between the services. Waiting lists for accommodation are rarely combined for the purposes of joint assessment and disposal.

In an adverse economic climate, departments tend to become inward-looking. Thus, although joint financing represents an important step in bridging the complexities created by two entirely different systems of financing services (taxes on the one hand and rates on the other), local authorities are increasingly cautious about its use. Joint financing represents only a temporary transfer of resources, and local authorities in the future may be required to continue paying for the recently devised new provisions. This anxiety increases in those areas where political control is subject to change in local elections. Over relatively short periods of time, a social service department may find its resources arbitrarily increased or diminished because of changes in local policies about public expenditure. While this is true of the National Health Service regarding changes in the policies of central government, the size of the service and the political strength of its professional lobby means that reductions are widely spread and have less local impact.

In the work of Joint Care Planning Teams established in 1976, a different kind of structural problem becomes apparent. Health services are often based on the allocation of beds to specific illness groups; specialization within medicine is similarly based. In social work, particularly since 1971, client group specialization has, in part, been superseded by casework, group work, and community work. Thus the quality and dimensions of needs assessment differ considerably within the two professions. A doctor may believe that a social worker lacks adequate understanding of the needs of an individual client; equally, a social worker may feel that medical assessments lack the broad understanding of the contextual issues in an individual case.

Differences between professional status and attitudes may also inhibit the achievement of cooperation. Doctors remain independent professional contractors within the health service. Their powers and freedoms are considerable. Social workers are essentially local government employees to whom certain responsibilities legally vested in the local authorities have been delegated. A social worker's power lies less in professional expertise than in hierarchical position within a bureaucratic structure.

The two professions also have different starting points in their assessments of need. A doctor makes an expert diagnosis and unilaterally prescribes the treatment. In contrast, a social worker's concern for "welfare" raises complex issues concerning the nature of this expertise, because every citizen is in some respects an expert. Thus, to a doctor, a social worker will frequently appear to be indecisive, while, conversely, a doctor may appear to be dogmatic. This professional difference is exacerbated by differences in the size of the caseloads and resulting differences in the speed of professional actions: A family doctor is responsible on average for 2500 patients; a social worker, for 35 clients.

Age differences also may influence the possibilities of effective liaison. A family doctor may be of any age after qualification, and general practice is regarded as a respected medical specialty. Field-based social workers are often relatively young, partly because of the rapid movement of older staff into administrative posts following the reorganizations of the last ten years. Social workers sometimes find doctors unapproachable, partly because of these differences in age and experience. Related to this and other differences in professional status, the assumed right of one profession to challenge the opinions of the other is notably lopsided. This is particularly evident in the admission of patients to mental hospitals: Although, under certain legal requirements, the final decision is vested in social workers, they will need a very high degree of self-assurance and moral courage (irrespective of the social validity of their opinion) to challenge the assertions of a consultant psychiatrist.

Furthermore, the tasks of the professions have different terminal points. A hospital doctor discharges a patient on completion of medical treatment, often irrespective of the wider social consequences of that discharge. The shortage of hospital beds and long waiting lists of patients seeking hospital treatment have shortened the length of hospital stay. This inevitably increases pressure on the domiciliary services of local authorities. Conversely, some patients, particularly the old and the mentally disordered, remain longer in the hospital because of the lack of alternative local authority accommodations. Once again, different professional perceptions of joint responsibilities may mitigate against cooperation. It is difficult to measure the relative performances of services by reference to their joint responsibilities when objectives have not been jointly defined. What is interpreted as a demand for service may become more a function of the limited availability of help rather than of the experience of human need. Some potential goodwill between professional workers dissipates because of lack of adequate guidelines on the performance of their reciprocal tasks.

CONCLUSION

Much of this chapter has implied that the rationale for seeking closer collaboration between health and social services lies in the pursuit of agreed-upon policies of community care. Community care represents more than just an alternative to institutional care. It constitutes a philosophy which is commonly held by both services. It argues that the reference point of their achievements should be the needs of the patient/client rather than the administrative and professional interests of the services.

Close cooperation is essential if people are to experience a coherent system of support. Collaboration alone cannot solve all the difficulties of providing such a system; both services endure a shortage of resources. The greater their commitment to alleviating felt need, the greater the resource issue is regarded as a major difficulty. However, collaboration could be advanced by enlarging the understanding in each profession of the attitudes, approaches, and administrative practices of the other. Little of this awareness has been incorporated into the basic training of either profession.

Second, more use could be made of interservice liaison appointments. These have been introduced at the middle management level in many social services departments. As suggested earlier, a similar liaison/attachment system at the level of the primary health care team has been beneficial in some local areas.

Third, arrangements might profitably be made by social services departments for all medical referrals from a particular hospital, clinic, or medical practice to be channeled to one team of social workers, regardless of differences in their official geographical catchment areas.

Fourth, a visiting medical or nursing adviser could be linked to a specific social service setting, such as a residential institution, day care facility, or area team.

Fifth, greater use could be made of Joint Care Planning Teams to strengthen their negotiation between the professions by the development of guidelines for practice in problematic situations, such as mental health admissions and discharges.

Finally, as each service recognizes its potential contribution to the development of community care, professional roles and tasks are bound to become blurred. This has begun to happen regarding the roles of social workers, health visitors, and community psychiatric nurses. Some flexibility of professional boundaries can be achieved without necessarily implying the loss of professional status and integrity.

REFERENCES

BAYLEY, M. J. (1973) Mental Handicap and Community Care. London: Routledge & Kegan Paul.

CASTLE, R. L. (1976) Case Conferences: A Cause for Concern? London: NSPCC.

Central Health Services Council and Personal Social Services Council (1978) Collaboration in Community Care—A Discussion Document. London: HMSO.

Department of Health and Social Security (1979a) Report of the (Jay) Committee on Services for the Mentally Handicapped. London: HMSO.

——— (1979b) Joint Financing Report. HC (79) 18, LAC (79) 11 (October).

——— (1977a) Joint Care Planning: Health and Local Authorities. HC (77) 17, LAC (77) 10 (May).

——— (1977b) Priorities for Health and Personal Social Services in England. A Consultative Document. London: HMSO.

——— (1976) Joint Care Planning: Health and Local Authorities. HC (76) 18, LAC (76) 6 (March).

——— (1975) Better Services for the Mentally Ill. Cmnd. 6233. London: HMSO.

——— (1974) Report of the Committee of Inquiry into the Care and Supervision Provided in Relation to Maria Colwell. London: HMSO.

——— (1971a) Establishment of Joint Consultative Committees. NHS Reorganisation Circular, HRC (74).

——— (1971b) Better Services for the Mentally Handicapped. Cmnd. 4683. London: HMSO.

Department of Health and Social Services and Welsh Office (1973) Report from the Working Party on Collaboration between the National Health Service and Local Government. London: HMSO.

HILL, M. (1980) Understanding Social Policy. Oxford: Basil Blackwell.

JEFFREYS, M. (1965) Anatomy of Social Welfare Services. London: Routledge & Kegan Paul.

Ministry of Health (1963) Health and Welfare: The Development of Community Care. Cmnd. 1973. London: HMSO.

——— (1962) Hospital Plan for England and Wales. Cmnd. 1604. London: HMSO.

SAINSBURY, E. (1977) The Personal Social Services. London: Pitman.

SARGEANT, T. (1979) "Joint care planning in the health and personal social services," in T. A. Booth (ed.) Planning for Welfare. Oxford: Basil Blackwell.

WILLCOCKS, A. (1967) The Creation of the National Health Service. London: Routledge & Kegan Paul.

9

ISRAEL

JOSEPH KATAN

THE ISRAELI SOCIOPOLITICAL CONTEXT

Health and social services in Israel function in a specific and unique sociopolitical context, and their structure, policies, and activities are influenced by its characteristics. Since its inception as an independent state in 1948, the Israeli sociopolitical context has been characterized by two main features: political and bureaucratic centralization, and dominance of political parties (Akzin, 1970).

Although these features have been weakened somewhat in recent years, they continue to constitute cornerstones of the state's political structure and to affect its organizational fabric. Several factors gave impetus to these trends toward centralization and politicization. First, from its inception, the state was beset with severe defense, social, and economic problems. The dominant conviction was that due to the complexity of these problems, they could be coped with only by a strong national leadership and centralized institutions rather than by organizations having localistic, sectorial or ethnic orientations. Second, the centralistic trends have not been counterbalanced

AUTHOR'S NOTE: *I would like to thank Yechiel Eran, Yehoshofat Harel, Ora Kahaner, and Baruch Ovadia for providing valuable information that was used in the preparation of this work. Special thanks are due to Dr. Dianne Vinokur-Kaplan for her assistance. However, their work bears no responsibility to its contents.*

by strong localistic tendencies; in fact, many towns and villages were founded after the establishment of the state and still lack local foci of identification. Furthermore, the majority of the Israeli population is composed of immigrants who arrived in the country after 1948 without economic resources or occupational preparation. Therefore, their absorption depended almost completely upon aid received from the absorption authorities, who usually represented central organizations.

Finally, Israel is a very small country; therefore, central control is feasible. Furthermore, this proximity facilitates easy and rapid access of the population to the big cities, the centers of political, economic, and cultural activity. These citizens identify more with the central political structure than their local institutions.

These tendencies toward centralization are reflected in the government's conception of its responsibilities and functions in welfare and health. Improving the well-being of the population is a national target, the achievement of which requires the collective efforts and massive involvement of central authorities. Adopting the main ideas of the "welfare state" and the growing government intervention associated with it was never seriously opposed by any political or public organization in Israel.

This avowed commitment to welfare did not diminish even after the general election of 1977, when the Labor Party (a Social Democratic party), committed ideologically to the welfare state, was removed from power after thirty years of control. It was replaced by an alignment of nationalistic-liberal parties with strong orientations toward a free-market economy. Still, the last four years have been marked by both an expansion of social legislation (minimum income guarantee, nursing care insurance, and a proposal for national health insurance) and continuous involvement of the government in different welfare and health programs.

This political environment could be conducive to the formation of an integrated system of health and social services and could facilitate the development of coherent national policies and long-range planning in these areas. However, the forces pushing toward national policies, central planning, and integration have been counterbalanced by other sets of factors pushing in the direction of service fragmentation and lack of coordination among them.

First, while tendencies toward political centralization constitute a key factor in the Israeli political system, the political center itself is not uniform. It comprises various national bodies such as central political parties, a strong national trade union (the Histadrut), and the Jewish Agency (representing the World Zionist Organization). This diversity in the center reflects the composition of the Israeli governments for the past thirty years. These were coalition governments drawn from different parties, with one party in a dominant role. The ministries dealing with social and health services, such as Health, Welfare, Labor, Housing, Absorption, and Education, were always in the hands of different parties or various factions within the same parties.

Control of these ministries by one party still does not guarantee cooperation among them. Ministries, like other organizations, develop their own guarded monopolies and autonomous aspirations. However, the distribution of the responsibility over welfare-related ministries among different parties aggravates the split among them and makes the creation of collaborative interministerial relationships a difficult, if not unsurmountable, task.

Diversification at the political center is reflected in the position and impact of the Histadrut (the Israeli General Federation of Labor), the largest and strongest trade union in Israel. The Histadrut's Sick Fund (Kupat Holim), not the government, is the largest medical care organization in Israel. The government itself plays only a minor role in this important area.

Second, local responsibility for the delivery of certain social services has a long tradition in Israel; it constitutes an existent and accepted phenomenon. Third, voluntary organizations engaged in the provision of services to populations in need have been always an integral part of Jewish communities throughout the world. This tradition found concrete expression in the development of many voluntary service agencies in Israel even before the establishment of the state.

The diversification of the political center, the operation of local services, and the functions of voluntary service agencies weaken the central government's ability to form an integrated national system of social and health services, or at least of establishing intensive collaboration among them. In addition, the government has shown basic reluctance to assume overall responsibility for the delivery of health and social services and to use its authority to ensure both central guidance of services and strong coordination among them. This approach by Israeli governments has been affected by political considerations, financial limitations, administrative constraints, and a basic conviction that local and voluntary organizations have a role in the social and health services arena.

Thus, the Israeli sociopolitical context is characterized by conflicting forces. While the tendencies toward centralization, bureaucratization, and politicization push toward greater and expanded government involvement, the split in the center among different parties and factions and the traditional roles played by voluntary and local organizations push toward decentralization and fragmentation of services. The impact of these various factors is described and analyzed in the following review of the structure and activities of the social and health service.

STRUCTURE AND ACTIVITIES OF
THE SOCIAL WELFARE SERVICES

Various organizations provide social services to different populations in Israel: the central government, local municipalities, the Jewish Agency, voluntary organizations, trade unions (especially the Histadrut), and other public and private organizations (see Macarov, 1975, 1978; and Neipris, 1978). The structure, objectives and main activities of these different factors and the interrelationships are discussed below.

The Central Government

Seven ministries offer direct social services: Labor and Social Affairs, Defense, Absorption, Education, Housing, Health, and the Office of the Deputy Prime Minister.

(1) The Ministry of Labor and Social Affairs. This ministry plays a key role in the welfare arena, although the main burden for the direct delivery of various social services is in the hands of local municipalities and various voluntary organizations. The ministry provides most of the budget of these organizations and supervises their activities. It develops social legislation, makes policies, and issues rules and regulations to guide the activities of the other organizations. However, the ministry is not just an indirect partner in the welfare arena; it also provides direct services to particular population groups. These include probation services to juvenile delinquents and rehabilitation services to the handicapped, retarded, and blind. Also, the ministry owns and operates institutions for juvenile delinquents and the retarded.

The ministry contains the following divisions and departments: Family and Community Services; Child and Youth Welfare; Rehabilitation; Care for the Aged, the Retarded, and the Blind; Vocational Training; Probation Services; Youth Protection; and Planning and Research. A body which operates within the framework of the ministry but has a special legislative status is the National Insurance Institute (NII, or Hamosad Le Bituach Leumi). Unlike the other units within the ministry, NII is financed through taxes paid by employers, employees, and self-employed persons.

The NII has a broad conception of its functions. It works toward locating vulnerable population groups in order both to protect them against the risks of poverty and distress and to prevent their emergence in the future. It seeks to realize these aims by developing different types of social insurance and income maintenance programs, by providing social work services, and by developing new types of services. In addition, it collects data and conducts studies on the situation of socially vulnerable groups in Israel and develops social policies and programs. The income maintenance programs aim at guaranteeing a minimum income to vulnerable groups in society. They include pensions for men at age 65 and for women at age 60, benefits for survivors (widows and orphans), work injury insurance, maternity benefits, children's allowances (from the first child), unemployment compensations, and general disability insurance.

The NII's rehabilitation branch employs social workers. It provides treatment and consultation to the insurees and helps them to plan their rehabilitation programs and to cope with the new circumstances they face after an injury or family loss. In recent years, the institute has extended its activities in a new sphere, the planning and implementation of special projects, whose main purposes are to create and provide innovative services to the constituencies of the institute (elderly people, the handicapped, widows) and to evaluate their outcomes.

Despite their affiliation to the same ministry, the relationships between the NII and the other ministry units are quite loose. These relationships are allowed by the independent legal status of the institute.

(2) The Absorption Ministry provides a wide range of services to new immigrants in the first stage of their stay in Israel. These services include assistance in housing and employment, provision of minimum income until the immigrant finds employment, and social-educational activities.

(3) The Education Ministry finances and supervises the activities of "street-corner" or detached community workers (few of them social workers) who are employed by local municipalities in an attempt to help detached youngsters reintegrate into society.

(4) The Ministry of Housing and Construction is responsible for initiating, financing, and planning homes for new immigrants, low-income families living in crowded apartments, young couples, and the elderly. The ministry is responsible for the operation of government housing and maintenance companies. It represents the government in government-municipal housing corporations operating in certain cities. Some of these companies have established community organization units whose main purposes are to maintain the houses and the quality of life

in neighborhoods and to provide their residents with necessary services.

(5) The Office of the Deputy Prime Minister coordinates government involvement in a new urban renewal program it initiated in 1977 called Project Renewal. This project has two interrelated objectives: to improve the physical housing conditions of residents in poor neighborhoods, and to develop a wide range of social and educational services designed to meet their various needs.

Other governmental bodies involved in the social arena include the Israeli Army, which utilizes social workers as mental health officers in various units, and Prison Authority, which utilizes social workers to provide treatment and rehabilitation to prisoners. The government also employs occupational welfare officers (some of them social workers) in most of its ministries. The activities of the Health Ministry in the social services arena are described later in this chapter.

The Local Municipalities

Despite the comprehensive involvement of the central government in various social welfare areas, the municipalities assume direct responsibility for the delivery of most welfare services. Every local authority is required by law to establish a social service department. Although they differ from one another in the comprehensiveness, diversity, and quality of their activities, local social service departments generally provide a basket of services that contain the following main components:

(a) eligibility determination for individuals and families to receive different kinds of financial and material aid, using the formal criteria issued by the central government (e.g., income maintenance payments, health insurance, and rent subsidies);
(b) consultation and treatment for individuals and families;
(c) linkage and referral of clients to other services;

(d) child welfare services, including adoption and placement of children in foster homes and institutions;
(e) services for the elderly, including treatment and consultation, meals-on-wheels, and assistance in nursing home placement;
(f) rehabilitation services to the handicapped, the mute, deaf, and blind; and
(g) community organization activities, including assessment of needs, planning of new services, and organizing neighborhood committees.

Since most of the financial resources for this wide range of services are allocated by the Ministry of Labor and Social Affairs, it plays a key role in guiding and supervising the activities of the local departments. This supervision has a threefold purpose: first, to guarantee the provision of certain basic services to different vulnerable population groups throughout the country; second, to ensure uniformity in the allocation of financial assistance, thereby avoiding unjust local variation; and third, to provide administrative and professional guidance to departments which face difficulties and need assistance.

Despite the government's involvement, local departments—especially the bigger ones—have considerable autonomy to initiate and develop new projects, to utilize different intervention techniques, and to put emphasis on provision of services to specific population groups. The differences in the departmental activities do not necessarily represent variation in population needs, but rather different approaches of workers, local political functionaries, and local groups.

The Jewish Agency (JA)

The JA's involvement in the social services field is especially evident in the provision of social services to new immigrants, and the treatment of youth, especially from new immigrants and low-income families. (The Jewish Agency in Israel is the executive body of the World Zionist Organization.)

The General Federation of Labor (Histadrut)

The largest trade union in Israel, this group has pursued from its inception a unique course of action. It has operated not only a traditional trade union seeking to improve the salaries and working conditions of its members, but it also functions as a human service organization striving to respond to the needs of its members. Operating in this framework, the Histadrut provides comprehensive health services to its members through Kupat Holim (Worker's Sick Fund), assistance in housing, and allocation of loans.

The Joint Distribution Committee (JDC)

In Israel, this has become in recent years a key factor in the welfare services arena. Although it does not provide direct services to populations (as it did in the past), it allocates extensive financial resources, professional guidance, and direction to the development of a wide range of existing services as well as new and innovative projects. (The JDC [American Joint Distribution Committee] is a Jewish Relief Organization supported by American Jewry through United Jewish Appeal and other agencies. It develops and maintains health welfare and rehabilitation programs for needy Jews in 25 countries. Its operations in Israel are conducted by JDC–Israel.)

Part of the assistance is channeled by the JDC through joint JDC-government associations established in recent years for the purpose of developing service to particular population groups. One example of this kind of collaboration is Eshel, the association for planning and development services for the aged in Israel. A considerable number of Eshel's activities are initiated and conducted by special local associations established in many communities throughout the country. These associations include local organizations providing social and health services for the elderly, local voluntary organizations, and representatives of the elderly population itself. While Eshel provides financial resources and guidance, the planning and implementation of community and institutional programs are conducted at the community level.

The collaboration between Eshel and the local association represents a unique combination and integration of national and local bodies. The success of forming this kind of collaboration between various local organizations, as well as between them and national organizations, might be attributed to the impact of the JDC and the strings it attaches to the allocation of financial resources to various programs (Eran, 1977).

Voluntary Service Agencies (VSA)

Voluntary organizations in Israel provide a wide range of services to various populations and play a central role in the delivery of certain special services (Leron and Spiro, 1980). For instance, women's voluntary organizations, most of them affiliated directly or indirectly with political and/or religious organizations, are responsible for the development and delivery of day care services for infants and young children. Child care is an example of a service almost fully funded by the government but actually run and controlled by voluntary organizations.

Another domain where voluntary organizations are active is providing services to citizens who suffer such handicaps as blindness, deafness, neuromuscular disorders, mental retardation, cancer, and chronic illness (Kramer, 1971). The VSAs provide a wide range of services to these populations, including treatment and consultation, development of educational and recreational programs, vocational training, linkage and referral services, and the establishment of hostels and other institutions (e.g., for the retarded and the blind). Some of these services are provided solely by these VSAs. Other services are provided by other organizations as well as the local social service departments.

These organizations are partially subsidized by the government. A study conducted on 15 of these organizations revealed that 14 were direct recipients of government funds. There is little evidence, however, that this support constrains the freedom of these organizations in both program decisions and their implementation (Kramer, 1971).

A third and unique type of voluntary organization is the multitude of small, parochial, community-linked organizations operating throughout Israel. These intimate, small organizations are generally affiliated with synagogues or linked to ethnic groups; they provide for the economic and social needs of their members. They tend to operate independently and avoid formal links with public organizations (Salzberger and Rosenfeld, 1974).

Any review of the complicated, diversified, and comprehensive welfare system in Israel is incapable of revealing all its unique facets and components. Its major characteristics are as follows: (1) the involvement of a wide range of organizations, governmental, municipal, public and voluntary, in the delivery of services; (2) the diversity, variety, and comprehensiveness of services provided to the population, resulting in few social problems remaining uncovered (social service programs account for a substantial part of the gross national income); (3) the absence of central planning and guidance; and (4) the lack of coordination among services at the national and local levels, leading to overlap and duplication of services.

STRUCTURE AND ACTIVITIES OF
THE HEALTH SERVICES

Unlike its considerable involvement in the welfare arena, the central government plays only a partial role in the health arena. The key factor in this sphere is a number of nonprofit sick funds. The largest and most influential of these is the one belonging to the Histadrut.

The Histadrut's Sick Fund provides comprehensive medical services to 70 percent of the Israeli population. Several other small sick funds provide these services to 22 percent of the population, leaving approximately 8 percent of the population not covered by a comprehensive medical insurance. These figures are based on data provided by the Ministry of Health; other sources indicate that the percentage of the population covered by the sick funds amounts to 95 percent. In addition to these sick funds, several other organizations provide certain limited health care services; the health ministry, local municipalities, Hadassah, until 1975 the JDC, and a few voluntary and private organizations. (For a full discussion of the political implications of the Israeli health services structure, see Arian [1981] and Sharkansky and Radian [1981].)

The continuous existence of the current structure since the establishment of the state reflects the reluctance of "labor" governments that controlled Israel until 1977 to weaken the power of the Histadrut Sick Fund. The leadership of the Labor Party was convinced that the existence of this Sick Fund was a powerful way of ensuring the continued strengthening of the Histadrut, which was vital for stabilizing the political power of the party. The Labor Party was committed to the idea of full and comprehensive health insurance for the entire population, but it believed that this target might be achieved within the framework of the current system without introducing basic changes into it. In 1973, the Labor government submitted to the Knesset (Parliament) a National Health Insurance Bill guaranteeing full health insurance to every citizen through the existing sick funds. The proposal specified various regulations designed to ensure coordination among the different medical care services. At the same time, it allowed the sick funds to maintain their autonomy. The law did not pass, due to the strong opposition of some parties to allow the various sick funds—especially the one belonging to the Histadrut—to maintain their autonomy.

Following the 1977 elections, the newly formed government submitted a new health insurance bill to the Knesset. Like the old bill, the new one suggested basing the provision of health services on the existing sick funds. However, it deviated in three significant respects. First, it called for the establishment of regional health authorities, authorized to plan, supervise, and coordinate the health services in each region. Second, it specified that citizens pay their health insurance dues to the National Insurance Institute, rather than to the sick funds themselves; and third, it guaranteed the right of all citizens to select their own medical care services. This law passed on the first reading in February 1981. Its full approval and implementation undoubtedly would introduce a far-reaching reform in the structure of the health services. However, in the following review we relate to the health services as they are structured currently.

The Sick Funds

The largest and most influential sick fund, Kupat Holim, is run by the Histadrut. Membership in the Histadrut, open to salaried or self-employed workers, automatically bestows the rights of membership in the Sick Fund. Kupat Holim is a self-contained, autonomous organization within the labor union. It delivers services to members mainly in institutions owned by the Sick Fund and staffed by its personnel. The payment of dues to the Histadrut entitles members to comprehensive medical services (excluding dental services). The payments are progressive, based on the worker's income rather than the size of his family. (For a full description and analysis of the organizational structure of the Histadrut's Sick Fund, see Pizam and Meiri [1974].) About 60 percent of the dues collected by the Histadrut are allocated to the Sick Fund. Other sources of income are employers' contributions and government allocations, which now cover a considerable portion of the Sick Fund budget.

The medical care services of the Sick Fund are provided mainly through five interrelated frameworks:

(1) *Neighborhood clinics* are located in both urban and rural areas throughout the country and are essentially staffed by family practice physicians and nurses specializing in community and family medicine. They provide primary care, with a very minor emphasis on preventive activities. Kupat Holim also runs

several public health clinics which strongly emphasize national and child health. (2) *Regional professional clinics* serve a wide territory and provide specialized services in areas such as dermatology, geriatrics, gynecology, and family planning. In addition, they contain laboratories, clinics for physical and occupational therapy, x-rays, and dental care. (3) *Day hospitals* are a new type of medical service developed in recent years to provide full medical services to patients in their own community and to prevent their full hospitalization. The patient stays in the center during the day but returns every night to his home. (4) *Hospitals* care for members at 16 sites throughout the country. They include general, geriatric, psychiatric, and maternity hospitals. These hospitals also have outpatient clinics. (5) *Convalescent facilities* are designed for members who need a period of rest after surgery. Thus, the process of health care is a continuous one, being initiated by family physicians and pursued by the various specialists in the regional clinics and hospitals.

Other sick funds provide similar services with three main exceptions. First, due to their limited size, they have few neighborhood clinics and offer the primary care services mostly at the physician's residence. Second, since they do not own hospitals, they utilize hospitals owned by other organizations, or the government. Finally, the insurees pay their dues directly to the Sick Fund, and their membership does not associate them with any other organization.

The Ministry of Health

The Ministry of Health concentrates its activities in four main spheres that are only partly covered by the sick funds.

(1) *Preventive care:* Preventive services are provided mostly through mother and child centers (well-baby clinics). These neighborhood clinics are open to all pregnant women and young mothers and provide preventive care as a universal service. They are also responsible for providing preventive care services to

local schools, including health education, immunization, and medical checkups. Some of these centers also provide family planning counseling.

(2) *Hospitalization:* Government-owned hospitals contain about 50 percent of all hospital beds in the country. They range from general and maternity to psychiatric and geriatric hospitals, and provide both inpatient and outpatient services.

(3) *Mental health services:* Mental health services are provided through psychiatric hospitals and a number of community mental health centers (CMHCs) established in recent years in various regions of the country. The primary objectives of the CMHCs are (a) to provide mental health services within the community in order to reduce the demand for hospitalization and (b) to provide continuity of care to ex-patients in local settings.

(4) *Medical services to the elderly and the chronically ill:* These services are provided in Geriatric Hospitals as well as in patients' homes.

In addition, the ministry functions as the licensing body for the medical, pharmaceutical, nursing, and paramedical personnel and monitors the operation of hospitals and other medical institutions. In recent years, the ministry has made efforts to play a growing role in planning and coordinating the provision of health services in the country. These efforts, however, have achieved only partial success.

Local Municipalities

Local municipalities are in charge of sanitation services, cleanliness of streets, and supervising the hygiene of restaurants and foodstores. In addition, a few of the larger municipalities have established public health departments responsible for the operation of mother and child clinics, whose functions are identical to those of the government-owned centers. A few large municipalities, like Tel Aviv-Yaffo, own and operate city hospitals that provide inpatient and outpatient services.

Hadassah

Hadassah is the Women's Zionist Organization of America. It conducts a wide range of community services in the United States and Israel and played a pioneering role in developing a network of health services in Israel prior to the establishment of the state. Hadassah was responsible for the creation and development of an array of health care organizations, including five hospitals, mother and child clinics, services to schools, nurses' training schools, occupational therapy institutes, and a School of Medicine. It also introduced into the health system such innovative concepts as community health education and preventive services. In recent years, Hadassah has transferred the responsibility for most of these services to other organizations and concentrates most of its health activities at the Hebrew University and the Hadassah hospitals and medical school.

Voluntary Organizations (VO)

On the whole, the involvement of the voluntary sector in the health area is very limited. VOs are involved in three main ways. First is development and ownership of hospitals. This phenomenon is evident especially in Jerusalem, where all general hospitals belong to VOs. Second, they initiate various activities around specific medical issues. The Cancer Association, for instance, is involved in public education activities about the symptoms and early detection of this disease, rehabilitation counselling to cancer patients, and financial assistance to hospitals which enables them to purchase advanced medical equipment. The third area of VO involvement is activities of volunteers in hospitals.

Private Organizations

Private bodies are active in one area—ownership of hospitals. The Ministry of Health's figures indicate that 45 percent of the beds in psychiatric hospitals and 31 percent of the beds in geriatric hospitals belong to privately owned institutions. However, the hospitalization expenses in these hospitals are covered either by the government or the sick funds. Another phenomenon that should be taken into account in this context is the wide utilization of private physicians' services (especially specialists). Even members of sick funds often prefer to visit these physicians and to pay them for the service rather than waiting for the services provided by their own sick funds. The tendency to go to private physicians despite the financial expenses associated with it stems from several factors. The most striking among them are patient's mistrust in the quality of some of the public clinics' physicians, and their reluctance to wait for services. Dental services are not included in the medical insurance provided by the sick funds, and this service is provided mostly by private dentists in their own clinics.

In summary, the Israeli medical care system comprises mostly of nonprofit sick funds, owned and run by public organizations. The central government, local municipalities, and other public, voluntary, and private organizations play only a partial role in this system.

While there are no adequate and systematic evaluative studies on the operation of this system, most of its reviewers (Neipris, 1978; Doron, 1980; Arian, 1981) highlight the following features as its main positive attributes: (1) Good health is enjoyed by the general population, as reflected in both the low infant mortality rate and long life expectancy. (2) Over 90 percent of the population is covered by a comprehensive health insurance. (3) Some level of health service is available everywhere, even in the most remote areas, and to all sections of the population without discrimination according to national ethnic criteria. These services range from curative care at the village or neighborhood level to advanced specialized services at the regional and hospital levels. (4) The relatively low cost of health insurance removes potential economic barriers to the utilization of services by low-income groups.

This positive picture is challenged by counterarguments which focus on some of the central weaknesses of the current structure (Macarov, 1978; Neipris, 1978; Doron, 1979; Shark-ansky and Radian, 1981). First, the claim is made that the comprehensiveness of services is rather inadequate, due in part to the insufficient supply of certain specialized services and poor geographical distribution of physicians. Second, the fact remains that about 8 percent of the population are not covered by any health insurance. Third, the emphasis is on curative care, and inadequate attention is given to preventive and social services. Fourth, the image of the current services, especially in the largest sick fund clinics, is associated with queues, crowding, noise, and long hours of waiting for an appointment with a physician. Finally, there is a lack of coordination among the various health services.

There is a general consensus that basic improvements are required in five main areas: (1) introducing elements of national planning and central guidance into the health system; (2) improving the coordination between the various health services, thereby preventing duplication, overlaps and waste of resources; (3) strengthening the preventive and social aspects in the activities of the health services; (4) providing full health insurance to the entire population; and (5) guaranteeing equal distribution of quality services throughout the country. One of the most controversial questions is whether these objectives might be achieved within the framework of the current system or require a basic reform in its structure.

LINKS BETWEEN SOCIAL AND
HEALTH SERVICES IN ISRAEL

In principle, both the health and social services accept the importance and necessity of creating permanent linkages between the systems. This conviction is based on three main assumptions. First, physical, psychological, and social problems of individuals are interrelated and cannot be separated. The interaction between these problems therefore requires a certain amount of collaboration between health and social welfare organizations and their workers. Second, due to their intensive contacts with different populations in various stages of their lives, medical care organizations may detect psychological and social problems while social service agencies may identify medical problems of individuals, often in their early stage of development. Thus, interorganizational links between the systems can encourage referral of these individuals to the proper service where their problems might be adequately treated. Finally, collaboration among both systems may lead to better utilization of resources, such as physical facilities and manpower, and prevent duplication and overlapping services and waste of resources.

Certainly, health and social services have unique characteristics and functions that cannot be combined easily in one organization. Their total integration is therefore neither feasible nor desirable. However, the interdependence, the need to use the limited resources available to them in effective and efficient ways, and the possible contributions of each service to the other require that health and social services develop cooperative relationships.

In the following part of the discussion, we will describe various patterns of typical interorganizational linkages and analyze the factors that may affect their emergency. This discussion will serve as a background for a review and analysis of the interaction between health and social services in Israeli context.

Typical interorganizational relationships range as follows:

1. *Absence of any meaningful relationships.* Each organization acts according to its own interest, needs, and expectations without taking into account the policies and activities of other organizations.

2. *Exchange relationships.* Organizations develop exchange relationships of varying intensities, including such commodities as knowledge, information, clients, and equipment.

3. *Outstationing.* Workers of one organization are placed in another organization's facilities and provide services to its clients.

4. *Collaboration in joint programs.* Organizations develop and implement joint programs, such as joint collection of data and joint planning and implementation of projects.

5. *Coordination.* Organizations continue to operate separately but develop mechanisms designed to coordinate their activities.

6. *Integration.* Organizations operate together without any organizational separation. There are several possible variations of an interorganizational integration, ranging from separate professional departments within the same organization to interdisciplinary teams, in which different workers such as physicians, nurses, social workers, and other staff members work together.

The literature on organizational relationships suggests that on the whole, organizations tend to defend their territories, to operate autonomously, and to limit, if possible, their dependence upon other organizations. However, this unfavorable approach toward interorganizational cooperation, let alone integration, might be counterbalanced by several factors: (1) the existence of mechanisms of national planning and central guidance; (2) built-in requirements for interorganizational collaboration in national legislation and regulations; (3) the allocation of governmental financial support to organizations conditional upon their readiness to collaborate with other organizations; (4) ideological commitment by organizations to the value of interorganizational collaboration; (5) public criticism against duplication and waste of resources stemming from organizations' reluctance to coordinate their activities; and (6) professional socialization and training, which puts strong emphasis on the theory and practice of interprofessional and interorganizational collaboration.

To what extent do these factors induce interorganizational and interprofessional collaboration in the Israeli context? The fragmentation and diversification of the social and health service delivery systems do not provide an environment conducive to the creation and development of adequate interrelationships between social and health services. Israel has neither a national authority for social and health planning nor other national bodies capable of developing mechanisms of central guidance for integrated social and health programs. In one case, the government has formed an interministerial committee for social welfare composed of the ministries responsible for the welfare and health areas. This committee is useful as a framework for exchanging information, preparing legislation, and making recommendations. However, it has no power to dictate to the ministries any specific course of action or to compel them to coordinate their activities. It also lacks any supportive tools, such as research teams that may assist it in its activities and strengthen its position as a potential national coordinative body.

In addition to the absence of central planning and coordinative bodies, Israel has neither laws nor regulations that could back any initiative designed to compel organizations to collaborate with other organizations. Furthermore, since the government appears incapable of establishing proper interorganizational links within its own "house," it lacks the public legitimation to impose such demands on other organizations. The lack of adequate government initiative in developing sociomedical collaborative projects is undoubtedly affected by the lack of financial resources and the tendency to invest the limited resources available on items such as maintenance and acquisition of medical equipment and expansion of facilities rather than on innovative projects in the social arena.

In recent years, there has been growing public interest in the activities of welfare and health organizations and their effectiveness. This is reflected in editorials and complaints to the government ombudsman. However, this interest has not yet been translated into concrete pressures on these organizations to coordinate their activities. Cohesive client organizations that could put demands on organizations to change their policies and patterns of activity are almost totally absent from the scene.

The political structure, the fragmentation of services, and the absence of both national planning bodies and public pressures do not stimulate the development of viable relationships between health and social services. Nevertheless, most of these organizations and their professional workers are convinced—at least in principle—that health services must emphasize health

and not just disease, prevention procedures in addition to diagnostic and curative ones, and physical well-being together with
social and emotional well-being. Moreover, this belief in the
vital place of social dimensions in the delivery of health services
is deeply rooted in the development of health services in Israel.
It played a key role in the creation of the Histadrut's Sick
Fund, which, from its inception, was closely bound to a sociopolitical movement striving to achieve broad social objectives.
Its recognition by the union served as a main catalyst in the
development of innovative and pioneering patterns of community-based health services by Hadassah.

Another factor that might promote collaboration among
health and social services is the basic conviction of social workers, as well as other human service professionals, that such joint
efforts are vital for the delivery of quality services to consumers. This conviction is reflected, although to a limited
extent, in the education of social workers in professional
schools and in continuing education programs. Health professionals, especially physicians, are less receptive to these ideas.
However, there are some indications showing that they also are
becoming aware of both the place of social dimensions in the
delivery of health services and the necessity of introducing
social workers and other helping professionals into medical
settings. Some short training programs of students in medical
schools reflect this new trend (Osterveil and Ben-Dor, 1980).
Also, a special emphasis on the social dimension is reflected in
the new school of community medicine at Ben-Gurion University in Beer-Sheva. Thus, the forces constraining the possible
development of viable links between social service and health
organizations and workers appear to be counterbalanced by the
basic conviction of some organizations and professional workers
that such relationships are important and should be developed.

This variegated picture of forces pushing in various directions
reflects the types of relationships among social and health
services and professionals in Israel. While patterns of interprofessional integration emerged within various health organizations, the collaborative relationships between health and social

welfare organizations at the national and local levels remained loose and piecemeal. Some new forms of cooperation among certain health and social services, developed recently at the local level, signal the possible beginning of a new trend.

There are specific examples of links among these services reflecting different patterns of interrelationships that can be established: the activities of social workers in hospitals; the provision of social and educational services by the mother and child centers; and the involvement of community mental health centers. Adequate data do not yet exist on two other recently developed projects: the stationing of social workers in neighborhood sick funds' clinics and the provision of comprehensiveness services by interdisciplinary teams in the field of the elderly.

(1) Social work in hospitals. Social work departments now operate in most hospitals in Israel. There may be some disagreements and misunderstandings about the social workers' role in these settings, but their presence and active involvement in the delivery of services to patients and their families are generally accepted. They have become an integral part of the hospital staff. No systematic studies have been conducted as yet on the actual roles and tasks performed by hospital social workers and their relationships with other staff members. However, several reports written by social workers (Frankfeld, 1978; Alon et al., 1978; Rimon, 1974; Lowenstein, 1980; Laron et al., 1980), physicians and social workers (Kaplan-Denur et al., 1974, Osterweil and Ben-Dor, 1980; Oren and Druker, 1980), physicians, social workers and psychologists (Nofar et al., 1980), and physicians and psychologists (Zuriel and Katznelson, 1980) provide a picture of the activities of social workers and other helping professionals in a wide range of hospitals' departments and units dealing with patients suffering from disease such as pediatric leukemia, coronary disease, spinal cord injuries, cystic fibrosis, premature birth, hemophilia, and kidney dysfunction.

It appears that hospital social workers function in four main areas: the patients, the patients' families, the medical staff, and the patients' community. Relieving patients' distresses and wor-

ries in crisis situations, reducing their uncertainties and strengthening their own capabilities of coping with their problems, and
helping them to readjust to the new circumstances their disease
engenders constitute the main, although not all, objectives of
the social workers' activities. To achieve these objectives, they
develop a wide array of activities: They provide the patients
with necessary information and offer them moral and emotional
support, especially before operations and during painful treatments. In addition, they take part in planning the patients'
discharge, facilitating their reintegration into their family, and
linking them to community services when needed.

Patients' families constitute another central focus of social
workers' activity. A serious disease of one of the family members imposes a heavy emotional burden on the family, shakes its
balance of functioning, and may undermine its economic situation. In addition, this crisis situation may weaken the family's
own ability to cope with its problems and curtail its support to
the sick family member. The social workers' activities with
patients' families aim at reducing their tensions and anxieties,
enhancing their coping abilities, and helping them adjust to new
and unexpected circumstances. To achieve these objectives
social workers provide families with information, offer them
emotional support, deal with intrafamily tension and conflicts,
assess the family's economic and emotional needs, and link
them to resources available in the community. In addition,
social workers are engaged in organizing groups of patients or
patients' parents into mutual support organizations.

A third area of involvement is with the medical staff. Here
the main objectives are to strengthen the human dimension in
the staff activities, to help physicians relate to patients and their
families' emotional state, and to improve the communication
between them when necessary. In addition, social workers seek
to strengthen the medical team and to improve relationships
among its staff members.

The patients' communities are a fourth target of intervention,
especially when patients are released from hospitals and return

to their families, or when they continue to live in their communities, while being treated in a hospital. The social workers' main objectives in this sphere are to help patients reintegrate into their communities, to ensure continuity of care, to mobilize resources they need, and to increase the awareness of various services in the community to their special needs and problems. To achieve these objectives, social workers establish contacts with local social services, deliver information about patients and families' problems and needs, and link patients to services. The contacts established with the local services are based mainly on personal relationships between the hospitals' social workers and their colleagues in the local services, rather than on any formal interorganizational arrangement at the national or local levels.

As yet there are no adequate data on the way in which hospital social workers divide their time among these various activities. A review of the reports on their work suggest, however, that the lions' share of their time is devoted to working with patients and their families, while only limited attention is given to community-oriented activities. In recent years, social workers have been involved in new programs designed to provide medical services generally provided through hospitals, within the patients' own communities, either in day treatment centers where patients stay throughout the day or at the patient's own home. Such treatment arrangements create pressures and tensions that might be detrimental to the family's functioning and to the effective treatment of the patient. Social workers seek to relieve these pressures and to assist families to cope with them. They also are involved in activities designed to link these families to other services that might provide them with necessary coping resources.

In summary, social work departments operate as an integral part of the hospitals' organizational apparatus, and social workers appear to be embedded in their professional staff. The limited data available indicate that although there are cases of interprofessional conflicts and misunderstandings, social workers are generally accepted by physicians—the dominant profession in medical settings—and their activities are viewed as vital in the array of services provided to patients. The hospitals' social work departments represent a clear example of an integration of social work and health services. The social work services are provided by an internal organizational unit and workers that constitute an integral part of the hospital staff.

(2) Social service aspects in the activities of the mother and child centers. Mother and child centers are located throughout the country in urban neighborhoods and rural communities. They place a heavy emphasis on the social aspects of their activities, viewing them as a key factor in reaching their goal of preventive treatment designed to maintain and enhance national and child health. The following review of the way in which these social and educational aspects are intertwined in the activities of these primary health organizations is based essentially on reports about some of the centers located in Jerusalem. No adequate data are available on other centers. However, it is possible to assume that Jerusalem centers' success in combining health and social aspects have at least partly inspired other centers and influenced their activities.

In addition to the health services provided by these centers, they deliver social and educational services that may hardly be seen as belonging to the domain of a health organization. One of the main purposes of these educational and social services is to improve the parenting abilities of parents through their active involvement in the cognitive development of their infants. Nurses provide parents with information about cognitive development and guide them on how to communicate with their children and stimulate them. A strong emphasis is placed on developing viable and permanent interaction between parents and their children, through joint activities such as verbal communication, and the creating and playing of games.

While nurses are involved in the cognitive development of children and in strengthening the parenting abilities of their parents, social workers and social work students are involved with mothers who cannot benefit from the nurses' approach because of deficiency in their mothering capacity which leads to disturbances in mother-child relationships. Social workers and social work students use intensive casework methods in order to help these mothers to cope with their problem and to improve their mothering capacities (Hook, 1976, 1979).

In addition to these direct services, the centers also serve as informal information centers. Attracted by the centers' accessible location within neighborhoods and their strong community orientation, local residents use the centers whenever they need information about social services. The center staff refer them to the appropriate agency (Doron and Frankel, 1977).

While there are no systematic investigations on the success of these centers in combining health and social concerns, several studies indicate that these services are widely and frequently used by neighborhood residents. Furthermore, there is a very high level of client satisfaction with their activities: In fact, they constitute the most popular service in the communities in which they operate (Barzilai and Bar-Zori, 1975; Salzberger and Rosenfeld, 1974). Thus, the mother and children centers are another example of a medical care organization that provides health, social, and educational services in an integrated way. We have no adequate data that could shed light on the relationships between the centers and other health and social service agencies operating in the same communities. There are some indications, however, that, apart from referral, these relationships are partial and limited.

(3) The community mental health centers' involvement in the community. In the early 1970s, the division of Mental Health Services in the Ministry of Health produced a comprehensive plan to reorganize and reintegrate the mental health services in the country. The primary objective of this plan was to reduce the demand for hospitalization by providing a wide range of psychiatric services within the communities where people live. To this end, the establishment of CMHCs was proposed in different regions throughout the country. Several such centers have already been founded. The conception and objectives of these centers are anchored in the community

mental health movement, which places a strong emphasis on developing mental health services characterized by the following four ingredients: (1) location of services within a designated catchment area; (2) responsiveness to a wide range of human problems and community needs; (3) community involvement with strong emphasis on outreach; and (4) collaboration with other community services.

This broad perception of the CMHC's domain imposes certain prerequisites on its relationships with community organizations and groups. The center must be well-acquainted with the community's needs, problems and resources, political structure, the sociocultural background of its residents, and the networks of organizations operating within it. To what extent have these principles and objectives actually been adopted by the Israeli CMHCs and reflected in their activities? An examination of the ministry's proposals, as well as reports about the activities of several centers, suggest that both the Health Ministry's planners and centers' key staff members have adopted the community orientation approach and view it as an essential cornerstone in the centers' operation (Aviram and Brachott, 1978; Berzon et al., 1980; Eran, 1977; Kleinhauz and Beran; 1978, Reinhartz and Mester, 1978).

Kleinhaus and Beran (1978), reporting on the wide range of activities performed by the CMHC in Yaffo (Jaffa), emphasize its community orientation and describe its involvement in two main types of community activities: providing education and consultation to other local services, and organizing residents and coordinating human services in one of the area's neighborhoods. The consultation activities are designed to equip workers of other agencies (sick fund clinics, welfare department, mother and child centers, schools) with tools to enable them to detect individuals with behavioral and emotional problems and to treat them if they suffer from minor disturbances (with continuous guidance from the center's professional staff) or, when necessary, to refer them to the center for more specialized treatment. In addition, the center provides general education on mental health issues to various community groups. The activities car-

ried out by the center in one of the catchment area neighborhoods are not different in principle from those conducted by
community workers practicing in other agencies. They include
helping local residents to organize themselves in order to obtain
necessary resources and attempting to improve the coordination
among several service agencies operating within this area.

Through these various activities, the center seeks to
strengthen the capacity of the community to care for its members, and to allow the detection of problems in their primary
stages. It is further designed to inject in its residents a positive
image of the center, thereby helping to remove certain barriers
that usually deter people from using mental health services.
Several additional reports indicate that the Yaffo center's
involvement in the community is not an exception, but rather
represents the orientation of other centers as well (Reinhartz
and Mester, 1978).

A somewhat different look at the community involvement of
the Yaffo center is provided by an evaluative study (Aviram and
Brachott, 1978) which focused on two main issues: the amount
of time spent by the center's staff in community-oriented
activities, and the utilization of the center's community services
by other local services. The study's findings suggest that only a
limited amount of time was devoted to community-oriented
activities by center workers. The utilization of the center's
services by the local agencies varied a great deal. Intensive use
was made by 45 percent of the local health services but only 10
percent of the local social services. No intensive use of the
center was reported by local educational services. On the whole,
the findings indicate that while the center has established intensive relationships with a considerable part of the health services,
its relationships with both the social and educational services
remain loose. These findings suggest that there is a certain
amount of incongruency between the center's own perception
of its community involvement and its actual impact on the
community. They further indicate that the creation of viable
and continuous links among organizations requires overcoming
the traditional role conception of mental health workers.

A longer time perspective is probably needed in order to evaluate the extent to which an organization like CMHC that views collaboration with other organizations as one of its primary objectives is indeed capable of achieving it. It appears that the CMHCs' problem is not only to gain community recognition but even more to convince their own workers to put more emphasis on community-oriented activities.

(4) Stationing of social workers in sick fund's neighborhood clinics. Neighborhood clinics are one of the most heavily utilized public services in Israel. Therefore, they maintain intensive and continuous contact with most of the local population in the area where they operate. The medical clinics constitute a setting in which not only medical but also social and psychological problems might surface. Furthermore, medical problems in families may aggravate existing social problems and create new ones. The clinics might serve not only as an agency engaged in the delivery of medical services but also as an appropriate setting for the provision of certain social services.

It was this basic conviction that stimulated the social work department in the Histadrut Sick Fund, the Ministry of Labor and Social Affairs, and several local social service departments to develop a project designed to introduce social work services into local clinics and to use social services departments' social workers for this purpose. About 60 municipal social workers are now involved in the project. The specific tasks of these social workers are in a process of development. The limited information available indicates that they mainly provide consultation and treatment in family problems such as marital difficulties, relationships between parents and children, and so on—information about various resources available within and outside the community, and client referral services.

The range of tasks performed by these social workers probably will expand in the future and include more aspects of the clinics' activity, such as planning and developing preventive activities and enhancing the human dimensions in the clinics' activities. This project is one of the few examples of collaboration between organizations at the national and local levels. The project is in its preliminary stage, and it is still too early to assess its impact on the realtionships between the organizations and their workers and on the quality of services provided to the population.

(5) The provision of comprehensive services by interdisciplinary and interorganizational teams in the field of the elderly. This is a new project that was developed in recent years and operates in about 30 localities in Israel. The teams generally include physicians and nurses from local sick fund clinics, a public nurse from the local mother and child center, and a social worker representing the local social services department. This kind of composition allows the team to relate simultaneously to the health and social problems of the elderly. The purpose of the team is to identify elderly people that need assistance, to diagnose their situation and needs, to assess the resources available to them, and to plan a treatment program. When necessary, the team refers clients to appropriate services in and outside the community.

Data on the activities of these teams are still limited. It is too early, therefore, to evaluate this project. However, it reflects the possibility of developing collaboration among various organizations and professionals around specific issues.

SUMMARY AND CONCLUSION

Various medical care organizations (the Histadrut Sick Fund, the Ministry of Health, Hadassah) have developed social work units within their frameworks. These units are generally well-integrated into these health settings organizational fabrics. However, this effort has not been reinforced by parallel attempts to create viable and continuous links with social service organizations operating at national and local levels.

Recently, some new developments signal a possible change in this situation. These include the partial attempts of CMHCs to develop relationships with social health and educational services operating in their catchment area; the stationing of social workers in neighborhood sick fund clinics; and the involvement of interdisciplinary teams in the provision of services to the elderly. However, these are still sporadic, temporary, and unstable phenomena that have not yet fully developed. They might develop and expand, but they also might shrink and disappear. It is difficult to predict their outcomes as well as their possible course of development at this time.

Any effort to establish permanent and continuous links among health and social services within the Israel political and organizational context must overcome many barriers, such as organizations' guarded monopolies, a long tradition of fragmentation in the delivery of services, political interests inherent in the current structure of social and health services, professionals' traditional role conceptions, the absence of public pressures and client demands, and the lack of adequate resources. Some of these constraints might be viewed as insurmountable. However, the fact that certain interorganizational links recently have been created and developed indicates that initiatives taken by organizational executives and professional workers committed to the idea of interorganizational and interprofessional collaboration can produce positive results.

The crucial questions are, first, to what extent does the existence of collaborative interorganizational and interprofessional links in certain settings, and their absence in others, affect these organizations' responsiveness to population needs? Second, what is the most appropriate design of these links—for example, is the creation of social work units within health services better than the formation of links between health and social service organizations? Our own impression based on reports describing the activities of social service workers in health settings is that organizations like hospitals, CMHCs, mother and child centers, and neighborhood clinics that have introduced social services into their frameworks or developed collaborative relationships with external social agencies are more capable of providing better services to their clients than organizations lacking these components. It is still not clear that these various interrelationship designs better serve the needs of clients than other possible designs. More definite answers to these questions require systematic evaluative studies that would examine the concrete outcomes of these organizations' activities.

REFERENCES

AKZIN, B. (1970) "The role in parties in Israeli democracy," in S. N. Eisenstadt et al. (eds.) Integration and Development in Israel. Jerusalem: Israel University Press.

ALON, S., S. DUBOI, and N. ROSMAN (1978) "Social aspects of treatment of the spinal cord injured." Society and Welfare 1, 3: 256-267. (Hebrew)

ARIAN, A. (1981) "Health care in Israeli political and administrative aspects." International Political Science Review 2, 1: 43-56.

AVIRAM, U. and D. BRACHOTT (1978) "The visibility of a community mental health center: Israel," in D. Thursz and J. Vigilante (eds.) Reaching People: The Structure of Neighborhood Services. Beverly Hills, CA: Sage.

BARZILAI, Y. and R. BAR-ZORI (1975) "Attitudes towards testing facilities and deficiencies in health spheres from the standpoint of services for consumers." Social Security 8: 93-98. (Hebrew)

BERZON, M., U. AVIRAM, and E. DAROM (1980) "Evaluation of continuity of care in a community mental health center." Society and Welfare 3, 3: 269-283. (Hebrew)

DORON, A. (1980) "The ailing health services." Jerusalem Quarterly 14 (Winter): 82-93.

——— and E. FRANKEL (1977) "Information and advisory services in Jerusalem." Social Security 14-15: 103-115. (Hebrew)

ERAN, Y. (1977) "Community work in Israel." Mental Health and Society 4, 3-4: 229-244.

FRANKFELD, S. (1978) "Hemophelia and its physical, emotional and social aspects." Society and Welfare 1, 3: 239-255. (Hebrew)

HALEVY, H. S. (1964) "Health services in Israel: their organization, utilization and financing." Medical Care 2,4.

HOOK, S. (1979) "A contribution to good parenthood. An experimental project." Society and Welfare 2, 4: 441-449. (Hebrew)

——— (1976) "Introducing social work into mothers and children's centers." Soad 20, 5. (Hebrew)

KAPLAN-DENUR, A., G. FISHER, M. MOSES, and J. CZACKES (1974) "Diagnoses and therapy of families and patients on chronic hemodialysis." Mental Health and Society 1, 3-4: 251-256.

KLEINHAUZ, M. and B. BERAN (1978) "The Yaffo Community Mental Health Center." Mental Health and Society 5 (3) (1978). 304-313.

KRAMER, R. (1971) Community Development in Israel and the Netherlands: A Comparative Analysis. Berkeley: Institute of International Studies, University of California.

LARON, N., B. MENZER-LICHT, Y. ROTSTEIN, and N. VOGHERA (1980) "Abortion committees in Israel–A reflection of a social dilemma from the viewpoint of social workers." Society and Welfare 3, 3: 334-347. (Hebrew)

LIRON, R. and S. SPIRO (1980) "Voluntary agencies or agents of governmental welfare programs: the day camps for mothers of large families." Society and Welfare 3, 1: 66-87. (Hebrew)

LOWENSTEIN, E. (1980) Social work in a neonatal intensive care unit." Society and Welfare 3, 3: 296-311. (Hebrew)

MACAROV, D. (1978) "Service delivery at the neighborhood level in Israel," in D. Thursz and J. Vigilante (eds.) Reaching People: The Structure of Neighborhood Services. Beverly Hills, CA: Sage.

––– (1975) "Israeli social services: historical roots and current status," in D. Thursz and J. Vigilante (eds.) Meeting Human Needs. Beverly Hills, CA: Sage.

NEIPRIS, J. (1978) Social Welfare and Social Services in Israel. Policies, Programs and Issues in the Late Seventies. Jerusalem.

NOFAR, O., O. ARAN, N. BEIT-HALOCHMI, A. GALATZER, A. PERTZELEN, and Z. LARON (1980) "Marked short stature–psychological impact and therapeutic approach." Society and Welfare 3, 3: 325-333. (Hebrew)

OREN, A. and A. DRUKER (1980) "Chronic renal failure in children: experience in a pediatric hemodialysis unit." Society and Welfare 3, 3: 312-324. (Hebrew)

OSTERWEIL, D. and B. BEN-DOR (1980) "An attempt by a social worker to develop awareness of a personal relationship to patients." Society and Welfare 3, 4: 458-462. (Hebrew)

PIZAM, A. and I. MEIRI (1974) "The management of health care organizations–medical vs. administrative considerations: the case of Kupat Holim." Medical Care 12.

REINHARTZ, S. and R. MESTER (1978) "Israeli culture and the emergency of community mental health procedures: the case of the West Jerusalem Mental Health Center." Mental Health and Society 5, 5-6: 241-251.

RIMON, L. (1974) "Social work with children stricken by leukemia." Society and Welfare 2, 4: 450-456. (Hebrew)

SALZBERGER, L. and J. ROSENFELD (1974) "The anatomy of 267 social welfare agencies in Jerusalem: findings from a census." Social Service Review 48, 3: 255-267.

SHARKANSKY, I. and A. RADIAN (1981) "The Likud government and domestic policy change." Jerusalem Quarterly 18 (Winter): 86-100.

ZURIEL, S. and D. KATZNELSON (1980) "Psychological aspects of cystic fibrosis." Society and Welfare 3, 3: 284-295. (Hebrew)

10

UNITED STATES
Coordinating Services to the Aged

CHARLENE HARRINGTON and
ROBERT J. NEWCOMER

Favored constituents for health and social welfare programs in the United States, the aged, have benefited greatly in recent years. Unfortunately, current policies and programs have not alleviated poverty, illness, disability, substandard housing, or inadequate social services for millions of aged. The structural design and financing of the health and social welfare systems are responsible for many of these hardships and problems.

A variety of political and economic forces now threaten the gains in services and benefits for the aged. Hudson (1978) identified the "graying" of the federal budget, the increasing share of funds being allocated to the aged. It is a major factor bringing special attention to and attack on policies and programs favoring the aged. As state governments experience increasing fiscal strain and as taxpayers not only refuse tax increases but demand cuts, state policymakers examine ways to reduce total expenditures, targeting health and social welfare programs as areas for potential reductions.

At the same time, the new administration and the Congress are examining tax cut proposals and federal program reductions. The competition for limited public funds threatens those programs for the aged previously considered essential. Policymakers are reexamining these programs and proposing basic changes in public policy.

Recent proposals to restructure and reduce health and social welfare programs may have a significant impact on the aged. This chapter examines the current services for the aged with special attention to the major federal programs. Old Age Survivors Insurance (OASI) and Supplemental Security Income (SSI) are reviewed for special problems they create for the elderly. An examination of four major programs financing health and social services—Medicare, Medicaid, Social Services, and aging programs—concludes that the current health and social services system has major structural problems creating high costs, inappropriate services, and gaps in services for the aged.

BACKGROUND

An estimated 25 million people, or 11 percent, of the U.S. population, the aged, received favorable public policies and programs in the past because of their political legitimacy, utility, and potential power. The legitimacy is based on the belief that the aged should be supported. Political support for the aged builds on the group's ability to pursue political agendas and career goals. As the aged grow in proportion to the total voting population, their potential political power increases. And since the aged were considered to be ill and impoverished through no fault of their own, they were thought to deserve federal programs. Public sympathy and political support led to Social Security, Medicare, and Supplemental Security Income (Hudson, 1978).

The federal government is so committed to supporting the aged that 25 percent of the national 1978 budget was spent on this constitutency of 11 percent of the population. If present policies and demographics remain, this figure will rise to 40 percent by the year 2000 (Binstock, 1979). Thus, it is important to examine the health and social welfare system and the federal programs that finance it.

FEDERAL PROGRAMS

Federal efforts serving the aged were classified by the U.S. House of Representatives Select Committee on Aging (1977a) into 47 major programs, with up to 200 others providing assistance. The 1980 catalog of Federal Domestic Assistance lists 127 programs in the Department of Health and Human Services (HHS) which have direct or indirect benefits for the aged.

Current programs that benefit the aged can be grouped into two types: (1) categorical, designed to serve all aged individuals, and (2) generic, designed to benefit all age groups. The categorical programs of importance in this analysis are Old Age Survivors Insurance (OASI), Medicare, and the Older Americans Act. The generic programs examined in this chapter are Medicaid, Social Services (Title XX), and Supplemental Security Income (SSI).

SOCIAL SECURITY

In this section, attention centers on the five provisions of the social security system which have importance in the quality of life for the elderly in the United States. Each of these programs contains major sums of money but also has structural and policy defects.

Old Age Survivors Insurance

In 1980, the Old Age Survivors Insurance (OASI) program of the Social Security System provided $100 billion benefits to the aged. The current program is financed out of a social security payroll tax, which has a flat rate paid up to an earnings ceiling of $22,900. This system has been criticized as being regressive, falling heaviest on those with low incomes. There are gaps in the program for those who have not been in the wage force contributing to the system through payroll taxes. While there are wage-earning limitations on beneficiaries, there are no limitations on other pension sources. Benefits are paid to all aged regardless of need (U.S. Department of Health and Human Services, 1981b).

Of all sources of income in 1979, in the U.S., for persons aged 65 or older, 50 percent came from social security, 10 percent from private pensions and 10 percent from retirement savings (U.S. Congress, Senate Special Committee on Aging, 1980). Even though the OASI program benefited 30.9 million aged and their dependents in 1980, the benefit levels were so low that many found the average of $341 per month inadequate (U.S. Department of Health and Human Services, 1981b). Those dependent upon social security as their only source of income live in poverty. Other aged persons, not eligible for benefits because they did not pay into the system, are forced to rely on SSI.

One serious concern with the program is that funds currently paid into the system pay for current beneficiaries rather than being reserved or invested for the use of future payees. This approach raises questions about the soundness, equity, and investment value of the program. The Board of Trustees of the social security fund reported 1980 that under the present conditions the fund would be insufficient to pay benefits by late 1981 or 1982 (U.S. General Accounting Office, 1980a). As the number of older persons increases by 8 million in the next 25 years and the proportion of working population to aged declines, there will be increased difficulty in financing the social security system as currently designed.

The social security system is under intensive review. Potential changes include increasing the age for full benefits and financing from the general fund (U.S. General Accounting Office, 1980a). Adequate for the population of 1935, when it was started, the system needs major restructuring now that a greater proportion of the population depends on it. However, there are major political problems with changing the system because it threatens the benefits for those who have already paid into the fund. Although changing such a basic "safety net" program is politically unpopular, some leaders advocate restructuring it to a guaranteed annual income program for the aged (Binstock, 1979).

Supplemental Security Income

The problem of low income caused by inadequate retirement support is magnified by the impact of recent inflation rates on fixed incomes. Many aged live in poverty, in spite of Social Security benefits and considerable improvements in income levels in the past twenty years. In 1979, the median annual income for families headed by a person aged 65 years and over was $10,141, half that of families with younger household heads (U.S. Congress, Senate Special Committee on Aging, 1980). The median income for aged individuals was $4,303. The poverty rate for the aged climbed from 14 percent in 1978 to 15.1 percent in 1979.

Supplemental Security Income (SSI), Title XVI of the Social Security Act, is a federally funded program providing income maintenance to persons who are over 65, blind, or disabled and whose income and assets fall below federal poverty standards. An income maintenance program, SSI was established in 1972 to federalize the Old Age Assistance program. About half of the states provide additional supplemental income to those who qualify for SSI. In 1980, almost 1.8 million persons ages 65 and over received $233 million in federally administered SSI payments (U.S. Department of Health and Human Services, 1981b).

There are three major problems with the current SSI program. First, there are disincentives for the aged to live with relatives or friends (Rigby and Ponce, 1980). If a beneficiary lives with relatives or friends, the individual's SSI benefits are reduced by one-third. This discourages group and family living arrangements which could assist the aged in living independently. It prevents the social benefits which might be enjoyed by not living alone. Such a policy may encourage early institutionalization, costing the government more in the long run through other funding sources, such as Medicaid.

A second problem arises because states have discretion in establishing income levels and standards for supplemental funds. The states vary considerably in the amount of funds they provide to the aged. This creates substantial inequities. Payments vary depending on a number of factors, such as geographic and living arrangement differences, and may provide for emergency or special conditions. Nine states provide no optional state supplementation for basic needs. Other states do not provide supplements for special needs. In 1980, the average level of state-administered state supplementation benefits varied from $20 in Wyoming to $172 in Virginia for those aged individuals living independently and alone (Rigby and Ponce, 1980). The federally administered programs' average SSI payments to the aged ranged from $72 in Maine to $207 in California in 1980. In addition, when the SSI program was developed, it established mandatory minimum state supplementary payments for those states to maintain individual recipients of aid to the aged, blind, and disabled at their December 1973 income level, so that no individuals would have decreased benefits under the new program.

The most serious problem is that Supplemental Security Income levels plus state supplementation, while raising most individuals above the official poverty line, are still inadequate to meet the basic minimum living standards for food, clothing, shelter, and heat. The functionally disabled and ill aged who must purchase health and social services are not able to do so within the limited income received. Such aged must depend on the health and social service system to provide the supports they cannot afford to purchase under the limited SSI allocations.

Medicare

Medicare, Title XVIII of the Social Security Act, adopted in 1965, is probably the best-known program of health insurance for the elderly and the disabled in the United States. About 28 million people, 90 percent aged 65 or older, were enrolled in the Medicare program in 1979 (Gibson, 1980). Medicare is federally administered and financed for all persons eligible for social security payments, without respect to income. The program pays 74 percent of its total expenditures for hospital services and another 22 percent for physician services. Payments for nursing home services account for only 1 percent of the expenditures, and home care expenditures are less than 1 percent of the total. The remaining 3 percent of Medicare expenditures pay for professional services, eyeglasses, and appliances (Gibson, 1980).

Medicare has two health services. Medicare Part A, Hospital Insurance Program (HI), financed from Social Security Trust Funds from employer and employee contributions, finances inpatient hospitalization, skilled nursing home care, and home care after a hospital stay. Beneficiaries must pay a deductible before Medicare will reimburse hospitals and nursing homes and pay co-insurance for those services over the limit (U.S. Department of Health, Education and Welfare, 1979a). Medicare, Part B, Supplementary Medical Insurance Program (SMI), is financed through general federal revenues and deductibles. Those eligible pay a $60 deductible and 20 percent co-insurance for most services. Part B pays for necessary physician services, outpatient therapy, some medical equipment and supplies, home health care visits, and rural health clinic services (U.S. Department of Health, Education and Welfare, 1979a).

Medicare is federally administered and therefore is not linked closely with health programs administered by the states (e.g., Medicaid). Unlike Medicaid, Medicare is designed as a broad program for all elderly and disabled, rather than for all poor persons. Consequently, the Medicare program, with its broad eligibility and financing, is not specifically targeted for those who are the most needy. Because of its service limitations and co-payments, Medicare pays for only 42 percent of the aged's health expenditures. Medicaid, private payments, and insurance make up the remainder. The total 1979 program expenditures exceeded $29 billion for 28 million enrollees, 90 percent of whom are aged 65 or over (Gibson, 1980). Those on Medicare who spend sufficient funds on health care expenses may "spend down" to the income level where they then become eligible for Medicaid benefits. As a greater proportion of the aged are unable to meet their costs of health and social services within their own income, the number of aged forced into the Medicaid program increases.

Medicaid

Medicaid, Title XIX of the Social Security Act, enacted as a companion to Medicare in 1965, is a program for the indigent. For this state-administered program the federal government contributes between 50 and 78 percent of the funds, according to per capita income levels (Gibson, 1980). Under federal guidelines, the states have the discretion to develop eligibility standards, benefit coverage, provider qualifications, payment schedules, and administrative structure. All states except Arizona voluntarily participate in the program and must cover the "categorically needy": those persons who are eligible for SSI and AFDC (Aid to Families with Dependent Children in which one parent is the absent, aged, blind, disabled, incapacitated, or unemployed). States have the option to cover the "medically needy"—those persons who are not eligible for SSI or AFDC but with low incomes not adequate to pay medical expenses. Thirty-three states and territories cover the "medically needy" (Gibson, 1980; Hawkins and Rigby, 1979). For the three million Medicare beneficiaries who are poor and cannot afford to pay their deductible, co-insurance, or premiums, Medicaid law requires that states pay these costs (Gibson, 1980). As those aged with Medicare cannot meet their medical expenses, they then become eligible for the Medicaid program. In this respect, the two programs become closely related.

Social Services, Title XX

Title XX of the Social Security Act was established in 1974 to consolidate social service programs. States were required to provide at least one service for each of the five program goals: economic self-support, personal self-sufficiency; protection from abuse, neglect, and exploitation; prevention of inappropriate institutionalization; and arrangement for appropriate institutional care. Each state must provide at least one service to meet each goal of the program. Under Title XX, Congress provides funds to states according to their per capita incomes at the rate of 75 percent matching to 25 percent in state funds. States are required to prepare a state plan and to include at least all recipients of AFDC and SSI. States may also program services to persons with incomes up to 115 percent of the state's median income, and must charge fees for persons whose income exceeds 80 percent of the state's median income. States have the option of declaring uniform eligibility for aged under Title XX; some have done this (Gelfand and Olsen, 1980; Gilbert et al., 1979).

The program goals call for the maintenance of economic self-support and self-sufficiency and preventing or reducing inappropriate institutional care by providing community-based care, home-based care, or other forms of less intensive care (Field et al., 1978). The program is directed in part to particularly vulnerable populations, such as the aged and the disabled young. It provides homemaker and chore services. Other services offered include protective services for adults and children, information and referral, family planning, employment education and training, health-related family counseling, day services for children and adults, transportation, legal, adoption, and youth services, housing, and home-delivered and congregate meals. In 1979, the estimated national Title XX budget of $3.9 billion was used to serve about 20 million clients (Kilgore and Salmon, 1979).

Data are not available on the number of aged served by Title XX programs. In fact, data on eligibility, services, expenditures, and providers are difficult to obtain on a national level. In 1978, states spent an estimated $481 million (13 percent of the total Title XX expenditures) on home-based health services to 1.5 million people (Wolff, 1978). It can be assumed that the aged and disabled are the primary beneficiaries.

Older Americans Act

The Older Americans Act (OAA) of 1965, reauthorized in 1978, funds an array of services for persons over age 60. The act has several titles for different services and established a network of state and area agencies on aging to plan for a comprehensive and coordinated delivery system for social services to the aged. It provides funds for community service projects to develop coordinated comprehensive service systems. Monies are available for social services such as information, referral, homemaker services, and transportation. Additional services include nutrition education, counseling, research, demonstration projects, and training. These programs have considerable overlap in focus and goals with the Title XX Social Service program (Gelfand and Olsen, 1980).

HEALTH AND SOCIAL SERVICE SYSTEM

Like other population groups, the aged require medical, health, and social services. They are particularly vulnerable to functional disability which can be caused by chronic illness. As estimated 13.5 percent of the noninstitutionalized population has some degree of activity limitation. This becomes more prevalent as age increases.

The aged, without informal support systems such as relatives and friends, are not likely to rely on the health and social service systems. They may lose their social support systems with the death of spouses, relatives, and friends. The availability of support is also diminished by limited family income, mobility among family members, and increased participation of family members in the labor market. In addition to support systems, adequate income is an important factor in encouraging independence and decreasing reliance upon the health and social service system (U.S. Department of Health and Human Services, 1981a).

The aged use a variety of health and social services. These can be classified by the setting in which they are rendered, ranging

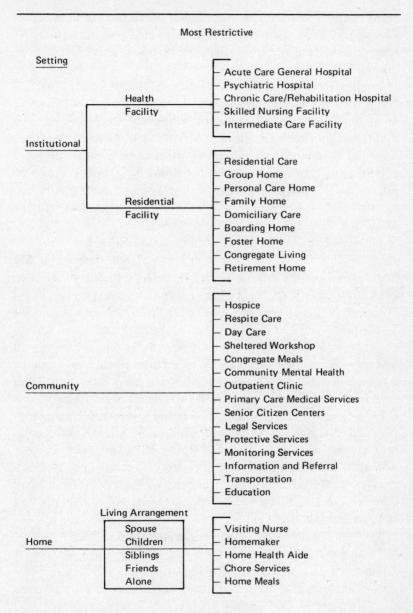

Figure 10.1 Health and Social Service System for the Aged and Disabled in the U.S.
Modified version of Brody and Masciocchi (1980: 1197).

from institutional services to community services to home care. Figure 10.1 provides a listing of services arranged from the most restrictive setting (a hospital) to the least restrictive setting (the home).

Health facilities are usually licensed by states to provide medical, nursing, and therapeutic services. Hospitals offer the most intensive medical services, while the chronic care and rehabilitation hospitals focus on the less intensive services designed to restore individuals to maximum levels of physical activity functions. There are approximately 19,000 skilled and intermediate care facilities providing 24-hour nursing care services to over 1.3 million residents in the U.S. (U.S. Department of Health, Education and Welfare, 1979c).

Often licensed by the state, residential facilities provide assistance with activities of daily living, supervision, and room and board, but no nursing services (U.S. Department of Health, Education and Welfare, 1976). Estimates were that in 1976, 600,000 persons aged 65 and over lived in such facilities. Community services include a range of health and social service programs. Hospice services are designed for the terminally ill and may be offered in a variety of settings, including home or hospital. Respite care usually is provided on a short-term basis to relieve caretakers for a period of time. Day health programs offer a range of services such as nursing, occupational therapy, physical therapy, and other rehabilitation services in a community setting on less than a 24-hour basis for those who are not fully independent (U.S. Congress, Senate Special Committee on Aging, 1976). There are approximately 700 adult day care programs in the U.S. (U.S. Department of Health and Human Services, 1981a).

Sheltered workshops provide occupational, educational, or recreational services in a supervised setting on less than a 24-hour basis. Congregate meals are those provided in a group setting outside the home for the elderly who cannot prepare their own meals. Community mental health services, outpatient clinics, and primary care medical services are offered outside of a hospital. Senior centers provide recreational, educational, and other services for the aged. Legal services, public protective services (adult conservatory or guardianship services for those not capable of making independent decisions but without private guardian), information and referral services, monitoring services (such as friendly visitors), transportation, and educational programs are all important services for linking the aged to existing programs. Also, they assist the aged in maintaining their independence and avoid institutionalization (Wolff, 1978; Brody and Masciocchi, 1980). Home care services are offered to those who are ill or functionally disabled. These include periodic and intermittent skilled nursing care, rehabilitation, and some person care services in the home. Home health care is usually provided by visiting nurses or their assistants, called home health aides, and can include professional services such as occupational, physical, and speech therapy. Homemaker and chore services include meal preparation, house cleaning, laundry, errands, yard work, repairs, shopping, financial management, and other such personal care services and assistance with activities of daily living. Definitions of these programs vary by funding agency and by state.

Despite this vast array of health and social services for the aged, not all services are available at the time and place needed. Families and friends still provide the bulk of long-term care services to the aged in the United States. It is estimated that 60 to 80 percent of the care for the impaired elderly is provided by relatives and friends who are uncompensated for their care (U.S. Department of Health and Human Services, 1981a). The health and social services system could not assume additional care for the aged without additional funding and correcting some of the system's inefficiencies and structural problems. These are discussed in the following section.

Even with the numerous home- and community-based services in the United States, the dominant approach to care of the aged continues to be institutionalization. Although only about 1.5 percent of the aged population was institutionalized in 1910, this figure grew to 5.7 percent in 1950 (Estes and Harrington, 1981). Of those institutionalized in 1950, 45 percent lived in boarding houses, 31 percent in homes for the aged and nursing homes, and 20 percent in mental hospitals. Many of the aged were moved from mental hospitals into nursing homes in the 1960s with the funding of Medicaid. The pattern of institutionalization has continued so that 7.5 percent of the aged were living in institutions in 1970, but a substantial proportion of these were in nursing homes (U.S. Department of Commerce, 1973). Many states are attempting to develop alternatives to institutions under their Medicaid programs, yet these have not had a significant impact on the rates of institutionalization.

OBSTACLES TO EFFECTIVE SERVICE DELIVERY

There are three major categories of obstacles to effective service delivery in the United States. Federal constraints limit program effectiveness and efficiency. These constraints include the current requirements for high cost reimbursement for institutional services, restrictions on reimbursement for noninstitutional services, and the medical model for the health services program (i.e., Medicare and Medicaid). A second set of problems relates to the high degree of state discretionary authority allowed in the Medicaid, Title XX, and Title III programs. This discretion leads to service and eligibility inequities as well as program fragmentation within state and among state programs. At present, probably the most serious obstacles are the financial constraints on the programs themselves due to limitations on state and federal budgets. Financial limitations create funding shifts between programs, service reductions, and eligibility restrictions. While various techniques may overcome some of these structural and economic problems, the current approaches have not been successful in eliminating such obstacles.

Before discussing major obstacles in the efficient operation of federal programs, we must address the source of these problems. Feldstein (1980) posits two theories for principle causes of the unsatisfactory legislation and regulations leading to ineffective programs: (1) ignorance and incompetence on the part of the lawmakers or officials or (2) knowledgeable decisions based on interest group responses. Feldstein concludes that unsatisfactory publicly established programs were based on intent of the lawmakers to respond to the demands and interests of special health pressure groups. The major health pressure groups are the health associations representing providers of care (e.g., American Medical Association, American Hospital Association), third-party payers (e.g., Blue Cross), and the educational institutions.

Estes (1979) also identified special interest groups in the "aging enterprise" as congeries of programs, organizations, bureaucracies, trade associations, providers, and professionals who serve or depend upon the aged for income, jobs and professional careers. Estes suggests that these groups define the nature of aging policies and programs to the advantage of their own interests and not necessarily those of the aged. Successful policy changes must include the special interests that designed the legislation and programs, by either modifying their goals or minimizing their impact.

Federal Constraints

High-Cost Institutional Services

The Medicare and Medicaid programs are oriented toward expensive institutional services. The Medicare program spent 74 percent of its 1979 allocations on hospital services and 1 percent on nursing home services. The Medicaid program spent 37 percent of its funds on hospital care and 41 percent of its budget on nursing home care. Thus, a total of 78 percent of the Medicaid $21.7 billion budget went for institutional care in 1979 (Gibson, 1980). Of the Medicaid expenditures for the aged, the percentage of dollars spent on institutional services is even greater: 11 percent for hospital care and 75 percent for nursing home care in 1978 (Fisher, 1980).

The basic reason for the use of high-cost institutional services is that current federal statutes require hospital services to be reimbursed on a reasonable cost basis. Most states reimburse on a retrospective basis so that reasonable costs are calculated on the program's share of the institution's total expenditures. These expenditures generally have no maximum limits; therefore, this reimbursement method provides incentives for hospitals to increase spending to increase their revenues. The reasonable cost reimbursement system has been criticized by federal and state legislators, officials, and researchers as being a primary cause of inflation in the health care system (Holahan et al., 1977). Because of the statutory basis for this practice, states do not have the authority to reimburse at less than hospital costs without doing so under the authority of a demonstration project approved by the Health Care Financing Administration. Statutory change to eliminate reasonable cost reimbursement will be difficult to accomplish.

Nursing homes were also required to be reimbursed on a reasonable cost basis until the federal law was changed in the 1980 Budget Reconciliation Act to allow states to set rates which they consider reasonable and fair. All other providers under both Medicare and Medicaid provisions can be and are paid at considerably lower rates (less than costs) set by the states.

Restrictions in Reimbursement for
Noninstitutional Services

A recent Department of Health and Human Services (1981a) study noted that 12 to 17 percent of the noninstitutional population are either bedridden or require assistance in the basic functions of daily living. Yet, only about one-third of the functionally disabled receive some form of governmental assistance. The major needs of this population include home care and in-home personal support services.

Restrictive policies under Medicare and Medicaid are the major obstacles to provision of home care services (U.S. Department of Health, Education and Welfare, 1979a). Current federal statutes for Medicare restrict reimbursement for home health benefits. Although the Medicare statute provides for 100 days of home health care per episode of illness, this provision has been rigidly interpreted by the federal administering agency. Only those aged who are able to be completely rehabilitated are considered eligible for this benefit; those who are chronically ill with little potential for rehabilitation are deemed ineligible. In addition, home health services are confined to nursing care; physical, occupational, or speech therapy; medical social services as directed by a physician; and part-time home health aide services. Medicare does not include personal, supportive or homemaking services. In addition, the statute requires patients to be homebound or in need of services at the skilled nursing level. This is quite restrictive.

The Medicaid program is less restrictive of home care services but is not being well-utilized. Federal regulations do not require that a beneficiary be homebound, require skilled or intermittent nursing care, or have rehabilitation potential. However, only two percent of the Medicaid budget is provided for other noninstitutional health services including home care. Most states restrict the provision of home care services by applying federal Medicare policies to Medicaid.

Many reports urge the establishment of alternatives to institutionalization. The U.S. Government Accounting Office (1979a) reported that many federal and state policies for the Medicaid program contribute to the excessively high costs of institutionalization, while denying appropriate services to many older people in need of care. The General Accounting Office (GAO) estimated that 75 percent of those in nursing homes neither need nor prefer nursing home care; admission could be avoided if necessary services were available in the community. Many reports have recommended that Medicaid policies be changed to provide noninstitutional services with broad access to such services as homemakers, respite care, and home care (Estes et al., 1981).

In 1979-1980, Congress appropriated $20.5 million for special initiative long-term care demonstration programs using funds from the Health Care Financing Administration and the

Older Americans Act Title IX model programs. Designed to assist the functionally impaired elderly, these demonstration programs were funded to stimulate system-level changes in the organization of the delivery system; to create a community structure to coordinate, to manage, and to arrange for delivery of long-term care services, and to collect data for policy development. Each program must provide access to a broad range of services such as homemaking, chores, and transportation (U.S. Congress, Senate Special Committee on Aging, 1980). This project addresses issues of funding interpretation and system fragmentation; it does not involve structural reform.

Medical Model Versus Social Model

Another major obstacle to integrating health and social services is that federal statutes establish some programs under a medical model and others under a social model. Medicare and Medicaid are designed as medical programs, although some social services are included. The programs are medical, since all services must be authorized or approved by a physician. Utilization controls placed on the program follow the basic premise that only the physician can authorize benefits for the eligible population. Even home health services, which have close links with social services, must be medical in nature for patients who would otherwise be in an institution; these must be authorized by a physician. Social services cannot be provided to home care patients without medical authorization to receive reimbursement by Medicare and Medicaid.

In contrast, social service programs can be authorized, purchased, and evaluated by program managers and cannot be authorized directly by private physicians. Social service programs, such as those funded by Title XX, have different types of managers, professionals, program criteria, and standards from those of health programs, even though the services may be the same as those established under the health programs. The artificial distinction between medical and social problems is an obstacle preventing the aged from receiving continuity of services. These distinctions contribute to fragmentation in reimbursement, service provision, and the actual services provided.

State Discretionary Policies

Three major state-administered programs give states primary discretion: Title XIX (Medicaid) and Title XX (Social Services) of the Social Security Act and the Older American Act. In these programs, each state has the discretion to develop and to determine, within the federal mandates, eligibility, benefit coverage, provider qualification, provider payment, and administrative structure. There are major inequities among states: many offer programs at the minimum level required by the federal law, while others extend programs beyond the minimal requirements.

Service Inequities

Service inequities among states characterize all three programs. For example, many states spend the majority of their Medicaid dollars on institutional services, offering few home care services. According to a survey of state Medicaid coverage of home health care, 23 states require recipients to be homebound; 23 states have a prior authorization requirement; 16 states limit the number of visits; and some states limit home health care to postinstitutional care. For example, in 1979, California spent only 59 percent of its total Medicaid budget on nursing home services compared to 77 percent in Texas (Newcomer et al., 1980). Only 10 states provide for the personal care services allowed under the federal Medicaid statutes as an optional service. This is a homemaker service usually provided in conjunction with home health aide services. Personal care services may provide states with an option to expand less intensive in-home care beyond the limits for such services under Title XX.

Spitz and Holahan (1977) documented the great variation in Medicaid expenditures. In 1979, Medicaid recipients over age 65 received an average of $952 of inpatient hospital expenditures in California compared to $338 in Texas (Newcomer et al., 1980). In 1974, the Medicaid expenditures per eligible varied from $86 in West Virginia to $1,322 in New York (Holahan et al., 1977). While it is difficult to rationalize the significant differences in services among states, standardization in services would require revision of the Medicaid statute defining the type, level, scope, and duration of minimum services.

Title XX offers a wide range of services, which vary considerably among states. Of the 1979 total program expenditures, 22 percent were for child day care, 14 percent for home-based services (of which most were probably for the aged), 11 percent for substitute services (of which only 2 percent were for adults). Housing, transportation, and health-related services were decreasing in expenditures while home-based services, day care for adults, and protective services for children were increasing (Kilgore and Salmon, 1979). Wolff (1978) found that $481 million (13 percent of the total Title XX services) were spent on home-based services for 1.5 million people in 1978. While at least one home-based service was available in all 51 states, these varied significantly. Since Title XX statistics are not kept by age, there is no accurate count of the aged services, although it can be expected that the aged receive a significant portion of the home-based services. Home-based services varied from .5 percent of the total budget in Oklahoma to 31 percent in California in 1978 (Wolff, 1978).

A study of seven states by the General Accounting Office (1979b) found that the percentage of expenditures for the SSI elderly varied between 3 percent in Ohio and 13.4 percent in New Mexico. Since Title XX is targeted for SSI beneficiaries, it is not serving a high proportion of those who are SSI elderly. This study found that services were generally directed toward helping the aged improve, maintain, and safeguard their functioning in their own home by providing health-related services, homemaker/chore services, individual and family counseling, transportation, and protective services. Unfortunately, service definitions vary across states because the Title XX program does not have standard service definitions, nor do states have guidelines on the scope, duration, and quality of services for the program. The study recommended that states set standards to assure suitable quality for these services.

While the federal reauthorization legislation for the Older Americans Act in 1979 required that at least half of the Title II funds be expended for health and in-home services, the states had the discretion to determine the proportion of funds allocated to each set of services (Estes et al., 1981). State and area agencies have different priorities for service programs. In 1979, some states devoted 46 percent of OAA Title III funds to home health, day care, and medical services, while others devoted only 22 percent (Estes and Newcomer, 1981). Such program differences between states and the changing nature of the programs create a complex, fragmented social services system.

Eligibility Inequities

In the Title XX program, eligibility standards vary considerably among the states. Thirty-nine states vary eligibility according to the service provided. Between 1976 and 1978, 14 states decreased eligibility standards and others have imposed nonincome eligibility requirements (Wolff, 1978). Between 1978 and 1979, 13 states lowered their maximum eligibility levels for services and others limited access to services (Kilgore and Salmon, 1979). The maximum income levels for Title XX also vary among states, so the question of equity becomes a serious one. For example, in Texas, only persons earning below 60 percent of the state median income are eligible for services, while California and Pennsylvania allow persons with incomes higher than the median to quality (Wolff, 1978; Newcomer et al., 1980).

Under Title XX legislation, elderly persons must be SSI beneficiaries or meet the state income criteria, while under the Title III Older Americans Act, all elderly are eligible for Title III services regardless of income. Therefore, persons eligible for one program may not be eligible for other programs because their income exceeds state requirements (U.S. General Accounting Office, 1979b).

Medicaid requires states to cover specific groups: all aid to families with dependent children (AFDC) and those receiving Supplemental Security Income (SSI). These groups are referred to as the categorically needy and are determined by complex means tests. Because of the different SSI eligibility options and the grandfathering of the program discussed in a previous section, Medicaid eligibility builds on these inequities in state SSI programs. In addition to the categorically needy, states may elect to include the "medically needy," those who did not exceed 133-1/3 percent of the maximum assistance payments for similarly sized families under AFDC (U.S. Department of Health, Education and Welfare, 1979a; Spitz and Holahan, 1977). Thirty-two states provide eligibility to the medically needy in one of the cash welfare program categories. Other states provide eligibility for those who are medically indigent, those who have income to pay their basic living expenses but cannot meet the costs of medical care, and thus they reduce their income below the medically needy maximum by spending down to that level. Only a few states—for example, Maryland, California, and New York—cover such individuals (U.S. Department of Health, Education and Welfare, 1979a).

Each state may require an individual to undergo a series of different and complex eligibility determinations for each of different programs, including Medicaid, Title XX, and SSI. But the most serious problem is that the same individual with identical characteristics is treated differently from state to state. The need for uniform nationwide eligibility criteria and procedures is clear to improve efficiency and monitoring of programs and to reduce the misuse of eligibility standards (Spitz and Holahan, 1977). But the cost of developing a program which would raise all the states up to the level of the highest state would be high. Cost is a primary factor inhibiting moves for standardization, and few would argue for reducing eligibility levels below what individuals currently receive.

Fragmentation of Services

The ideal national system of health and social services would include a continuum of programs from the most restrictive to the least restrictive settings (see Figure 10.1). Services would not overlap and would represent levels and types of programs for more intensive to less intensive by program type. Services would not duplicate, but would substitute for, each other at different levels for different types of patient needs. Unfortunately, the health and social service delivery system is not planned or organized on this type of basis but is fragmented into an almost incomprehensible arrangement.

The federally funded health and social service programs contribute to the irrational fragmented service arrangement. Medicare, Medicaid, Title XX, and the OAA all provide some home care services, but differences in benefits, eligibility, and service provision create overlap, duplication, and confusion. Each program has different definitions, range and duration of services, service providers, and reimbursement methods. Serious coordination problems are created by the different federal statutory requirements and different state policies and programs (U.S. Congress, House of Representatives, 1976b).

The Medicare system provides home health benefits for those who need skilled nursing care. Medicaid provides limited home health benefits and "personal care services" as an optional benefit. Title XX provides optional programs of homemaker, chore, home management, personal care, home-delivered meals, and home health aide services. The combined federal, state, and local expenditures for these programs totalled $1.1 billion in 1977; $458 million for 690,000 Medicare beneficiaries, $179 million for 300,000 Medicaid beneficiaries; and $491 million for 500,000 Title XX beneficiaries (U.S. Department of Health, Education and Welfare, 1979b). Implementation of recommendations that artificial distinctions between program titles be removed and standard definitions be developed has not yet been attempted.

Public agencies often purchase social and health services from the voluntary and private sectors. The resulting proliferation of voluntary agencies increases the variety and flexibility of programs but has many disadvantages. The purchase of such services compounds fragmentation and weakens accountability in the service network (National Conference on Social Welfare, 1979). The wide variety of community services described in Figure 10.1 makes it difficult for individuals to determine what services are needed, which are available, how to link into the appropriate services, and how to obtain reimbursement for the programs. Programs such as Title XX, which reported 1,313 services under 41 categories, make the problems for both consumers and professionals difficult (U.S. Department of Health, Education and Welfare, Office of Human Development Services, 1976).

Even though federal legislation requires coordination for the Title XX and Title III (OAA) programs, little evidence can be found that coordination is effective. Coordination can be defined as joint participation through an organized system to maximize program benefits and minimize duplication, overlap, and conflicts. One finding from a recent study was that only one out of seven states in the study provided any coordination between agencies providing social services under Title III (OAA) and Title XX (U.S. General Accounting Office, 1979b). Coordination problems were caused in part by the different eligibility requirements of the programs and the different organizational structures. Title III (OAA) has agencies in multicounty areas, while Title XX programs are generally operated by the counties. Thus, each Title III agency usually has to coordinate with several separate county-run Title XX agencies.

There was duplication of funds for some services and a shortage of funds for other services. There was duplication of needs assessments and a lack of joint planning (U.S. General Accounting Office, 1979b). Many problems have hindered linkage activities, including the complexity of the various programs, the rapid changes in policies and procedures, the absence of common geographic boundaries, and separate organizational structures. Linkages between programs are usually examined at three levels to ensure appropriate services to those with the greatest need: between the federal, state, and local level.

Program linkages have important agency benefits: providing complementary programs and services and lowering administrative costs. Coordination allows programs to devote efforts to primary objectives and to improve the efficiency and effectiveness of operations and services. This allows states and local programs to maximize their reimbursement dollars by placing services under the programs with the most favorable reimbursement rates. Various methods have been attempted to achieve linkage between programs. Some programs enter into agreements with state and local social service agencies to improve linkages. Others have provided cross-program training. Another approach has been to place the administrative structure of programs together under umbrella agencies or in the same locations.

One approach to improve linkages among programs is the establishment of information and referral agencies. Such attempts have little impact unless the various information and referral programs can be integrated at the local level. Such efforts have been weakened by the duplication, multiplicity, and specialization of the information and referral programs, which have themselves become fragmented (National Conference on Social Welfare, 1979).

Another method to improve coordination is the case management system in which an agency or program assumes responsibility. It either purchases services directly on an individual case basis or indirectly contracts for the case management services. Success in improving effectiveness and efficiency of services under a case management system depends on organizational structure, reimbursement procedures, and program incentives.

Social and health services are intricately related to income support programs, which provide basic subsistence to the poor. Social and health services complement income support programs, making linkage between the programs essential. If linkages are not made among income support, health, and social service programs, those who receive services may not necessarily be those most in need, but rather those who are best able to seek and obtain help for themselves (National Conference on Social Welfare, 1979). The primary purpose of linkages is to benefit clients, especially those in greatest need.

Financial Constraints

The third major obstacle now facing federal and state officials is that total expenditures for Medicare and Medicaid are too high (see Table 10.1 for expenditure patterns of all national health care programs). Hospitals are the major cause of the increased costs which are based on a number of factors, but the major one is that of price increases on service per use beyond inflationary increases. The primary cause of increases in hospital prices has been identified as the reasonable cost reimbursement requirement for hospitals built into the Medicare and Medicaid statutes (Holahan et al., 1977). Such reimbursement provides for payments retrospectively to cover whatever expenditures the hospitals make. This encourages increasing expenditures to increase the total revenues; there is little incentive for hospitals to be efficient and to minimize costs. Some states have developed special mechanisms, such as utilization reviews, prospective budgeting, and rate setting, in order to reduce hospital costs (U.S. General Accounting Office, 1980c).

The existing financing requirements discourage states from managing programs efficiently and results in excessive allocation of resources to health programs relative to social services and other programs. States react to matching in the Medicaid program by increasing expenditures. With open-ended matching programs, the more the states spend, the more federal revenue they receive. Those states with the most resources are better able to take advantage of the federal revenues from Medicaid, even though the matching programs vary based on per capita income. Those states with the greatest resources pay 50 percent of costs in the Medicaid program, while those with the least pay only 22 percent. Holahan et al. (1977) argue that the federal

TABLE 10.1   Estimated National Long-Term Care Expenditure Patterns for 1979 (in millions)

	Title XX[1]	AoA[2]	Medicaid[3]	Medicare[3]	Other Health[3]
Social Services[4]		197.0			
Home-based services	568.5				
Day care services— children and adults	864.9				
Protective services— children and adults	357.8				
Information and referral	116.9				
Legal services	39.0				
Family planning	80.0				
Home/congregate meals	23.8	272.5			
Services to expectant parents	7.5				
Adoption services	22.5				
Substitute care— children	267.4				
Housing	27.5				
Transportation	68.4				
Model projects		15.0			
Health-related services	96.7				
Hospital care			8,005	4,347	18,032
Physicians' services			2,218	1,203	2,000
Dentists' services			448	–	90
Other professional services			459	552	190
Drugs and medical supplies			1,225	–	194
Eyeglasses and appliances			–	249	159
Nursing home care			8,795	373	934
Other health services (home care)			528	97	3,273
Other	1,419.0	334.8			
Total	3,960.0	819.3	21,683	29,328	24,873

1. Kilgore, G., and G. Salmon (1979) *Technical Notes: Summaries and Characteristics of States' Title XX Social Services Plans for Fiscal Year 1979.* Washington, DC: U.S. DHEW, Office of Assistant Secretary for Planning and Evaluation, June 15.
2. U.S. Senate, Special Committee on Aging (1980) *Developments in Aging: 1979,* Part 1. 96th Congress, 2nd session, S. Rept. 613. Washington, DC: Government Printing Office, p.116.
3. Gibson, R. M. (1980) "National Health Expenditures, 1979." *Health Care Financing Review* 2, 1 (Summer): 1-36. Statistics include both federal and state expenditures for health care.
4. Social services includes home-based, information and referral, legal, and transportation services.

government should change its matching formula so that states with the highest income would pay an even greater share of the Medicaid program to discourage state spending. They also argue that program funding for Medicaid should be close-ended with some overall program limitations to encourage greater state efficiency in program administrative and monitoring fraud and abuse in the program. This approach is under consideration by the Reagan administration.

Title XX social service programs were changed in 1972 from their previous matching formula approach with no maximum limits to a closed-ended matching formula with a total federal allocation of $2.5 billion. In 1974, Congress established block grant funding for the Title XX program but kept the $2.5 billion ceiling (U.S. Congress, Senate Special Committee on Aging, 1980). The estimated expenditures for the program in 1978 were $3.7 billion, of which $2.5 billion was paid by the federal government even though the program has a 75-25 federal-state match. The federal expenditure limit was $2.9 billion in 1979. A study by the U.S. General Accounting Office (1979b) in 1978 found that under limited funding, the aged SSI recipients did not receive adequate services, since they were competing with other SSI groups for benefits. Homemaker and transportation services were extremely limited because the total financial resources for the program were inadequate.

In contrast to the open-ended funding of Medicaid, the closed-ended funding of social services encourages states to distort program funding and program priorities. Because of the limitations on social services, overall expenditures for the aged háve been directed toward high-cost hospital and nursing home services. If program funds were reallocated to social services as a substitute for high-cost medical services, there might be considerable savings to both federal and state programs. However, at the present time, if these funds were merged into one to give the states greater discretion to shift resources to social services, the danger would be that resource allocation would be shifted even more toward medical services. This would be a result of the powerful lobbies of the hospitals, physicians, and other health providers in contrast to those in the social service field. States are using several strategies to control costs, such as ending program expansion, reordering service priorities, changing client services, reducing services, and shifting funding sources.

Funding Shifts Between Programs

One major strategy used by states with funding constraints is to shift services to programs with more favorable reimbursement rates so that services can be continued (Millar et al., 1977). The different federal funding formulas for health and service programs invite program shifting by states to maximize federal reimbursement. Under Medicaid, states receive federal funds in a range of 50 to 78 percent based on each state's per capita income. The federal share for Title XX is 75 percent. It reaches 90 percent for the Administration on Aging.

As the size and scope of federal domestic assistance programs has grown, federal influence in state and local government has increased through control over funding, primarily through matching grants and maintenance of effort requirements. "Match" is defined as the minimum share of program costs for the grantees as a condition of receiving federal assistance and the maximum amounts of program cost paid by the federal government. Maintenance of effort provisions ensure that federal funds supplement existing state and local programs and do not act as a substitute for existing resources (U.S. General Accounting Office, 1980a). These federal requirements speed the cost of implementing programs and ensure state and local accountability and responsibility for programs to control spending.

Matching requirements have been developed on a program-by-program basis in a confusing and complex manner, with different matching rates and ways to meet the matching levels even within the same functional areas. The U.S. General

Accounting Office (1980a) reports that nonfederal match is required in 63 percent of the federal grant programs, accounting for 71 percent of the funds available to state and local governments. The different matching requirements lead grantees to distort their selection of federal grant programs to take advantage of more favorable match rates and conditions. Grantees are also likely to select lower nonfederal match programs when more than one program is available for a given project. This has induced state and local governments to reshape or distort program priorities (U.S. General Accounting Office, 1980a). Some programs with higher matching rates may be underutilized even though there may be community need.

Examples of interprogram funding shifts occur in day care and personal care services for the aged. These may be funded by either Title XX or Medicaid. Depending on the state's matching rate under Medicaid, it may be to a state's advantage to shift all day care and personal care services into the Title XX program. On the other hand, Title XX funds are limited by a ceiling, over which the state has to pay 100 percent of the costs. If a state cannot keep its Title XX program under the ceiling, then funds can be maximized by shifting day care and personal care services to Medicaid, which does not have a ceiling at the present time. If the federal government places a ceiling on the Medicaid program as proposed, states could attempt to maximize reimbursements by shifting service costs of the aged to the Medicare program because there are no limits on its reimbursements and no matching funds required.

When, to maximize the receipt of federal and state funds, services are shifted from one funding source to another, from one agency to another, and from one provider to another, fragmentation and confusion result for clients. Such shifts may affect the quality of service the client receives. For example, services provided under Medicare have fairly high federal standards which providers (e.g., nursing homes) must meet. Federal standards on providers under Title XX and SSI are minimal.

Eligibility Reductions

Some states continue to limit eligibility in the Title XX program by lowering the maximum income level for services or restricting availability of services. Between 1978 and 1979, 13 states lowered their maximum eligibility levels for services and eligibility levels for high-cost services or applied nonincome criteria for services (Kilgore and Salmon, 1979). Some states administering Medicaid programs have reduced eligibility as a means of controlling costs.

Medicaid has been a primary problem for states in terms of its increasing growth in creating fiscal strain and crisis. The program grew from $2.3 billion in 1967 to $12.9 billion in 1975 to the present $22 billion (Holahan et al., 1977). Periodic recessions which increase the level of unemployment and under-employment are also factors in increasing the number eligible for the Medicaid program and consequently the costs of the program. Recessions also decrease the state revenues, creating further fiscal strain. Holahan et al. (1977) showed the relationship between state fiscal strain and the Medicaid program cutbacks, particularly in eligibility during 1974-1975. They recommended policy changes to assist states with the greatest fiscal strain so that there would be greater equity in the Medicaid program by preventing cutbacks in eligibility and benefits. One approach is to provide capitation payments to states based on the number of eligibles in the program to bring about greater uniformity rather than to provide federal funds based on the current per capita income formula. One major approach to cost containment is limiting Medicaid eligibility. Some states have eliminated or have proposed to eliminate the medically needy and the medically indigent from the program because these are not mandated by the federal law. Other states have not raised the income eligibility level to keep pace with inflation, thereby reducing the number eligible for the program (Wolman, 1980). Reducing the number of eligibles from the programs adversely affects the aged and those most in need of services and their families. And there may not be overall cost savings. Such a policy approach may increase the health care costs of local governments or shift the entire burden for those deemed ineligible to the state. Thus, eligibility cutbacks may result in only marginal savings or shifting costs to the state.

Service Reductions

The U.S. General Accounting Office (1979b) study of Title XX programs in seven states in 1978 determined that only 3 to 33 percent of the aged SSI beneficiaries received social services under the program, even though services are mandated for all SSI beneficiaries. Those states serving the lowest percentage of SSI elderly had more elderly persons relative to their total populations than the other states. This study concluded that inadequate funding levels were partly the cause, forcing the aged to compete with other SSI groups for services. In order to increase the services to the aged, services to other SSI groups would have to be decreased. The GAO recommended that the allocations for the Title XX program be changed to the number of SSI eligible in the state's population instead of total population.

Some states have limited services to Medicaid recipients as a cost containment measure. A temptation of states suffering severe fiscal strain is to eliminate optional services and restrict the mandatory services. This approach may place hardships on those with the most severe disabilities (Spitz and Holahan, 1971). And since there is no rationality to the designation of optional and mandatory benefits, cutbacks in optional services and mandatory limitations may actually increase costs by shifting them to higher cost programs such as hospital care.

REAGAN ADMINISTRATION PROPOSALS

During 1981, the Reagan administration submitted to Congress a federal budget proposal which cut funding levels for many programs. The administration's policy is to group programs by categories under block grants to states. The overall effect is to give states greater discretion in the management and operation of programs within the block grant categories. The states would determine priorities, services reimbursement methods, and other policies previously defined for each categorical program.

The Reagan administration proposed that the Medicaid budget spending be capped at $100 million below the $16.2 billion allocated for 1981 and that only a five percent increase be allowed for 1982. The funds to states would continue to be allocated on a matching basis depending on state per capita income. To compensate for the federal reductions in Medicaid spending, the administration promised that states would be given additional flexibility to target services to the truly needy and to develop innovative methods for financing and delivering services (U.S. Congress, House of Representatives, 1981).

States must make difficult choices to save funds or pay for additional costs out of their own revenues, a highly unlikely option (Wolman, 1980). Since Medicaid expenditures have continued to increase at rates greater than inflation, the burden of containing costs will shift increasingly to the states. If cost-based reimbursement and freedom of choice provisions are removed so that states have the flexibility of contracting for services on a bid basis, states will be able to save a considerable amount of money. On the other hand, the dangers are that states will attempt to achieve cost savings by reducing eligibility and benefits, which would directly affect the aged. Critics of the proposal suggest that the Medicaid proposals will place the greatest hardship on the nation's poor and force arbitrary elimination of benefits and eligibility (U.S. Congress, House of Representatives, 1981). If the 1981 federal eligibility and benefits requirements are removed from the Medicaid program, the likelihood is that not only will reductions in expenditures per eligible person occur but the variability among states will become even greater.

Under the administration frameworks, states will encounter serious problems in holding costs below the proposed funding levels when inflationary costs are expected to be 10 percent. Strong incentives to control costs will encourage states to integrate programs more closely. Increased state responsibility and discretion may multiply differences and inequities in services among the states. If the programs are allowed to be selected by the states, within certain categories, those programs with the strongest organized constituencies—especially the providers—are most likely to be able to protect their funds. Programs with strong benefits and cost effectiveness might be removed entirely. In programs such as Title XX, the aged will be forced to compete with other needy groups and may receive even less than their already meager share.

The restructuring of the federal funding for health and service programs into block grants may allow for greater program integration at the federal, state, and local levels. On the other hand, dangers inherent in precipitating reductions and shifting fiscal burdens to states are great.

CONCLUSION

U.S. human services programs focus on costly institutional services and, as built-in constraints from federal statutes and regulations, restrict home and community-based services. At the same time, state discretionary policies allow service inequities, eligibility inequities, and fragmentation of programs among and within the states. Options to correct these problems include developing stronger linkages among existing programs and designing greater coordination in service delivery, funding, and eligibility between programs. The goal is to correct basic structural defects in the federal legislation of each program. Funding limitations at state and federal levels exacerbate structural problems. States seek to maximize program dollars by shifting services to those programs with the most favorable federal matching rates, thereby increasing program confusion. Financial constraints have led states to cut back eligibility and benefits, widening program inequities for the aged among the states.

Proposed federal reductions and policy changes give states greater reductions in eligibility and benefits. While public policymakers seek new ways to control costs, there is a willingness to make basic changes in the existing programs. However, fiscal pressures may encourage unsystematic and poorly devised approaches to correct existing problems.

REFERENCES

BINSTOCK, R. H. (1979) "A policy agenda on aging for the 1980s." National Journal (October 13): 1711-1717.

BRODY, S. J. and C. MASCIOCCHI (1980) "Data for long-term care planning by health systems agencies." American Journal of Public Health 70,11: 1194-1198.

BUTLER, P. A. (19XX) Financing Non-Institutional Long-Term Care Services for the Elderly and Chronically Ill: Alternatives to Nursing Homes. Washington, DC: Research Institute, Legal Services Corporation.

ESTES, C. L. (1979) The Aging Enterprise. San Francisco: Jossey-Bass.

––– and C. HARRINGTON (1981) "Fiscal crisis, deinstitutionalization, and the elderly." American Behavioral Scientist (July).

ESTES, C. L. and R. NEWCOMER (1981) Funding Practices, Policies, and Performance of State and Area Agencies on Aging. Final Report to the U.S. Administration on Aging. San Francisco: Aging Health Policy Center, University of California.

ESTES, C. L., P. R. LEE, C. HARRINGTON, L. GERARD, M. KREGER, A. E. BENJAMIN, R. NEWCOMER, and J. SWAN (1981) Public Policies and Long-Term Care for the Elderly: A Multibillion Dollar Dilemma. Berkeley: California Policy Seminar Institute of Governmental Studies, University of California.

FELDSTEIN, P. J. (1980) "The political environment of regulation," in A. Levin (ed.) Regulating Health Care: A Struggle for Control. Academy of Political Science 33, 4.

FIELD, T., R. MILLAR, and B. BENTON (1978) Effect of Title XX Implementation on the Allocation of Social Services. Washington, DC: Urban Institute.

FISHER, C. R. (1980) "Differences by age groups in health care spending." Health Care Financing Review 1, 4: 65-90.

GELFAND, D. E. and J. OLSEN (1980) The Aging Network: Programs and Services. Volume 8, Springer Series on Adulthood and Aging. New York: Springer Publishing Company.

GIBSON, R. M. (1980) "National health expenditures, 1979." Health Care Financing Review 2, 1: 1-36.

GILBERT, N., H. SPECHT, and G. NELSON (1979) Social Services to the Elderly: Title XX and the Aging Network. San Francisco: Institute for Scientific Analysis.

HAWKINS, S. C. and D. RIGBY (1979) "Effect of SSI on Medicaid caseloads and expenditures." Social Security Bulletin 2, 2: 3-14.

HOLAHAN, J. and B. STUART (1977) Controlling Medicaid Utilization Patterns. Washington, DC: Urban Institute.

HOLAHAN, J., W. SCANLON, and B. SPITZ (1980) "Public finance: impact of national economic conditions on health care of the poor." Effects of the 1974-75 Recession on Health Care for the Disadvantaged. NCHSR Research Summary Series, January.

——— (1977) Restructuring Federal Medicaid Controls and Incentives. Washington, DC: Urban Institute.

HUDSON, R. B. (1978) "The 'Graying' of the federal budget and its consequences for old-age policy." The Gerontologist 18, 5: 428-440.

KILGORE, G. and G. SALMON (1979) Technical Notes: Summaries and Characteristics of States' Title XX Social Services Plans for Fiscal Year 1979. Washington, DC: U.S. Department of Health, Education and Welfare, Office of the Assistant Secretary for Planning and Evaluation.

MILLAR, R., B. BENTON, T. FIELD, and S. EDWARDS (1977) The Impact of the Federal Expenditure Ceiling on Title XX Social Services. Working Paper 0990-20. Washington, DC: Urban Institute.

MORRIS, R. and P. YOUKET (1979) "Major options in long-term care: background and framework." Waltham, MA: University Health Policy Consortium, Brandeis University.

MYERS, B. A. and R. LEIGHTON (1980) "Medicaid and the mainstream: reassessment in the context of the taxpayer revolt." Western Journal of Medicine 132 (June): 550-561.

National Conference on Social Welfare (1979) The Future Relationship Between Publicly Funded Social Services and Income Support Programs. Final Report. Washington, DC: National Conference on Social Welfare.

NEWCOMER, R. J., C. HARRINGTON, and L. GERARD (1980) A Five-State Comparison of Selected Long-Term Care Expenditure and Utilization Patterns for Persons Ages 65 and Older. Working Paper No. 11. San Francisco: Aging Health Policy Center, University of California.

"The Reagan FY 1982 federal budget." (1981) Health Systems Report. 10, 10: 1-8.

RIGBY, D. E. and E. PONCE (1980) U.S. Department of Health and Human Services, Office of Policy, Social Security Administration. The Supplemental Security Income Program for the Aged, Blind, and Disabled: Selected Characteristics of State Supplementation Programs as of October, 1979. Washington, DC: Government Printing Office.

SCANLON, W. J., E. DiFEDERICO, and M. STASSEN (1979) A Framework for Analysis of the Long-Term Care System. Washington, DC: Urban Institute.

SPITZ, B. and J. HOLAHAN (1977) Modifying Medicaid Eligibility and Benefits. Washington, DC: Urban Institute.

U.S. Congress, Congressional Budget Office (1977) Long-Term Care for the Elderly and Disabled. Washington, DC: Government Printing Office.

U.S. Congress, House of Representatives (1978) Conference Report No. 95-1618: Comprehensive Older Americans Act Amendments of 1978. Washington, DC: Government Printing Office.

U.S. Congress, House Select Committee on Aging (1981) Analysis of the Impact of the Proposed Fiscal Year 1982 Budget Cuts on the Elderly. 97th Congress, Briefing Paper. Washington, DC: Government Printing Office.

——— (1977a) Federal Responsibility to the Elderly: Executive Programs and Legislative Jursidiction. 95th Congress. Washington, DC: Government Printing Office.

——— (1977b) Fragmentation of Services for the Elderly. Hearings, 95th Congress. Washington, DC: Government Printing Office.

——— (1977c) National Crisis in Adult Care Homes. Hearings before House Select Committee on Aging, 95th Congress, 1st Session. Washington, DC: Government Printing Office.

U.S. Congress, Senate Special Committee on Aging (1980) Developments in Aging: 1979. 96th Congress, 2nd Session, Senate Report, Part I. Washington, DC: Government Printing Office.

——— (1977-78) Health Care for Older Americans: The "Alternatives" Issue. Parts 1-7. Washington, DC: Government Printing Office.

——— (1976) Adult Day Facilities for Treatment. Health Care and Related Services. 94th Congress, 2nd Session. Washington, DC: Government Printing Office.

U.S. Department of Commerce, Bureau of the Census (1973) Persons in Institutions and Other Group Quarters: Subject Reports. Series PC-2, 4E. Washington, DC: U.S. Government Printing Office (1973).

U.S. General Accounting Office (1980a) Implementing GAO's Recommendations on the Social Security Administration Programs Could Save Billions. Report to the Congress of the United States by the Comptroller General. Washington, DC: Comptroller General of the United States.

——— (1980b) Proposed Changes in Federal Matching and Maintenance of Effort Requirements for State and Local Governments. Report to the Congress of the United States by the Comptroller General. Washington, DC: Comptroller General of the United States.

——— (1980c) Rising Hospital Costs Can Be Restrained by Regulating Payments and Improving Management. Report to Congress by the Comptroller General of the United States. Washington, DC: Comptroller General of the United States.

——— (1979a) Entering a Nursing Home—Costly Implications for Medicaid and the Elderly. Report to the Congress by the Comptroller General of the United States. Washington, DC: GAO.

——— (1979b) State Programs for Delivering Title XX Social Services to Supplemental Security Income Beneficiaries Can Be Improved. Washington, DC: Government Printing Office.

——— (1977) Home Health—The Need for a National Policy is Better Provided for the Elderly: Report to the Congress by the Comptroller General. Washington, DC: Comptroller General of the United States.

U.S. Department of Health and Human Services, Health Care Financing Administration (1981a) Long-Term Care Background and Future Directions. Washington, DC: U.S. Department of Health and Human Services.

U.S. Department of Health and Human Services, Social Security Administration (1981b) "Current Operating Statistics." Social Security Bulletin 44, 3: 29-100.

U.S. Department of Health, Education and Welfare (1979) Home Health Services Under Titles XVIII, XIX, and XX. Report to the Congress pursuant to P.L. 95-14 (April 1979—Revised November 1, 1979).

U.S. Department of Health, Education and Welfare. National Center for Health Statistics (1976) Inpatient Health Facilities as Reported from the 1973 Master

Facility Inventory Survey. Vital Health Statistics, Series 14, No. 16, DHEW Publication No. (HRA) 76-1811.

U.S. Department of Health, Education and Welfare. National Center for Health Statistics (1979c) The National Nursing Home Survey, 1977 Summary for the United States. Publication No. (PHS) 79-1974. Hyattsville, Md.

U.S. Department of Health, Education and Welfare. Office of Human Development Services (1976) Social Services U.S.A. Publication No. 77-03300.

U.S. Department of Health, Education and Welfare. Office of the Secretary, Task Force on Long-Term Care/Community Services (1978) Major Initiative on Long-Term Care/Community Services Reform: Report of the Task Force.

U.S. Office of Management and Budget, Executive Office of the President (1980) Managing Federal Assistance in the 1980's: A Report to Congress. Washington, DC: U.S. Executive Office of the President.

U.S. Office of Management and Budget, Executive Office of the President (1980) 1980 Catalog of Federal Domestic Assistance. Washington, DC: Government Printing Office, 1980.

WOLFF, E. C. (1978) Technical Notes: Summaries and Characteristics of States' Title XX Social Services Plans for Fiscal Year 1978. Washington, DC: Department of Health, Education and Welfare, Office of the Assistant Secretary for Planning and Evaluation.

WOLMAN, H. (1980) State and Local Governments Strategies for Responding to Fiscal Pressure. Washington, DC: Urban Institute.

11

STRENGTHENING HEALTH AND SOCIAL SERVICE LINKS
International Themes

ROGER A. RITVO

The theory and practice of linking health and social services begins at the endpoint of both systems: the person in need. The details of how the international community approaches this concern provides an understanding of the differences. Government programs, professional ideologies, political concerns, financial arrangements, and social structures differ across each country described in this anthology. The similarities are as striking as the uniqueness of each national effort.

One of the clearest themes connecting each of the preceding chapters is the historical separation of health and social services. Whether we are discussing the Danish or the French approaches, legislative efforts to meet human needs had the subtle effects of beginning a split which endures today. Given this history, it would be difficult to reverse or alter such trends in the short term. Thus, like any well-planned change effort, a long-term strategy is needed. As a first step, problem recognition must occur. Who suffers because of the split between these services? Does it reduce service effectiveness? Would such linkages increase the efficiency of such services? Would increased professional interaction enhance the implementation of health and social welfare policies and programs? Without identifying a need for change, the status quo will remain. Such efforts require data for support. One theme connecting the discussions in this book is the relative lack of successful models which can be adapted to meet a specific national need. Could French policymakers draw from the Swedish or British experience? Probably yes, but with major modifications. Each nation has its own traditions, its own heritage, its own value system, and a differing set of service needs and infrastructures.

Given these unique histories and traditions, there are several themes which characterize more than just one or two of these efforts to link health and social services. This final chapter focuses on four major areas: role of government, professional concerns, financial issues, and consumer expectations. The central theme of this discussion lies in the optimistic analysis of these efforts. Much has been accomplished; more will occur. Despite the specific problems, the thrust and direction remain constant in pushing for greater cooperation, collaboration, and linkage.

THE ROLE OF GOVERNMENT

Each of these chapters has pointed out the continuing, central role of the various national governments. Whether in Denmark, Sweden, France, or Canada, without federal intervention little occurred. However, it is possible that leadership at a state, county, or provincial level could occur. Certainly these governmental officials are closer to the clientele than their national level peers. As political constituencies, these are the beneficiaries of service. However, little progress was made at the local, municipal, county, state, or provincial level without federal involvement. The reasons may center on financial factors, fear of failure, or an unwillingness to experiment or challenge the existing structures, norms, and patterns of delivery, even on a limited basis. Whether other reasons exist is of less concern than the reaffirmation of the fact that a national-level commitment often provides a needed catalyst for change. Without the willingness, commitment, and participation of a nation's leadership, its professional associations and major organizations, failure and an inability to experiment result.

Herein lies the dilemma. Unless federal intervention occurs, little cooperation develops. Yet it is often the regulations, rules, and constraints of this same government that impede linkage. While seemingly contradictory, the evidence exists. Governmental structures, differential involvement of the health and social welfare experts in public policymaking positions, and uneven eligibility standards contribute to this paradox.

Governmental structures often reinforce the inability of health providers to work in concert with their social welfare practitioners. The U.S. Department of Health and Human Services is a classic reinforcer of this dichotomy. There are major administrative posts for health, social security, human development services, and health care financing. While not inherently weak, this structure is not matched with an equal integrative process. The bureaucracy funds programs in its own area; it evaluates program performance with few measures of service coordination or cooperation. The problems encountered in the programs to deinstitutionalize the mentally ill provide ample evidence. Securing cooperation from the health, mental health, and social service providers gave local agency administrators a major concern. Such federal structures exist in Israel, Sweden, Denmark, France, and Canada. These bureaucratic divisions make sense from a legislative and organizational perspective. They do not aid in development of sound collaborative policies and programs.

As Holst and Ito noted in their review of the Danish approach, social workers rarely hold public policymaking positions. This void is not a reflection on the medical profession. Social service policies have long been developed by non-social workers, often without the input or advice of the delivery professionals. This is not true of the medical professionals. As policy options are developed and considered, the medical profession finds itself well-represented. Occasionally, the decision makers are physicians; more often the medical associations provide consultation. This imbalance of roles at the national level perpetuates and reflects the imbalance in status. A clear example of this disparity is the National Association of Social Workers (NASW), which has only one paid full-time lobbyist in Washington, D.C. This overworked, singular advocate for social workers must follow health, social security, child abuse, alcoholism, aging, and a myriad of public issues of concern to NASW members. For an association with over 80,000 professionals, it could assume a greater leadership role in developing public policy alternatives and more collaborative approaches to health and social services. The American Medical Association has one of the largest political action committee contributions to candidates for public office. This disparity may explain why some needed social services are excluded from public programs, while medical care under physician approval and guidance is reimbursed. These examples reinforce the societal power of the medical profession in many of the countries discussed in this volume.

An additional problem in developing the needed programs and policies to enhance linkage between health and social services is that each set of programs uses different definitions of eligibility. Without a system of universal coverage, categorical efforts will divide services: Medicare will care for the elderly; Medicaid will focus on the poor; some programs will serve rural residents, while others will attempt to focus resources on disadvantaged or depressed areas. By dividing and subdividing a national population into myriad categories and groups, any potential for linkage fades. Means tests, age limits, residential criteria, demographic factors, and marital and family status comprise the more common set of classification schemes. Each of these segments is a population, so it also creates the necessary conditions for specialists. As such, those codifications block interprofessional collaborations and impede cross-sector linkage. In the United States, the battle of federal versus states' rights lead in part to Medicare being a national program, while Medicaid was relegated to the states. Unless stricter requirements are mandated, Arizona will not have a program and eligibility variances in the other states will continue. For uniformity and consistency, a strong case for a single national criterion can be made. Clearly, problems of regional cost-of-living variances must be addressed. But, short of universality, means tests would appear likely to remain as a major determinant of eligibility.

In sum, government involvement is unquestioned. The issues of the present focus more on the technical and structural aspects, not the philosophical ones. In every country described in this book federal involvement is deeply ingrained in its national consciousness. Modifications, not redirections, are needed.

PROFESSIONAL IMPERATIVES

The roles and functions of the professional service providers cut across many chapters of this book. For, if linkage will occur, it must occur at the delivery level. Thus, professionalism, professional education, professional associations, and new professional practices will all affect, and be affected by, increased efforts for collaboration.

One glaring omission in each analysis of these several approaches lies in professional education of the service providers. Whether physicians, nurses, or dentists, the health care education segments its students. Different socialization processes create empires of professional practice. For the social welfare providers, this holds true as well. Schools of social welfare suffer some of the same stigma that society places on their clientele. For example, in Denmark and France, schools of social welfare are not an integral part of the university system. They exist as a mid-level vocational training enterprise. This status differential reflects a structure of professional hierarchies where health care delivery personnel often relate to their social welfare colleagues as a boss relates to a subordinate. At one time, the social worker in the Danish hospital needed a "prescription" from the attending physician prior to a pre-discharge visit with a patient. Such buffers in practice result from an educational system where such attitudes are fostered or left unchallenged. This unequal status in the educational hierarchies becomes reality in practice and service delivery.

One of the hallmarks of professional development in recent years has been the advent of the specialist. Additional training in medicine has created a situation where the family practitioner was almost extinct. This trend characterizes both health care and social welfare. As medical practice has evolved with neonatologists, geriatric internists, and child psychiatrists, social work has moved on similar lines. Curriculum development creates specialists in health, alcoholism or the aged. While not inherently counterproductive, such trends reinforce the structural distinctiveness of professional practice, thereby creating additional barriers to linkage. The movement in England to use the generic approach to the provision of social services has its counterpart in medicine with the growing awareness of the need for more family practice physicians. This has been documented in numerous studies and is now a possible course for the future. This trend toward greater specialization is a luxury of developed nations. In those countries with inadequate care and services, the concern about an oversupply of specialists would be a source of amusement; insufficiency dominates distribution. But for the national approaches described in this review, it is a problem. The generalist reorientation in British social services is analogous to the family practitioner's growth. The family practitioner in Denmark is the logical focus for collaborative efforts in primary health care delivery.

The role of the professional association has received minimal attention in this review of international approaches to link health and social services. One major function of any professional group is to define the minimal entry requirements for that profession. In the United States, through the American Medical Association or the Association of American Medical Colleges, standards for medical education are developed. The analogue fails when applied to social services. While accreditation standards in the United States provide a framework for social work education, each institution retains the discretion to develop its own curriculum. The policy statements for social work education are so wide that the undergraduate and graduate programs can adapt these requirements to their own needs. As noted elsewhere in this book, the educational systems have not become catalysts for change. In fact, they probably do more to reinforce the status quo than their membership.

In those nations where professional associations become the agents for collective bargaining agreements, the concern for linking health and social services is apparently low. Professional issues within a field will, and should, dominate those concerns that cut across professions. Wages, salaries, fees, and complements of service take precedence over team approaches to delivering care, experimental organizational arrangements, and alternative payment schemes. As a fact of professional existence, these issues will tend to inhibit linking health and social services without a major restructuring of the professional association's mandates, an unlikely event.

Beyond the confines of health and social service providers, there are other options. The Israeli, Danish, and U.S. analyses referred obliquely to the role of nursing. This profession may have a potentially greater role in establishing cooperative working relationships between medical and social service providers. In the institutional setting, the nurse often becomes the linking pin (Likert's terminology) for interprofessional communication. In this vital role, the nurse gains enormous power. Beyond the confines of the medical center and its rigidities, the home nurse assists the same clients in the same setting as does the social welfare practitioner. It is an almost natural alliance, with the problems of incongruent status requiring attention.

The developing use of industrial social workers reverses a trend of medical domination of the referral process. By focusing on the workplace, the problems of job stress, fatigue, "burnout," and alcoholism can be diagnosed and treated before they become acute medical and emotional problems. In these settings, the trained social worker can be the point of entry for care. Such efforts in the United States and Denmark are growing and data for evaluative purposes should emerge soon. The French have made significant progress in the field of industrial social work. This use of the workplace reinforces one of the theories connecting the chapters of this book: using defined and reachable population groups.

Thus, the education, status, and associations of professional providers play an important role in enhancing collaborative programs. These are most difficult to change since they are attitudinal and perceptual. Legislated efforts will succeed only when behavioral modifications are implemented. This requires a long-term strategy.

FINANCIAL ASPECTS

One common element of each analysis contained in the book is the concern for funding health and social policies. In countries such as Denmark, Sweden, and Finland, it appears that program concerns and human needs dominate fiscal constraints. In others, such as England and France, the tendency is to modify need by eligibility standards. In the United States, these tests became exclusionary by their very nature. In this section, attention centers on the role of insurance funds and the categorical funding approach.

One approach for the future directions of service linkage centers on the decisions of the federal governments in fiscal control. It seems clear from those discussions that cost containment dominates experimental integration. There is little doubt that efficiency rules effectiveness in these public arenas. The countries in this book were included because they are all rather well-developed, they have health and social welfare systems which rank among the world's best, and, at some level, they have attempted to respond to the concept of linkage. Each of these industrialized countries has a stable governmental structure. But one of unintended consequences of this similarity is the havoc in national economics that characterizes this sample. The artificial economics of the oil-producing nations has altered employment patterns, lifestyles, and tax and social structures in these nations. As the cohort of elderly live longer, they will draw more heavily on each nation's social programs and health services. As the age categories shift to an older population, the problems grow more acute. It did not surprise many observers to learn that, in 1980, the average age of the U.S. population was above 30, the first time in recent memory this had happened. These trends are not unrelated; they converge to demand change. While some may demand a fundamental, sweeping alteration, such radical restructuring is neither warranted nor appropriate. A more incremental strategy will succeed, if it meets certain criteria. As evidenced in the national analyses, a financial mechanism must allow integration to occur without penalty. Reimbursements which constrain linkage should be replaced with incentives for integrated practice. The professional health and social planning committees need information and representation from diverse groups.

Categorical funding mechanisms often impede such program linkages by using monies and expenditures for limited purposes. Integrative programs are constrained. The current concerns of many mental health administrators are illustrative. As alcoholism treatment programs expanded in the early 1970s, many efforts became linked to, and offered through, mental health facilities. Although housed in a mental health center, the alcoholic patient client/services were funded by non-mental health monies. Such a split required separate accounting systems with separate staffing patterns. These programs received funding from "soft" money, thereby keeping their existence and continuity in jeopardy. It is difficult to enhance medical and social interventions when a program's viability is threatened and is cumbersome to manage.

The use of categorical grant programs reinforces the split between health and social service professionals. It impedes the development of a holistic approach to patient care and service. As the community health center experience in Canada illustrates, the holistic approach is an experiment outside the normal service delivery system. The categorical grants and payment mechanisms preclude general implementation of this approach and philosophy.

Private and public insurance funds often inhibit such interdisciplinary cooperation, since a primary diagnosis often precludes payment for needed support services. A medical diagnosis would assure payments for care; the medical control of this process often reduces the role of nonmedical personnel. This is an acute problem in alcoholism treatment programs; the medical concerns should not be isolated from the social treatments. Service programs for the elderly encounter similar problems. Medical and psychosocial concerns are not distinct; one can become the root of the other.

The role of experimental programs in enhancing cooperation and linkages must not be understated. On one hand, such efforts are evidence of the concern for the problem. They represent attempts to respond to a known problem by concrete interventions in service delivery. On the other hand, these efforts are often relegated to the stockpile of social experiments and demonstrations. The Swedish, Canadian, and Finnish efforts fall into this category.

There is little evidence in the several chapters of this book of a high level of concern for linkage of health and social services in the public planning bodies. While this could be an omission in the data presented, it is more likely an oversight in the planning process. Since social planning often incorporates the existing structures, financial arrangements, and service delivery patterns, it is incremental and not a catalyst for broad social change. Given the history and traditions of the split between health and welfare, social planning and legislation will meet resistance if it attempts to be a leader rather than to mirror existing practices.

The Reagan administration's approach to human services contains two basic elements: reduced spending by the federal government and decentralization in administration. The curtailing of federal expenditures by 25 percent will force analysis causing nonentitlement programs to suffer. The model appears to be an attack on those programs which serve the neediest and least politically powerful. For example, the constituencies for alcoholism, drug, and mental health services cannot compete against the basic biomedical research community. The argument of the top leadership of the Department of Health and Human Services centers on the philosophy that the original reasons for federal involvement in these programs was solely for developmental purposes. Now that alcoholism programs have become a part of the human service delivery system, federal expenditures can be phased out. The development of mental health centers has proceeded to the point that federal funds can be withdrawn. There is a solid basis in law and in congressional intent for this position, despite the hardships it will cause in the short term.

This reduction in federal funds leads to the second element in the Reagan approach: decentralization. Using a block grant approach, the concept involves giving the states increased latitude to spend money on locally determined needs. Thus, if Ohio placed a high priority on its mental health center program, it would have the resources to do so. In this same approach, Indiana could fund alcoholism programs with its money. The major problem is the formula for funding. The approach is to reduce nonmilitary federal expenditures in fiscal year 1982. If approved by Congress, each state will receive, in fiscal year 1982, 75 percent of the fiscal year 1981 allocations to organizations, within boundaries. When this 25 percent reduction occurs in conjunction with 10 percent inflation, the real decrease is 35 percent. Few states have the resources to make up the difference; thus, major cuts are inevitable. This atmosphere of program reductions, termination notices, and curtailed service will negate many of the efforts at service linkage. It is inevitable, with increasing pressures and few categorical constraints, that services will be funded at the expense of research; programs will receive monies that once funded educational institutions. These are short-term "solutions," leading to a reduced public effort and commitment in human services in the United States. Is this the meaning of the 1980 elections in the United States? A strong case for the affirmative position is being made in the United States and other countries. The gains which have been made in service linkage shrink under the threat of service elimination.

CHANGING SYSTEMS

There are many strategies for change, change that would enhance the linkages between health and social services. The issue for many countries is not the lack of strategies or mechanisms to reach this goal, but rather their inability to adopt this as a priority. But for those national programs and efforts in the private sector that believe in the values and benefits of this collaborative and cooperative framework, the methods vary. One of the more successful interventions is to use the linking professionals, those service delivery personnel in each sector whose regular work maintains contact across professional lines and ideologies. Examples include alcoholism counselors, some health nurses, researchers, planners, and program managers. These jobs have the benefit of an existing system of contacts in numerous spheres of human service delivery. They serve as bridges and as communicators of information across professional boundaries. The inherent risk is that these same people may tend to be regarded as marginal by their peers, a situation that would reduce rapidly and significantly their power to link anything. These individuals may get caught in the trap of deviance, which, when once defined, becomes a self-perpetuating cycle. If the credibility of the collaborative professional is reduced, failure will result. Such failures increase the likelihood of future results of the same kind, thereby maintaining and reinforcing the status quo.

Vested interests in the status quo prevent increased cooperation and linkage between these two sectors. The concept of a consumer movement centers on accessibility, quantity, and quality of services within each sphere of activity. There is no such thing as a strong consumer movement for integrated service delivery. Unfortunately, it is only a calling of theoreticians, researchers, and academics. That does not mean such efforts are incorrect; it does not imply that they are doomed to be so in the future. It does mean that continued efforts are required to make the concepts a reality. Community mental health was an alien concept forty years ago; time, energy, resources, and education can be successful catalysts of change.

Lack of an organized consumer movement may well be a major obstacle to change. None of the preceding national analyses stressed the importance of the recipient's belief that service delivery cooperation would be of benefit. In fact, several chapters avoid the client's perspectives totally. One view is that it accurately reflects the existing service delivery system: specialized, fragmented, and uncoordinated. In this framework, client expectations are rarely heard. In fact, they are often unspoken. The patient is a tacit third party. A second perspective holds that clients do not realize what they are missing. In this mode, the client realizes something is wrong but has little or no information on which to act. A third alternative is that the patient knows what the choices are and opts for the current system. This view would account for the fact that consumers are more concerned about rising costs than approving an experimental demonstration to link the health and social services delivery systems to the alcoholic. No matter which of these three views dominates, the net result remains. The role of the recipient of service as a change agent is minimal.

Professionals, public officials, and service delivery managers would probably prefer that this situation remain. No politician wishes to confront an antagonistic constituency. Only a masochistic professional wants to hear that service is ineffective. No manager wants to hear that services are inefficient. Each of these groups has a vested interest in the status quo, making them an unlikely catalyst for change or action.

Therefore, public officials, the professional community, the managers, and the consumers of service seem satisfied enough with the status quo not to become advocates for the widespread development of new approaches. If costs are controlled, either by a real reduction or by a slowing down in their growth rate, then a major source of dissatisfaction will be eliminated.

One subtle theme cutting across these chapters is the class distinctions in each country. Only in the analysis of the Canadian system did the issue emerge directly. By definition, the affluent can afford health care services in abundance. By law, social security is universal. By economics, the poor must rely on public services and resources. Thus, it often falls to the middle class to chart the course for the future. The current debates about rising costs reflect the middle-class income earner's concerns.

For the poor, such dependence on public services can be seen as a prelude to repression. Through this filter, linking health with social welfare policies opens a pandora's box of misinterpreted efforts. Efforts to increase cooperation and collaboration between these systems could be interpreted as a mechanism of social control. It could imply a method of those in power to increase their hold on the lower class. Thus, even beneficial motives would be viewed as malevolent intentions of the elite upper class.

Are the social welfare policies of France, Denmark, Sweden, England, and the United States used as a form of repression? Do public sector health programs add to the status inequities in Canada and Israel? While there are those who believe this is part of a socialist approach, the history and development of these programs reveals a different interpretation. Originated as a response to intolerable conditions, social programs were an effort to alleviate a specific problem. While it would be foolhardy to argue that such policies were aimed at the causes of a problem, they did aspire to remove the most visible manifestations of the poor condition. One of the totally unplanned consequences of these socially responsive programs is the fragmentation of services that exists today. As social and health policies developed, the pattern remained similar, in that public officials responded solely to the crisis of the moment. This reactive process characterizes many national efforts described herein.

PARADIGM FOR CHANGE

Any system must incorporate the following principles if it will be able to link health and social services successfully:

- build on community acceptance,
- build on client participation,

- be supported by an effective system of cross-referrals,
- maintain continuity of care,
- as functional, use a holistic approach to service,
- have a strong outreach component, and
- have a secure financial base.

This list succinctly summarizes many of the successes documented in this book. If a change in a service program has community acceptance and the input of the intended beneficiaries, its chances for success increase. In the arena of health and social welfare programs, systems of cross-referrals are mandatory for increased linkages. If a control system were added to ensure that referrals occur, increased linkage could result. Use of the holistic approach is not without debate. But this concept is naturally allied to increasing linkages across systems. If a strong community outreach program can be implemented, the system will be enhanced. And, of course, adequate funding in the short term and secure funding in the long term are prerequisites for service delivery and public confidence.

In the discussions of service linkage for health and social welfare programs, three starting points have emerged. One option is to begin by defining the problem to be addressed. This approach stresses that a behavioral or physical need exists and seeks to solve the concern. An alternative approach defines a population group and determines the needs of this cohort of individuals. A state or county geopolitical territory illustrates this concept. Finally, a third option views the individual and attempts to diagnose need and treat or refer the person to the proper source of care and service. These three approaches and starting points for problem analysis lead to differences in policy development, organizational management, and service delivery. Figure 11.1 represents a nine-cell grid of this idea.[1]

For the first cell, the policy implications of a *problem-focused* approach, several important questions arise. This approach seems to characterize current policymaking efforts in many countries. If one defines alcoholism as a problem, then

FOCUS	POLICY	MGMT.	PRACTICE
PROBLEM (Behavioral)			
POPULATION (Children, aged, poor, is MS geographical area)			
INDIVIDUAL NEEDS			

Figure 11.1   Social Problem Analysis Grid

public policies develop to focus resources on this problem. Social legitimacy arises from such public definitions and policy. Through the policy process, targeted resources can be utilized to "combat" such problems; the "war on poverty" illustrates the point clearly. The problem definition approach provides for easy definitions of eligible populations and allows for clear determination of eligibility standards.

When the problem definition approaches become reality for agency managers, they have several benefits. Often, such new programs can be appended to the existing organizational structure: a mental health clinic, a renal dialysis unit, or an emergency medical center. In terms of agency finances, such new structures can be added to a line item budget with requisite staff additions. And when added, such efforts can adapt to new data collection efforts on the quantitative numerics of clients served, units of care provided, and other such information to document program utilization. At the service delivery level, specialists can be hired in the new program area. When referrals are made, the practice professionals serve. Treatment outcomes on this level often center on the reduction or elimination of present symptoms.

But this problem approach reinforces the traditional separation of health and social services. It avoids a holistic approach to services. It continues to reinforce the split between medical and social service needs. It assumes a narrow range of causes for problems by limiting treatment and service modalities. By focus on symptoms and treatments, it provides no incentive for innovation or creative problem-solving. It is dependent on a well-informed referral network. Without such a system, inappropriate client visits will occur, thereby decreasing service efficiency and effectiveness.

The *population-based approach* to human services policy increases the likelihood of more holistic concepts. It may enhance a broader perspective of human needs to replace the problem focus. Since it is not bound by the cause-intervention-effect mentality of the former approach, using a population group as a unit of analysis has the potential of increasing professional interaction in policy development.

At the organizational level, departmental distinctions blur, being replaced by a program focus. For many, this means that the line item budget yields to the program budget. A complement of personnel is required, staff who can and will work toward a team approach. Outreach programs often emerge as an acceptable mechanism to inform a community of program availability. These services tend to be more decentralized; the community mental health centers and the health clinics in Denmark, Canada, and the United States used a medical and psychiatric facility as a support, not a hierarchical control system.

Services often move to the location of the clients: clinics in schools for adolescents, home health care for the elderly. Practice training and professional education require a more generic approach, such as the British model, rather than the specialist approach which characterizes other nations. The role of the family practitioner reflects this concept, whereas the specialist physician mirrors the problem focus. While the role of the "reformed" problemholder was important in the former approach, (e.g., a former alcoholic and a former drug user) these new providers have a decreased role in services when a population at large is the unit of analysis.

When the unit of analysis shifts to the *individual*, the public policy process becomes obscured. It is difficult, if not impossible, to set national priorities based on the needs of all individuals. For an agency administrator to cope with and respond to the needs of all individuals who arrive expecting services is unrealistic. It is beyond available resources of both the agency and the community. For the practitioner to respond is equally unrealistic.

Of these three approaches, the population at large concept comes closest to assisting service linkage. It can avoid much of the duplication that arises from the problem-specific approach. It allows interprofessional collaboration and information exchange. It encourages interaction between professionals in training and education. It allows for the development of new roles which can become linking personnel. Home health aides, community health educators, and social workers in discharge planning roles illustrate these creative staff functions. While this approach is far from the main focus of most of the national efforts described herein, it is an emerging theme in Sweden, England, and Israel. While the United States has reviewed these notions in Congress and through public discussion, public policy in health and social services still responds to the problem focus. It seems that such a frame of mind will continue for the near future.

THE FUTURE

"Health For All By The Year 2000" symbolizes the World Health Organization's commitment of energy and resources for the rest of this century. Its definition of health is broad enough to include physical and emotional states. Yet, with the exception of William TenHoor's review, mental health was rarely mentioned in the national reviews of this volume. This does not reflect the charge to the authors, for neither editor defined the topics. Rather, it probably reflects the reality of a medical-psychological state of health division. This unfortunate dichotomy becomes another obstacle in linkage of health and social services. Mental health treatment throughout the world has moved beyond its institutional and custodial traditions. The care and rehabilitation of the mentally ill presents an excellent opportunity to use health providers and social welfare professionals in complementary roles. For nonresidential clients, the mental health system is a community-based outreach effort. Such programs succeed when they can incorporate the work of both fields. Whether in mental health clinics or halfway, transition houses, the collaborative efforts of the two systems (health and social services) increase the potential for successful treatments.

Following this, little attention was given to alcoholism and drug rehabilitation programs, other arenas of linkage in some countries. Certainly, these are not the glamorous medical issues of our times. They do not command the respect and public attention given to heart transplants, but they exist in great numbers. As the underside of medical and social welfare practice, funding for these programs in several countries is under scrutiny. Yet, drug treatment and counseling programs combine the medical and social service providers in clinics, schools, universities, and churches, representing another example of effective interaction.

The meaning of these myriad examples is clear. Linkages occur in greater numbers than one might first believe. In each country described herein, there are programs and policies aimed at this cooperation. Financial and other incentives enhance linkage. Thus, the apparent threat of cooperative efforts breaching new ground is unreal. If there were concerns about decreasing professional autonomy, the examples cited would seem to disprove that problem. If there were concerns about developing unworkable programs, successful models exist. And if there were concerns about the increasing costs of new programs, available evidence appears to negate this worry.

Another lesson from these national examples centers on the need for a specific population for which service linkage can become the basis for program modification. As Harrington and Newcomer vividly documented, the numerous government programs for the elderly produce gaps and overlaps. By using an age criterion complemented by a means test, these programs replace service with eligibility concerns. The financial determinations use planning and policymakers' time more than necessary. As this book goes to press, public debate in the United States centers on how to "save" the social security system, not how to make it more comprehensive. Given the constraints of this approach, solutions will be implemented, such as interfund borrowing, raising the age of retirement with full benefits, and narrowing the definition of disability. None of these "solutions" to "save" the system responds to the need for an integrated service system. Rather, they respond to the need to "save" the political figures who must react to the problems. Few can forget former President Carter's 1977 declaration that said social security is fiscally sound through the middle of the twenty-first century, a statement that took only 1,000 days to disprove.

The different approaches described in this book reflect the uniqueness of each nation's history, traditions, and value systems. The rugged individualism and frontier spirit of the colonial period of the United States formed the framework of many social policies, or lack thereof, today. For the Danes, the word *kommune* means city, but it also reflects the communal assistance programs which implement their national policy. In Israel, the bonds of a struggle of existence, coupled with a small territory and population base, increase the scope of human service programs. The altruism of the French extends for almost 300 years, albeit for the destitute. If the human rights doctrine of all the democracies discussed in these chapters has one thread, it is that health care and social security as a concept must be offered. The programs differ, but they are not incompatible to the philosophy. Linkages are an important next step to enhance these efforts. Further efforts in each country will occur and will undoubtedly build on past successes.

NOTE

1. The author would like to acknowledge Professors Arthur Blum and Howard Goldstein for their assistance in developing this framework.

NOTES ON THE CONTRIBUTORS

JACQUES FOURNIER is a Senior Advisor to the President of the French Republic. He teaches at the Institute for Political Studies in Paris, Bordeaux, and Grenoble. He has authored several books and scholarly articles.

CHARLENE HARRINGTON is Adjunct Associate Research Sociologist at the Aging Health Policy Center, Department of Social and Behavioral Sciences of the University of California in San Francisco. She received a B.S. in nursing from the University of Kansas, an M.A. in community health nursing from the University of Washington, and a Ph.D. in sociology from the University of California at Berkeley. Dr. Harrington's special interests include health policy research on Medicaid, Medicare, and health care delivery systems. She is a co-principal investigator on a study of long-term care for the California Policy Seminar, and coordinates two research projects on the correlates of long-term care expenditure and service utilization. Dr. Harrington serves as a consultant to numerous health organizations and is a member of a number of professional associations including the American Health Planning Association, the Western Gerontological Society, and the American Public Health Association.

MERL C. HOKENSTAD, Jr. is Dean and Professor at the School of Applied Social Sciences, Case Western Reserve University in Cleveland, Ohio. He holds a Ph.D. in social policy and planning from Brandeis University, an M.S. in social work from Columbia University, and a Certificate in Educational Management from Harvard University. Dr. Hokenstad has served as a Visiting Professor in Comparative Social Policy at Stockholm University in Sweden and a Visiting Scholar in Comparative Social Work Education at the National Institute for Social Work in London, England. Long active in international organizations, he is currently a member of the Board of Directors for the International Association of Schools of Social Work and the Cleveland International Program. Professor Hokenstad's publications include a book and several journal articles in the areas of comparative social welfare policy and human services education.

ERIK HOLST, M.D., is Chairman of the Institute of Social Medicine, School of Medicine, University of Copenhagen. He also serves as the Danish Co-Director of the University of California (UCLA/University of Copenhagen) Joint Center for Studies of Health Programs. Professor Holst has served as president of numerous professional organizations, including the Danish Union of Academic Professionals, the Danish Association of Junior Hospital Physicians, and the Danish Medical Association. He has served as editor-in-chief of the *Danish Medical Journal* and as a member of the editorial board of the *Scandinavian Medical Journal.* Dr. Holst's activities in the international health community include work on the 25th World Health Assembly and service on several commissions (psychotropic drugs, health statistics, health education, and social sciences). A prolific writer, Erik Holst's work has earned him a position on the French Ministry of Education's National Center of Scientific Research Health Committee.

HIROBUMI ITO is a research associate at the Institute of Social Medicine of the University of Copenhagen. He received his B.A. in sociology from the University of Copenhagen and his M.A. in German/Scandinavian studies from the Washington University, St. Louis. A Ph.D. candidate in sociology at the University of Copenhagen, his research interests are historical and comparative medical sociology. Mr. Ito is involved in a number of research projects, including an analysis of the development of health and social policies in Scandinavian countries, declining patterns of infant mortality in Western European countries, and the problems of coordinating health and social services in Denmark and Japan, with a particular focus on the care of the elderly.

JOSEPH KATAN is Senior Lecturer at the School of Social Work, Tel Aviv University. He earned his M.S.W. at the University of Michigan and his M.A. in sociology and education at the Hebrew University of Jerusalem. After receiving a Ph.D. from the University of Michigan, Dr. Katan studied community organizations and social change processes in Israel. He has served as Chairman of the Israeli Association of Schools of Social Work, as Director of the School of Social Work at Tel Aviv University, and as a consultant to the Family and Community Services Department of the City of Jerusalem. Professor Katan has been a Visiting Professor at the School of Applied Social Sciences, Case Western Reserve University, and the School of Social Work of the University of Michigan. Dr. Katan has published over a dozen articles, chapters in books and public reports.

ROBERT J. NEWCOMER is Adjunct Associate Professor, Department of Social and Behavioral Sciences and Deputy Director of the Aging Health Policy Center at the University of California in San Francisco. Dr. Newcomer's experience in aging and health planning ranges over employment in private consulting, government, and university teaching and research. Areas of substantive expertise are housing for the elderly and the continuum of care, the subject of two books. His interest in the continuum of care focuses on case management, policy incentives on quality of care, and service utilization. He is currently Principal Investigator on a study of self-help and advocacy for the underserved elderly, and is Co-Principal Investigator studying state discretionary policies and long-term care. Dr. Newcomer is active in professional associations, including the American Planning Association, Urban and Regional Information Systems Association, American Public Health Association, the

Gerontological Society, and the Western Gerontological Society.

NICOLE QUESTIAUX serves as Minister of National Solidarity for the French Government. She teaches social policy courses at the Institute of Political Studies in Paris, Bordeaux and Grenoble, and has co-authored two books and numerous articles.

ROGER A. RITVO is Associate Professor and Assistant Dean at the School of Applied Social Sciences, Case Western Reserve University in Cleveland, Ohio. In addition to the Ph.D. in organizational behavior from Case Western Reserve University, Dr. Ritvo received an M.B.A. in health care administration from George Washington University. He served as a Senior Policy Coordinator in the Immediate Office of the Secretary of the Department of Health and Human Services on the staff of both Patricia Roberts Harris and Richard S. Schweiker. As a Fellow of the World Health Organization, he has conducted research on the health planning system in Denmark. Professor Ritvo's publications include works on international approaches to linking health and social services, hospital governance, technology transfer, and program evaluation.

ERIC SAINSBURY, Professor of Social Administration at the University of Sheffield, has experience as a schoolteacher, probation officer, family casework supervisor, and lecturer in social work. His research interests center on the organization of personal social services and "consumer" studies of social work. He has served as Chairman of the Social Work Education Committee of the Joint University Council for Social and Public Administration, is a member of the Central Council for Education and Training in Social Work, and was scientific adviser to the Chief Scientist at the Department of Health and Social Security. He is associated locally with various statutory and voluntary services and is a Justice of the Peace. His principal publications are *Social Diagnosis in Casework* (1970), *Social*

Work with Families (1975), *The Personal Social Services* (1977), and *Social Work in Focus* (1982).

KARIN TENGVALD is Professor of Public Health at the University of Linköping, Sweden. Her main research areas include poverty and social policy issues, as well as the fields of health maintenance and health policies. Dr. Tengvald earned her Ph.D. (sociology) from Uppsala University and for several years belonged to the faculties of the Department of Sociology, Uppsala University and the School of Social Work and Public Administration, University of Stockholm. She has also been a research fellow at the Swedish Council for Medical Research and consulted with governmental agencies at local and central levels.

WILLIAM J. TENHOOR is Senior Policy Coordinator for the Office of Human Development Services in the Immediate Office of the Secretary of the Department of Health and Human Services. He holds a Master of Social Work degree from the University of Illinois. As Deputy Chief of the Community Support and Rehabilitation Branch at the National Institute of Mental Health, he was instrumental in designing and implementing two major federal demonstrations directed toward the reform of the system of care for the chronically mentally ill. He also directed a psychiatric halfway house program, worked with major community foundations, conducted research on public/private sector relationships, and has written several articles.

GEORGE TSALIKIS is Associate Professor and Director of the Masters Programme in Health Administration at the University of Ottawa. He studied political science and public administration in Athens, Greece and social administration at the London School of Economics, where he wrote a Ph.D. thesis under the supervision of Professor R. M. Titmuss. He held senior positions in the Greek Ministry of Health and Social Services. He taught sociology, social history, and social policy (health, education and welfare) in Greece and in Canada, where he also acted as consultant and researcher for various governments and organizations. His current research focuses on the relationship between social theory and social policy. Dr. Tsalikis serves as a trustee at the Sandy Hill Community Health Clinic in Ottawa and is a consultant to the Ministry of Health in Zimbabwe.

GEORG WALLS is Assistant Professor at the Institute of Social Policy of the University of Jyväskylä, Finland. Dr. Walls received the Doctor of Social Sciences degree from the University of Tampere. His research interests include analysis of the cooperation between health and social welfare personnel in delivery of primary care services. Formerly Acting Professor in Sociology at the Åbo Akademi in Turku, Dr. Walls's current teaching and policy analysis concerns power and influence in social welfare in Finland.